BRITISH PROPAGANDA AND NEWS MEDIA IN THE COLD WAR

International Communications
Series Editor: Philip M. Taylor

This is the first comprehensive series to tackle the fast-expanding subject of International Communications.

This multi-disciplinary subject is viewed as a field of enquiry and research that deals with the processes and impact of the transfer of information, news, data and cultural products as well as other forms of transborder communication between nation-states within the wider context of globalisation. As such it is not only a field of study in its own right but also directly connected to international history, international politics, international affairs and international political economy.

Most writers in these more 'established' fields are agreed that communications have come to play an ever more significant part in relations between states at the political, economic, diplomatic, military and cultural levels. This series will show *how* communications serves to influence those activities from the points of transmission to those of reception.

Enormous breakthroughs in communications technologies – satellite communications, computer-mediated communications, mobile personal communications – are now converging, and the possibilities which this might present are forcing a reconsideration of how established patterns of inter-state relations might adapt to, or be influenced by, this latest phase of the information age.

Debates relating to international regulation, censorship, public diplomacy, electronic democracy, cross-cultural communications and even information warfare all reflect the sense that communications are transforming the nature and practice of government, education, leisure, business, work and warfare. Information has become the lifeblood of this globalising set of patterns.

Books in the series reflect this phenomenon but are rooted in historical method, even when tackling more contemporary events. They are truly international in coverage. The range of books reflects the coverage of courses and teaching in international communications and they are carefully aimed at students and researchers working in this area.

Books available in the International Communications series:

Propaganda, Censorship and Irish Neutrality in the Second World War
By Robert Cole

Nazi Wireless Propaganda: Lord Haw-Haw and British Public Opinion in the Second World War
By Martin Doherty

British Propaganda and News Media in the Cold War
By John Jenks

Forging Peace: Intervention, Human Rights and the Management of Media Space
Edited by Monroe E. Price and Mark Thomson

British Propaganda in the Twentieth Century: Selling Democracy
By Philip M. Taylor

British Propaganda and News Media in the Cold War

John Jenks

Edinburgh University Press

© John Jenks, 2006

Edinburgh University Press Ltd
22 George Square, Edinburgh

Typeset in Ehrhardt by
TechBooks International Delhi, and
printed and bound in Great Britain by
Biddles Ltd, King's Lynn, Norfolk

A CIP record for this book is available from the British Library

ISBN-10 0 7486 2314 0 (hardback)
ISBN-13 978 0 7486 2314 3 (hardback)

The right of John Jenks
to be identified as author of this work
has been asserted in accordance with
the Copyright, Designs and Patents Act 1988.

Contents

Acknowledgements

This work began as a dissertation at the University of California-Berkeley and depended on generous grants from the Mellon Foundation, UC-Berkeley's history department, the university's Humanities and Social Sciences Research Grant Program and the Centre for German and Western European Studies. For that stage I'd like to thank my dissertation committee – chairman Anthony Adamthwaite, Susanna Barrows, Diane Clemens and Thomas Leonard – for their advice and direction. Fellow graduate students, scholars, writers and researchers on both sides of the Atlantic helped develop it through their comments and suggestions. In the US I would especially like to thank Laura Belmonte, Jim Cane, Stacey Cone and Michelle Tusan, and in the UK I would like to extend the same thanks to Margaret Bryan, Ruth Dudley Edwards, W. Scott Lucas, James Oliver and Tony Shaw. Archivists in dozens of libraries and private collections helped me through seemingly endless piles of documents. They have my eternal gratitude.

Dominican University's Faculty Research Grants were invaluable at two key moments – allowing an additional visit to the British archives in 2002 to examine the latest releases from the Foreign Office's Information Research Department, and giving time for focused thinking and writing in 2004. Feedback from colleagues at the regular faculty colloquia lunches gave me new ideas and interesting twists on old ones. Members of the Association for Education in Journalism and Mass Communication's history division gave valuable criticism on early drafts of the work at several conferences. My students' questions have helped me think in different ways about propaganda and news media. And my chair, Ric Calabrese, has always offered moral support, insight and sage advice.

Finally, I must thank my family for the support in what must have seemed to them an interminable process. My parents, in-laws, brother and sister came through at vital times. Leah and Daniel kept it real. And Jennifer made it happen in a thousand different ways.

Abbreviations

Abbreviations Used in the Text

AFL	American Federation of Labor
BBC	British Broadcasting Corporation
BPC	British Peace Committee
BSCF	British Society for Cultural Freedom
CCF	Congress for Cultural Freedom
COI	Central Office of Information
CRO	Commonwealth Relations Office
FO	Foreign Office
ICFTU	International Confederation of Free Trade Unions
IPD	Information Policy Department
IRD	Information Research Department
IUS	International Union of Students
LPS	London Press Service
MI5	Security Service
MI6	Secret Intelligence Service
NATO	North Atlantic Treaty Organisation
RFE	Radio Free Europe
TUC	Trades Union Congress
USIA	United States Information Agency
VOA	Voice of America
WFTU	World Federation of Trade Unions
WPC	World Peace Council

Abbreviations Used in the Notes

BBC WAC	British Broadcasting Corporation, Written Archives Centre
BBK	Beaverbrook Papers
CCF	Congress for Cultural Freedom
DBPO	Documents on British Policy Overseas
FRUS	Foreign Relations of the United States
NARA	National Archives and Record Administration
PRO	Public Record Office

Introduction

Knowledge and power are closely linked, a truism that just about everyone from Francis Bacon to Edward Said has recognised. In this book I examine knowledge as news and the news media. News is not synonymous with information, but is rather 'new information about a subject of some public interest that is shared with some portion of the public'.[1] News obviously fills a basic human need, and is essential for the functioning of global business and democratic government. At the same time the control, suppression, dissemination and manipulation of news can be important for gaining and maintaining hegemony, both domestic and international.

Historically news has had multiple functions in the exercise of power, both within Britain and as an extension of British power overseas. Since the mid-nineteenth century Britain had a strong tradition of press liberty. The growth of journalistic professionalism and its claim to objectivity gave the press greater credibility, the emergence of an advertising-supported mass circulation press made the media profitable and their presumed influence over the newly enfranchised masses made them powerful. Monopoly public service radio later added to the mix. By the mid-twentieth century Britain was saturated with news media – commercial, political and public service.

Early theorists of this mass society spoke of a mechanical 'engineering of consent' on major social and political issues through the press and other institutions.[2] It was not that simple, however. Later theorists building off the work of Italian Marxist Antonio Gramsci have instead spoken of a hegemonic process by which the dominant blocs in a society such as schools, churches, businesses and news media 'negotiate' with each other and the broader population to establish a 'common sense' view of the world and specific problems in it. For Gramsci and many of his interpreters the hegemonic process was essentially about continued capitalist domination that made the working class accept the status quo as the natural 'common sense'.[3] But the ideas have value far beyond that context. In this work we see that journalists in the early Cold War generally did not avoid certain stories and sources for fear of the government or losing their jobs; they accepted the hegemonic common sense about Communism and the Soviet Union and probably never even considered challenging it.

A similar process happened with American journalists in the Vietnam War. Early on the journalists all shared unquestioned core assumptions and avoided 'deviant' interpretations of America, Communism and the war. The boundaries, however, shifted as the war ground on and the American establishment split. Journalists' reporting took more excursions into the 'sphere of deviancy' through coverage of things like American atrocities against Vietnamese civilians.[4] Hallin's study helps illuminate the British shift in an opposite direction – away from an indulgent view of the Communist world and toward a sceptical if not downright hostile interpretation of it. It also helps explain how some journalists found themselves stranded as the political tide turned.

But in Britain in the 1940s and 1950s the government had sharp tools to reinforce those boundaries of acceptable discourse and behaviour. The D-Notice censorship system, the British Board of Film Censors and the occasional threat of prosecution let the press and the public know the consequences of straying too far. Government propaganda helped point to the desired facts and filled in the gaps left by censorship and self-censorship. The blurred boundaries between war and peace during the Cold War could often tempt the government to push for the more stringent controls associated with total war.[5] Journalists' acquired reflexes from 1939–45 often let them get away with it. This legacy of total war and the exigencies of Cold War – particularly propaganda – kept the British media tightly self-disciplined when it came to the Soviet Union and Communism. But in the mid-1950s the system broke down, beginning with the thaw following Stalin's death, and continuing through the Geneva summit and the debacle at Suez in 1956.

Overseas British power and media influence have long been intertwined. British economic and information hegemony reinforced each other through-out the decades of Britain's global dominance in the nineteenth century.[6] Critics in the 1970s identified British, French and particularly American news media as dominating and distorting information flows in the Third World, and called for a more equitable New World Information and Communication Order. It never happened. The movement's champions in UNESCO chose, perhaps unwisely, allies in the Communist bloc and Third World dictatorships, and Britain and America counterattacked furiously. But other critics building on Immanuel Wallerstein's world systems theory and Herbert Schiller's theory of media imperialism have analysed the persistent patterns of domination, subordination and control in global media flows.[7] They cannot simply be dismissed.

Two world wars and an international depression had eroded Britain's ability to project power, but the global media system it had built in the nineteenth century and the propaganda expertise it had honed in the two world wars gave it inordinate influence over global news media discourse. After 1945 the British government sought to use this influence and expertise, often in conjunction with the newly arrived Americans, to defend its still extensive strategic interests. The British preferred private entities such as Reuters, but increasingly turned to the quasi-official BBC and British Council and fact-based propaganda – overt, covert and mixed – both to supplement the increasingly anaemic private news sector and to keep up with the burgeoning American and Soviet propaganda machines. The successful exercise of this system – private, public and subsidised – in the Cold War strengthened it and thus helped Britain preserve inordinate prestige, power and influence in the global media. Going into the twenty-first century British news media were second only to the Americans in truly global power and prestige, despite Britain's quite substantial tumble as a global economic, political and military power.[8]

These national and international stories cannot be told in isolation. As the hub of the world communication system London was where these two forces came together. And that is one of the major themes of this book: the blending of domestic and international propaganda and media in the struggle against the Soviet Union during the early Cold War. The Cold War further complicated any domestic-foreign dichotomy by combining traditional Great Power rivalry with aspects of an 'international civil war' in which the news and information shaping the beliefs of Scottish trade unionists, French intellectuals and Third World students were all in contention and frequently in common circulation. This is sometimes expressed in the cliché 'a battle for hearts and minds' but is better thought of as a struggle for dominance in information and perceptions. For example, was the peace movement an authentic expression of worldwide revulsion against nuclear weapons, or a Soviet ploy? The news and information that shaped public perception could answer that question and tilt the advantage to the Anglo-American or the Soviet side.

Propaganda, Journalism and Censorship: Some Observations

Writers have described censorship and propaganda as two sides of the same coin. Censors choke off specific information and ideas, propagandists supply information and symbols to persuade, often giving misleading picture.[9]

Taken in isolation censorship is straightforward – 'suppressing the circulation of information or opinions offensive to the values of those representing the censor'.[10] Censors have a multi-faceted and potentially open-ended job. At its most basic censors try to suppress specific information that could be of immediate value to an enemy. They also look hard at what could potentially be useful to an enemy, and what could potentially damage home morale, allied harmony or diplomatic sensitivities. The retired admirals who ran British censorship in the Cold War ostensibly worried just about security censorship, but the boundaries frequently proved to be blurry.

Propaganda, however, is a slippery word that has frequently eluded definition. Some writers look at the intent of the propagandists, others look for evidence of lies, concealment or rhetorical dishonesty, and some consider almost any persuasive speech and writing to be propaganda. But one of the best overarching definitions of propaganda, however, is based on what it does:

It exploits information; it poses as knowledge; it generates belief systems and tenacious convictions; it skews perceptions; it systematically disregards superior epistemic values such as truth and understanding; it corrupts reasoning and the respect for evidence, rigor and procedural safeguards; it supplies ersatz certainties.[11]

It is clear that whether the British government called its propagandists in-formation officers, public relations consultants or publicists they were in the business of propaganda. True, British propaganda was not nearly as thorough-going, mendacious or blatant as that of its totalitarian contemporaries, but it clearly fits the definition. The British government's propaganda – whether overt or covert – preferred accurate facts with which to build its cases. This wasn't truth for truth's sake, but an expedient strategy to make the propaganda more persuasive and credible. When the truth was inconvenient and it was more expe-dient to dissemble, omit, and obscure, the propagandists did not hesitate to do so. The British propaganda case in the early Cold War comes off comparatively well, largely because its main adversary – Stalin's Soviet Union – so grossly dis-torted the facts and obsessively hid the damaging truths about itself. Britain's fact-based approach was likely to have been more effective than exhortation, based on research that showed, as media researcher Bernard Cohen pointed out, the media might fail in telling people what to think but they succeed admirably in telling people what to think about. This was especially true on issues where readers had little or no first-hand knowledge, such as foreign affairs or the nature of the Soviet Union.[12] Thus, British propaganda could be factual and effective, and credibly pass itself off as disinterested knowledge; it was often accepted as such and took its place in the news media, libraries and bookstores of the world. (Cold War propagandists divided their work into 'white', which was overt, factual and acknowledged; 'grey', which was fact-based but without acknowledgment or attribution; and 'black', which was often false and deliberately deceptive as to its origins. Covert propaganda was the term used to encompass both 'grey' and 'black' propaganda.)

Journalists had a wary relationship with propagandists, no matter what they called themselves. Propagandists needed journalists to prepare the audience with enough basic knowledge to absorb the propaganda, and then to spread their information in a credible medium. Journalists needed information, and often the government's propagandists were the only ones who had it, but resented the manipulation that accompanied it. It can be helpful to think of truth, journalism and propaganda as points on a continuum. Truth is at the disinterested end of the continuum, propaganda operates on the other, instrumental end. Journalists gather facts and fit them into patterns along this continuum – at their best they work toward the truth, at their worst or at their most desperate or corrupt they gravitate toward propaganda.

Despite many well-documented lapses, most journalists in the Anglo–American tradition generally saw themselves as professionals holding up certain standards – accuracy, fairness, independence and a fidelity to the facts – which they grouped under the rubric of 'objectivity'.[13] This tradition has influenced journalists throughout the world, especially in Britain's former dominions, colonies and cultural spheres of influence. This professional ethos gave mainstream British journalists a basis for resisting government intervention and the most blatant state propaganda. But long-term structural developments in journalism and the deferential and patriotic habits developed during World War II made journalists more vulnerable to British-style Cold War propaganda.[14] Some of the most important developments include:

- The 'beat' structure and specialist correspondents. Journalists covered powerful institutions and depended on them for a constant and reliable flow of news. Over time and by necessity beat reporters tend to identify to some degree with the views of their sources. They could not afford to antagonise the institutions to the point at which the news flow was threatened.
- The credible source. Not all news sources are created equal, partly due to the beat structure and partly due to sources' differing access to accurate information that can fit within journalists' broad conceptual framework. Generally sources close to power – in the 1940s and 1950s particularly state power – were considered more reliable than those distant from it.
- Accessibility. Journalists find it easier to report information that's easily accessible. In the early Cold War it was virtually impossible for correspondents to freely access and report on the USSR, but there was always easily accessible information from the Foreign Office News Department or Information Research Department.
- Framing. Journalists have developed rough templates for packaging news whether it is a diplomatic summit, political expose or murder. Almost anything can 'fit' into one of the fairly limited number of templates. Both journalists and their readers recognise and often demand these 'frames'.[15]

Historiography

The history of censorship, propaganda and media during the Cold War has generated a number of different currents and sub-fields, though the interdisciplinary work necessary for the field has not developed as vigorously as it should have.

In the area of British Cold War propaganda history journalists Paul Lashmar and James Oliver's *Britain's Secret Propaganda War* used recent Public Record Office releases from the FO's Information Research Department (IRD) to good measure, but the book has gaps and overemphasises lurid 'dirty tricks'. They argue that British propaganda was powerful, malign and out of control.[16] Andrew Defty's *Britain, America and Anti-Communist Propaganda 1945–53* closely examines the IRD and its relationship to the Americans. He uses this relationship to argue that the Cold War defined British propaganda, and that propaganda became Britain's chief method of fighting the Cold War.[17] Tony Shaw's *British Cinema and the Cold War: The State, Propaganda and Consensus* concentrates on one medium and argues that British films had a key role in shaping public attitudes toward the struggle with the USSR. The government knew it and had a hand in shaping those films.[18] Susan Carruthers' *Winning Hearts and Minds* examined propaganda and media manipulation within Britain in the context of

British colonial counterinsurgency, concluding that the government's efforts to shape discourse to support government actions had a mixed success. Philip Taylor's broad survey *British Propaganda in the Twentieth Century: Selling Democracy* contains an important chapter on post-war developments in which he describes how government sought to use propaganda to deal with overall British decline.[19] Much additional literature on Cold War propaganda and state-media relations has focused on press coverage of tension with the USSR.[20]

Although Defty, Lashmar and Oliver concentrate on the IRD, other literature on that department has gone through a number of phases. The first public knowledge of the department came soon after the Foreign Office closed it in 1977 when investigative journalists traced the department's origins and development.[21] A few works followed in academic journals during the following eighteen years, and renewed journalistic attention came with the release of the IRD's records for 1948 and 1949, in 1995 and 1996, respectively.[22] Stephen Dorril's sprawling book *MI6: Inside the Covert World of Her Majesty's Secret Intelligence Service* pulls together a great deal of information in a highly critical account of all the British state's secret activities, and their friends, allies and minions.[23]

Other researchers have covered much of the open propaganda through long-available sources. John Black's *Organising the Propaganda Instrument* was probably the most thorough of those early accounts.[24] Caroline Anstey took that framework and added archival flesh to the story of Britain's post-war attempt to woo the United States through propaganda on a range of issues – the need for economic aid, the British case in Palestine and the Soviet threat.[25] More recently Gary Rawnsley has looked at BBC propaganda in the second half of the Cold War and has edited a wide-ranging study of Cold War propaganda in the 1950s.[26] Tony Shaw has analysed the Suez crisis, probably the most divisive foreign policy issue in the 1950s, perhaps in the entire post-war era.[27]

Outline

This book unfolds in roughly chronological order. It starts with a quick sketch of Britain's news strengths and weaknesses in the years preceding the Cold War, and then looks at the creation and maintenance of a Cold War consensus and borders of acceptable discourse. The rest of the book examines the creation and operation of the main covert propaganda agency, the Information Research Department, and examines three cases in depth – the denigration of the Soviet-backed peace movement, use of Soviet defectors in propaganda and the campaign to expose the USSR's system of forced labour.

Chapter 1 sets the stage for the Cold War. It describes how Britain came to dominate the world news system in the nineteenth century and to develop covert and overt propaganda and information management techniques in two world wars. Growing media influence at home led the state to step up manipulation and management through public relations. Abroad, new power bolstered Britain's influence at a time when it was weakened and overstretched. The state kept a strong BBC international presence, helped prop up the Reuters news agency, and built a strong information supply system for the Foreign Office's expanded worldwide network of Information Officers.

Chapter 2 analyses the gyrations of British propaganda and media from the 1941 forging of the Anglo–Soviet alliance, through the wartime honeymoon and into the post-war deterioration of the relationship. It takes it up to Britain's acknowledgement of a Cold War in January 1948. The media and government worked warily with each other and with the Soviets. In a little less than three years the British media developed a Cold War consensus of Soviet intransigence and British virtue, and the government prepared for a propaganda barrage to sell that message to the rest of the world.

Chapter 3 looks at journalism censorship and debate about suppression to see how the consensus held together, and how the government was willing to use harsher methods to keep the news and commentary within proper bounds. Britain's shift to a Cold War state of mind in the late 1940s stranded a number of journalists and commentators beyond the margins of acceptability. Some whose left-wing views or Russophilia had been acceptable to mainstream media employers during the war found themselves in difficult situations as hostility with the Soviets increased. Some recanted, some quit (or were fired) and a few went over to the Communist cause. The government used the clubby D-Notice self-censorship system and threats of prosecution to keep more difficult news and journalists in line.

Chapter 4 goes inside the IRD and describes its organisation and how it generated and packaged news for the media and its other clients. Despite the cloak-and-dagger image most of the IRD's work was trawling through the published records of the Communist world looking for evidence of hypocrisy, lies, crime and failure, then carefully supplementing those results with material provided by defectors, intelligence agencies and overseas missions. This cornucopia of propaganda was packaged in more than a dozen different formats for audiences ranging from anti-Stalin Communists to Quaker pacifists.

Chapter 5 concentrates on the IRD's wary yet persistent relationship with journalists and publicists. The department was determined to stay in the background but built strong relationships with London-based journalists, the BBC's overseas services, news syndicates and hundreds of foreign journalists who depended on tips and facts from friendly information officers at British diplomatic posts around the world. This way the IRD hoped that its favoured facts and interpretations would circulate widely and percolate into 'common sense' views about the Soviet Union and Communism.

Chapter 6 outlines how the IRD depended on a number of partners, most importantly the United States propaganda system. The British Foreign Office recognised early on that a close partnership gave it unequalled influence over the massive, well-funded but sometimes clumsy American propaganda machine. The IRD also found that its propaganda could work best once it had been circulated through independent bodies, so developed a wide variety of state-private partnerships with unions, churches and advocacy groups thus removing the stain of original sin of state sponsorship.

Chapter 7 concentrates on the most serious Soviet propaganda challenge in the early Cold War, the peace movement that became the World Peace Council. The entire British government and its network of partners mobilised to expose and cripple the movement, especially when it was slated to have a major congress on British soil in 1950. This effectively de-legitimised in the news media and wider society the Soviet's peace group, but also most independent and non-Communist groups as well.

Chapter 8 looks at the IRD and its allies inside and outside government and how they went on the offensive early on using Soviet defectors and evidence of a massive forced labour system in the USSR to debunk the Soviet myth of a 'workers' paradise'. The IRD used British diplomats at United Nations meetings to ventilate the issue, and kept up contacts with a range of private figures such as the French anti-Stalinist David Rousset to keep up the pressure and arguably hasten the decline of the Soviet forced labour system.

The book ends in 1955, just after the thaw following Stalin's death but before the Anglo–French debacle at Suez, which led to a revamping of Britain's global propaganda strategy. By 1955 the Soviet-backed peace movement was on the run but the non-aligned movement had yet to revive. The Soviet forced labour system was shrinking and the USSR was opening up – a little. The IRD had moved past the crisis atmosphere of the early years and was settling into a pattern of reflexive anti-Communism that it would keep up to 1977. Inside Britain the media had been willing to cooperate to an extraordinary degree, but by the mid-1950s the cooperative self-censorship system was showing its cracks.

Notes

1. Mitchell Stephens, *History of News* (Fort Worth: Harcourt Brace, 1997), p. 4.
2. Terence Qualter, *Opinion Control in the Democracies* (New York: St Martin's Press, 1985), pp. 19–29.
3. Stuart Hall, 'The rediscovery of ideology: the return of the repressed in media studies' in Michael Gurevitch, Tony Bennett, James Curran and Janet Woollacott (eds), *Culture, Society and the Media.* (London: Routledge, 1982); Todd Gitlin, *The Whole World is Watching: Mass Media in the Making and Unmaking of the New Left* (Berkeley: University of California Press, 1982), pp. 249–82.
4. Daniel Hallin, *The 'Uncensored War': The Media and Vietnam* (Berkeley: University of California Press, 1986).
5. Susan Carruthers, *Media at War: Communication and Conflict in the Twentieth Century* (New York: St Martin's Press, 2000), pp. 11–15.
6. Herman Schwartz, *States versus Markets: The Emergence of a Global Economy*, 2nd edn (Houndmills: Palgrave, 2000), pp. 71–8.
7. Thomas McPhail, *Global Communication: Theories, Stakeholders, and Trends* (Boston, MA: Allyn and Bacon, 2002), pp. 8–21; Herbert Schiller, *Mass Communications and American Empire*, 2nd edn (Boulder: Westview, 1992).

8. Jeremy Tunstall and David Machin, *The Anglo-American Media Connection* (New York: Oxford University Press, 1999), pp. 77–90.

9. Philip Taylor, 'Censorship in Britain in the Second World War: An Overview' in A. C. Duke and C. A. Tamse (eds), *Too Mighty to be Free: Censorship and the Press in Britain and the Netherlands* (Zutphen: De Walburg Press, 1987).

10. Nicholas Cull et al., *Propaganda and Mass Persuasion: A Historical Encyclopedia, 1500 to the Present* (Santa Barbara, CA: ABC/Clio, 2003), Entry for 'Censorship', p. 70.

11. Stanley Cunningham, *The Idea of Propaganda: A Reconstruction* (Westport, CT: Praeger, 2002), p. 4.

12. Joseph Klapper, *The Effects of Mass Communication* (New York: Free Press, 1960), pp. 55–7; Bernard Cohen, *The Press and Foreign Policy* (Princeton: Princeton University Press, 1963), pp. 12–15.

13. Tunstall and Machin, *The Anglo-American Media Connection*, pp. 73–6; Jean Chalaby, *Invention of Journalism* (Houndmills, UK: Macmillan, 1998), pp.133–40.

14. See, Jeremy Tunstall, *Journalists at Work: Specialist Correspondents: Their News Organizations, News Sources and Competitor-Colleagues* (London: Constable, 1971); Philip Schlesinger, *Putting Reality Together: BBC News* (London: Constable, 1979). Other studies, based on the American news media, discuss many common practices and important parallels to British journalism. See, Herbert Gans, *Deciding What's News: A Study of CBS Evening News, NBC Nightly News, Newsweek and Time* (New York: Vintage, 1980); Gitlin, *The Whole World is Watching*; Hallin, *The 'Uncensored War'*.

15. Robert Darnton, 'All the news that fits we print', in *The Kiss of Lamourette: Reflections in Cultural History* (New York: Norton, 1990).

16. Paul Lashmar and James Oliver, *Britain's Secret Propaganda War* (Stroud: Sutton Publishing, 1998).

17. Andrew Defty, *Britain, America and Anti-Communist Propaganda, 1945–1953: The Information Research Department* (London: Routledge, 2004).

18. Tony Shaw, *British Cinema and the Cold War: The State, Propaganda and Consensus* (London: I. B. Tauris, 2001).

19. Philip Taylor, *British Propaganda in the Twentieth Century: Selling Democracy* (Edinburgh: Edinburgh University Press, 1999).

20. Alan Foster, 'The politicians, public opinion and the press: the storm over British military intervention in Greece in December 1944', *Journal of Contemporary History* 19 (1984); Alan Foster, 'The British Press and the Coming of the Cold War', in Anne Deighton (ed.), *Britain and the First Cold War* (London: Macmillan, 1990); Alan Foster, 'The Beaverbrook Press and appeasement: the second phase', *European History Quarterly* 21 (1991); Tony Shaw, 'The British popular press and the early Cold War', *History: Journal of the Historical Association* 83 (1998).

21. 'Death of the department that never was,' David Leigh, *The Guardian*, 27 January 1978; 'How the FO waged secret propaganda war in Britain,' Richard Fletcher, et al., *The Observer*, 29 January 1978; 'Ministry of Truth,' *The Leveller*, March 1978.

22. See, W. Scott Lucas and C. J. Morris, 'A very British crusade: The Information Research Department and the beginning of the Cold War', in Richard Aldrich (ed.), *British Intelligence, Strategy and the Cold War, 1945–51* (London: Routledge, 1992); Susan L. Carruthers, 'A Red under every bed? Anti-Communist propaganda and Britain's response to colonial insurgency', *Contemporary Record* 9 (1995); Hugh Wilford, 'The Information Research Department: Britain's secret Cold War weapon revealed', *Review of International Studies* 24 (1998); and Andrew Defty, '"Close and continuous liaison": British anti-Communist propaganda and cooperation with the

United States, 1950–51', *Intelligence and National Security* 17 (2002). Some examples of the journalistic coverage include: 'Celebrity team used in secret anti-Soviet campaign,' Nicholas Bethell, *The Times,* 17 August 1995; Stephen Dorril, 'The puppet masters,' *The Guardian*, 18 August 1995.

23. Stephen Dorril, *MI6: Inside the Covert World of Her Majesty's Secret Intelligence Service* (New York: Touchstone, 2000).
24. John Black, *Organising the Propaganda Instrument: The British Experience* (The Hague: Martinus Nijhoff, 1975); Frances Donaldson, *The British Council: The First Fifty Years* (London: Jonathan Cape, 1984).
25. Caroline Anstey, 'Foreign Office efforts to influence American opinion, 1945–49.' (Ph.D. diss.), London School of Economics and Political Science, 1984.
26. Gary Rawnsley, *Radio Diplomacy and Propaganda: The BBC and VOA in International Politics, 1956–64* (London: Macmillan, 1996).
27. Tony Shaw, *Eden, Suez and the Mass Media: Propaganda and Persuasion during the Suez Crisis* (London: I. B. Tauris, 1996).

Propaganda, Media and Hegemony:
The British Heritage

British power, prestige and media reach had been obvious and self-evident in the mid-nineteenth century. Reuters and the British journalism model followed the cables and the flag and both circled the world. At home ferocious battles to suppress radical 'unstamped' newspapers had given way to a laissez-faire system that favoured 'responsible' highly capitalised newspapers. But war, economic decline, foreign competition, and the growth at home of a complex state and a mass reading and listening public would shake that comparatively cosy world by 1945. Britain's leaders responded by subsidising Reuters, establishing quasi-official BBC overseas services, and developing sophisticated overt and covert propaganda. At home opinion control developed through censorship and wartime propaganda that morphed into the public relations professions.

Casting the Global Net

Power and news go together. When London began its rise as a centre of finance and commerce in the late seventeenth century it developed a business communication network through personal connections, coffee houses, the posts and the press.[1] The news industry and British capitalism expanded hand-in-hand. Access to rapid and accurate information – through the financial press, for example – was a key component in the global success of the City-based financial service sector.[2] The government recognised this advantage.

By the mid-nineteenth century Britain was poised for a global news and information takeoff. The invention of the telegraph and the subsequent development of submarine telegraph cables boosted the already successful City into a world-dominating role and made London the hub of a global cable network. Although the cables primarily carried commercial and financial information – the system's limited carrying capacity and prohibitive rates minimised international news – they did enable the development of the global news agencies, such as the London-based Reuters news agency. Two factors helped Reuters thrive: the City's increasingly powerful role in global capitalism, and the explosive growth of the newspaper press, especially in Britain, and its appetite for foreign news.[3] Agreements with French and German agencies allowed Reuters to dominate much of the world. The London press also served as a template for newspapers throughout much of the empire, much as the BBC later became a model for broadcasting systems. As the colonial media matured, London remained the centre, with journalists and proprietors shuttling between their colonial homes and Fleet Street, a pattern that would continue through the 1960s.[4]

The almost wholly private system began to depend more on government aid during the years before World War I – for strategic cable constructions, Reuters' subsidies, and mobilisation of white Dominion journalists.[5] The legacy of power and the government backing paid off in 1914–18. Britain first crippled Germany's ability to communicate by cutting its submarine cables and destroying remote radio stations. That forced most cable and radio communication through the British system, allowing a universal censorship system that targeted a full range of communication.[6] Reuters Managing Director Roderick Jones simultaneously ran the government's cable and wireless propaganda, including an Official Service for straightforward government propaganda and a less straightforward *Agence-Reuter* service that gave a government twist on ostensibly independent news.[7]

A few British leaders recognised after the war that Britain's weakened position meant the country needed official reinforcement to project British ideas, influence and products overseas. The government experimented with several propaganda organisations before setting up in 1934 the British Council to promote British culture. Radio provided another tool. By 1932 the quasi-official British Broadcasting Corporation was using short-wave to link London to the Dominions with the English-language Empire Service. The BBC started foreign language broadcasting in 1938, beaming Arabic programmes to the Middle East.[8] As European diplomacy grew tenser, the British expanded the Foreign Office's British Official News Service and increased the number of information officers at overseas missions.[9]

Throughout the interwar years American news agencies were putting pressure on Reuters, and state-subsidised French and German agencies were selling news at below market costs.[10] Bottom-line pressures and an increasingly tense international situation led to a July 1938 'gentlemen's agreement' between Reuters and the government. The government subsidised Reuters to bolster its service to the Balkans, Middle East, and Far East. In exchange, Reuters let the Foreign Office suggest areas and types of coverage and, more importantly, gave them the right to veto Reuters' choice for its next managing director. A boardroom coup in February 1941 upset this deal. Jones' FO-approved successor, Christopher Chancellor, reorganised Reuters as a trust, brought in the national newspapers for new capital and loudly proclaimed its independence from the government. But that government continued to subsidise the agency quietly by granting Reuters preferential cable rates.[11]

In World War II British power over the cable system – and the cutting of German and Italian cables – once again meant Britain could censor beyond the boundaries of the empire through Cable and Wireless' London headquarters and scrutinise foreign traffic passing through the British system elsewhere.[12] Neutrals such as the United States increasingly depended on censored British news of the war. Other strategic, but unprofitable areas got their news from ostensibly independent government 'news agencies'. The Cairo-based Arab News

Agency supplied news in English and Arabic about the Arab world to Arab media. Britanova covered the Balkans and Near East.[13]

During World War I the Foreign Office's War Propaganda Bureau, better known as Wellington House, quietly developed the signature style of British propaganda. It selectively packaged seemingly accurate facts in books, pamphlets and articles that were indirectly distributed to elite foreign audiences. Some were anonymous; others were written by top British intellectuals and authors whom Wellington House had recruited. In addition, the government also planted news articles in foreign presses, bought up newspaper distributors and subsidised friendly foreign publicists. Other, more notorious, propaganda relied on unverified hearsay and innuendo, chiefly on the subject of German atrocities.[14]

World War II saw many of the same British propaganda techniques in neutral countries, especially the USA in 1939–41. The New York-based British Security Coordination worked with pro-British American front groups, planted news stories and damaging rumours and ran a short-wave radio station in Boston and subsidised a news agency to carry its propaganda.[15] In Europe the spread of German power forced the British to rely more on subversive and psychological warfare techniques in occupied Europe. The BBC became extremely important in reaching these markets, as did 'black' stations broadcasting disinformation to German troops. Control over propaganda was split among often feuding agencies – the Political Warfare Executive, the Special Operations Executive and the Ministry of Information – but the BBC managed to keep its statutory independence while expanding rapidly.[16]

Building and Policing a Domestic Consensus

Throughout the second half of the nineteenth century the British government's involvement in communications and the press had been mixed. The Royal Post Office took over the domestic telegraph and telephone services as public utilities, but the press was largely free in the era of laissez-faire, and lifting of the various stamp taxes had helped create a new-style, highly capitalised 'responsible' press.[17] The rise of a mass-circulation popular press and growing elite doubts about public rationality began to change the equation. Democracy and mass society were facts of life, but they needed to be properly guided by experts for the best results.[18]

War jitters and spy scares caused the government to reassess laissez-faire press freedom in 1911, creating the Admiralty, War Office and Press Committee (D-Notice Committee) and pushing through the Official Secrets Act. The committee brought military and press representatives together for cosy self-censorship. The military men would tell the committee what newspapers should not publish, the committee would usually agree and send out discreet D-Notices to the press describing the information and advising them not to print it. There was no direct penalty for violators, but those who strayed from the cosy D-Notice system always had to worry about the club behind the velvet curtain – the Official

Secrets Act of 1911.[19] The law punished any unauthorised release or publication of any official information and has been used inconsistently and capriciously over the years. The main function of this law, and the even more stringent 1920 update, was to intimidate journalists and their potential government sources.[20]

Wartime brought a new level of scrutiny and growing use of propaganda to mobilise the population. In the First World War news was restricted at the front, censored at headquarters and limited by D-Notices and advisory letters, but most newspapers needed no prompting to print sanitised and distorted accounts of the fighting.[21] In the Second World War the Ministry of Information, after initial bungling, discovered that the British public had 'a very high degree of common sense'. It shifted from emotional exhortation to more prosaic and effective forms of propaganda – explanation, instruction, interpretation and especially news. Minister Brendan Bracken understood that the MOI could be most effective by ensuring a continuous and voluminous flow of news to gratified journalists. And he was willing and able to fight the service ministers for it. By the end of the war the MOI, press, and public were 'working smoothly in harness'.[22] The *Newspaper World* pointed out that the British press knew much more than it printed and that it 'is loyal and trustworthy in things that really matter'.[23]

In World War I the Defence of the Realm Act covered those outside the pro-war consensus by prohibiting the spreading of 'false or prejudicial reports' resulting in any disaffection or interference with diplomacy, military recruitment or the prosecution of the war and later became even more draconian. Raids, seizures and bans on overseas circulation further limited dissent.[24] In 1939–45 similar emergency regulations again limited dissent. The government suppressed the fascist *Action* newspaper in 1940, the Communist *Daily Worker* in January 1941 and seriously considered shutting down the critical and mass-circulation *Daily Mirror* in 1942.[25] Even after the war began to turn in Britain's favour the government continued to keep a vigilant eye on press dissent. A right-wing Polish-language weekly, published in Britain, had been sharply critical of the Soviet Union to the increasing irritation of the Soviet embassy. In an attempt to smooth relations with the Soviets, Foreign Secretary Anthony Eden pressed for it to be banned in early 1944. It was.[26]

Dailies, Weeklies and the BBC: Post-war State of Play

By mid-century Britain was a media-saturated island. The public service British Broadcasting Corporation ran with considerable autonomy a radio and television monopoly, movie studios churned out cinema newsreels on current events and a plethora of newspapers and weekly journals were published on Fleet Street and in the provinces. Reuters handled foreign news while its domestic contemporary, the Press Association, handled the strictly British news.

After the war paper rationing kept issues small but advertising profits high, while a Royal Commission on the Press hunted for evidence of bias and monopoly. Daily circulation had gone from 17.8 million in 1937 to 28.5 million in 1947, but annual surveys beginning in 1940 showed that public perceptions of inaccuracy and bias meant they influenced fewer people.[27] When readers had little first-hand experience of a subject such as foreign affairs, however, the newspaper could still be influential.[28] Management, content and style varied widely among national newspapers:

- The *Daily Express* had perfected the formula of eye-catching design and upbeat sensationalism to become the country's top-selling newspaper by the 1940s. Owner Lord Beaverbrook's hands-on management style gave an idiosyncratic look to news and views – he was a Churchill confidant and a tireless Empire booster, but he also admired Stalin, distrusted the USA and consistently hired left-wing journalists. Beaverbrook ran his *Sunday Express* and *Evening Standard* in similar ways.[29]

- The *Daily Mirror* featured left-wing populism, sharp design, bawdy cartoons and snappy writing, and was growing quickly. Although criticism of the conservative establishment was common, 'serious' news was not the *Daily Mirror*'s specialty. The *Daily Mirror* controlled the *Sunday Pictorial*.[30]

- The TUC and Odhams Press jointly controlled the *Daily Herald*, and after Labour's 1945 victory the *Daily Herald* became a loyal supporter of government foreign policy. If its coverage deviated too much, a phone call from Foreign Secretary Ernest Bevin would stop a major foreign policy story.[31]

- The *News Chronicle* sought to avoid sensationalism and to bring serious news to its readers.[32] Neither the owners, nor the chairman nor even the editor decisively controlled the newsroom; the result was an occasionally unfocused paper that was usually farther to the left on Cold War issues than the owners would have liked.[33]

- The Camrose family ran the *Daily Telegraph* on a day-to-day basis and emphasised straight news presented in a grey, rigid style informed by consistent Conservative politics. It was a success. In April 1947 the *Daily Telegraph* was selling 1 million copies a day.[34]

- *The Times* had a special position in British journalism because of the widespread expectation that it would support the government's foreign policy. This gave the impression overseas that it was a quasi-official government organ, and led to ill-tempered disputes when the government and *The Times* diverged, as they did in the 1940s. *The Times* also had extensive on-the-spot coverage of diplomatic and foreign news.

- The *Manchester Guardian* in 1945 sold only 58,000 copies a day but had a worldwide reputation for accuracy, thorough reporting and forthright Liberal editorials.[35]

- The Kemsley family owned a stable of undistinguished and cautious newspapers and the 'quality' *Sunday Times*. The *Sunday Times* highlighted serious news, features and reviews. The Kemsleys also owned the *Daily Graphic, Sunday Graphic, Sunday Chronicle,* and a chain of eighteen provincial papers.[36]

- The cooperatively owned *Reynolds News* had a long history of radicalism, which it continued, along with the standards of sex, crime, and gossip, throughout the early Cold War. The diffuse, non-commercial ownership gave de facto control to the staff, who provided *Reynolds News* readers with serious news and a Cold War view that was distinctly friendly to the Soviet Union well into the early 1950s.[37]
- The Sunday *Observer* attracted more dynamic and cosmopolitan correspondents and writers than any other British newspaper in the post-war years. The *Observer* provided in-depth, independent coverage of serious issues of high politics and seriously challenged the *Sunday Times*' claim to be the top 'quality' Sunday paper.[38]

Among periodicals the weekly political press still carried a great deal of influence despite their small circulations. During the Attlee years the *New Statesman and Nation* provided critical left wing news and opinion that frequently enraged the government while *Tribune* was usually more supportive. On the right *The Spectator* led for the Conservatives while *The Economist* gave news and commentary with a right-wing Liberal perspective. Among general interest magazines, *Picture Post* carried the most clout.

The BBC had grown in size and stature during the war. In a 1946 White Paper the government evaluated the BBC and confirmed its autonomy in domestic broadcasting and – to a qualified extent – in overseas broadcasting. The BBC was required to consult with the government to produce overseas programming in 'the national interest'.[39] On the domestic side the BBC split programming into three distinct strands: a standard Home Service, a plebeian Light Service and an elite Third Programme.

Before television became widely established the biweekly cinema newsreels were an important source of visual news images. By the late 1940s the newsreels were 'venal and bad journalism' and not even very good entertainment. One major cinema chain found them too boring to show in its regular line up.[40] The government also had a low opinion of the newsreels.

> (COI film expert John) Grierson describes the newsreel editorial person as a combination of childlike innocence, gross corruption and a stupidity only slightly concealed by low animal cunning. They're said to be very susceptible to flattery and responsive to any set of circumstances that will enable them to feel that they are being specially favoured and 'let into' state secrets.[41]

Despite their poor journalistic quality, British newsreels managed to provide visual information for much of the world by regularly exchanging footage with other countries' newsreel companies. The companies also had a thriving business exporting and re-dubbing British newsreels in the Commonwealth, colonies, and other spheres of British cultural influence.[42] The government could easily influence the newsreel companies through the COI.[43] The Foreign Office subsidised newsreel cameramen's trips to the Middle East and paid for the newsreel companies to include film of naval manoeuvres to publicise the Brussels Pact in 1949.[44]

Post-war Censorship, Propaganda and Spin

In 1945, after six years of total war, the government was deeply involved in the news and information business. They retreated from some of the most intrusive habits – mandatory cable censorship and emergency legislation – but kept many of the other war-bred measures. To bolster British influence overseas the government maintained overt propaganda through the Foreign Office, an expanded BBC overseas service and quiet aid to Reuters. Domestic propaganda initially revolved around Labour's reconstruction and nationalisation programmes. Censorship continued to keep information out of the public sphere and allegedly away from unfriendly foreigners.

The D-Notice resurfaced a few months after VE Day, as the trade press had expected it would, for 'highly confidential service matters'.[45] Tight wartime guidance had conditioned the press to look for cues on how to handle military issues; the service ministries were happy to oblige them. Chief wartime censor, the genial Admiral G. P. Thomson continued as secretary of the committee. Even the Communist *Daily Worker* was 'very willing to co-operate' in the revised self-censorship.[46] At the first 'sensible and amicable' meeting the military men told the journalists that they merely wished to be consulted about certain security issues and assured them that the committee would not become 'any modified form of censorship in peacetime'.[47] Most British journalists shared a consensus with the service representatives – some information had to be withheld in the national interest. They just sometimes disagreed about how much information should be held back.

Government public relations had been growing steadily during the interwar years, accelerated sharply during the war and stayed at a high level in the post-war years. At Downing Street Prime Minister Clement Attlee appointed socialist journalist and MOI news chief Francis Williams as his public relations adviser.[48] Ministry public relations officers organised specialist correspondent groups, who alone would be invited to regular briefings.[49] The Foreign Office News Department under the leadership of William Ridsdale used a similar system and the department's close relationship to the diplomatic press corps to influence coverage. A guide on media management, delivered to the interdepartmental Russia Committee in 1946, serves as a valuable clue on the department's operations and how it viewed the press. In this document the News Department broke down its news brokering functions into five main categories, based on the importance of the news and the publicity desired:

- An inconspicuous leak to one newspaper. This would not attract much interest but would be on the public record and thus could later be cited by the Foreign Office.

- A more important leak, made with the intention of catching the attention of other newspapers both within Britain and abroad and giving 'rise to inquiries which can be answered in such a way as to suggest that the information is given reluctantly'.
- Multiple leaks to diplomatic correspondents who would then publish without any indication that their stories were 'inspired'. These leading diplomatic correspondents 'can be taken into closer confidence as to the facts'.
- Leaks to the news agencies, primarily the Press Association, 'whose correspondents can be relied upon to present it without attribution in a form approved by us'.
- Indiscriminate individual leaks attributed to 'informed quarters'. The two most general methods were press conference releases attributed to a 'Foreign Office spokesman' or 'official circles' and official press releases supplemented by press conferences and individual interviews.

The news department was confident in their abilities to manipulate the press: 'Information passed to the press by this means is inevitably presented with a varying degree of emphasis which is controlled by the News Department in the light of their consultations with the other departments'.[50]

The wartime agencies handling propaganda – MOI, PWE and SOE – were dissolved quickly after the war. MI6 took over SOE remnants while PWE personnel and functions tended to gravitate toward the Foreign Office.[51] The Labour cabinet followed through with coalition plans to break up the MOI. The cabinet would supervise public relations through a pair of ministerial committees – one for domestic work, one for overseas.[52] Individual ministries would look after their own public relations and the newly created Central Office of Information would handle the detail of both overseas and domestic propaganda, concentrating on productivity and export drives at home, and 'projection of Britain' abroad.[53]

The domestic public relations agencies had plenty of enemies. Journalists disliked them because they interfered with access and tried to both manipulate and spoon feed them. Conservatives disliked them because they saw government 'public relations' as pushing Labour Party propaganda at considerable taxpayer expense. Also, they didn't think the COI and the ministerial public relations officers did a very good job.[54]

Post-war Global Media Reach

The British government was deeply committed to maintaining Britain's great power status after the war, and a large-scale media influence was almost as essential as military power in achieving that goal. Britain's legacy gave it an advantage, but the government had to work hard to keep from losing it. The Foreign Office coached and subsidised Reuters, and financed ostensibly independent regional news agencies for areas where Reuters could not compete. The government capitalised on the reach and credibility the BBC had acquired during the war and tried to maintain as much of the key elements as possible. But their relative weakness combined with the increasing competitiveness of American, Soviet and nationalist news sources meant that the British would turn toward government propaganda – overt and covert, grey and white – to maintain British influence. This need was recognised early on. In the official, secret, history of the PWE put together in early 1947, author David Garnett noted that propaganda, as part of political warfare, was inevitable.

> The increase of popular education, the development of wireless
> broadcasts and television, or advertising and the study of mass psychology,
> make it probable that psychological pressures of various kinds will be
> increasingly applied by one country to another. Indeed, these pressures are
> to-day being applied particularly in the form of 'wars of nerve'.
> In any war in which the USSR or the United States are involved,
> political warfare is almost certain to play a large part, for the Russians will
> wish to make full use of the Communists in every country as agents for
> propaganda and subversion, and the Americans believe in Psychological
> Warfare, if only as a variety of advertising.[55]

Britain was still an important world news centre in 1945 despite its precipitous decline as a Great Power. Reuters called London home, as did more than twenty other independent agencies and syndication services.[56] The imperial cable, radio and transport infrastructure made London a logical point from which to cover or transmit world news. Half of the American Associated Press' world news passed through London in the early 1950s because of the speed and low price of the cable and radio communication.[57]

At victory Reuters faced mixed horizons. It was the leading member of an exclusive club, with 200 full-time staff abroad, service to 3,000 foreign newspapers and a 500,000-word flow through London every day.[58] There was no substantial European competition: the German DNB was defunct and the French Havas/AFP was in a painful transition. But the agency worried about competition from its own government's secretly subsidised news services during post-war months. Chancellor worried enough to write to Bevin and argue that Reuters' reputation for independence could help it better represent British interests. 'In simple terms I can express it in this way – is Britain to have a REUTERS or a TASS?'[59] The American Associated Press, United Press and International News Service were poised for global competition – loudly calling for a 'free flow' of information and end to government subsidies, which would benefit them.

The American pressure led Reuters to renegotiate its deal with the government. The transmission subsidies ended, but under the new Radcliffe-Chancellor Agreement the Foreign Office would pay artificially inflated subscriptions totalling £35,000.[60] This included some £8,500 'for the use of the service in special ways and outside the scope of the Radcliffe-Chancellor agreement'.[61] This combined with Chancellor's strict austerity policy helped Reuters survive, but not thrive. By 1947 the government's subscriptions to Reuters had settled at some £30,000 a year. But the Foreign Office had increasing doubts as to the strength and effectiveness of Reuters and began reassessing its relationship to the agency as the Radcliffe–Chancellor agreement neared its end and international tensions increased. After a canvassing, British diplomats reported that Reuters correspondents were often low-paid and low-quality, and frequently were not respected by journalists and opinion leaders in their host countries. Consequently, the Foreign Office concluded British-oriented news was often not competitive with that from other news agencies, especially in the Middle East and Latin America.[62] The Foreign Office's prescription called for better quality Reuters representatives in more locations and a willingness for the agency to accept short-term losses in unprofitable but strategic bureaus.[63] That cost money, which Reuters did not have.

The Foreign Office were considering a high-level approach to the Reuters' board to 'make them see the error of their ways and get them to improve their services' in October 1948.[64] Reuters had known about the probe (and had complained) but, just as in 1938, Reuters themselves made the first move. Chancellor wrote to information supervisor Christopher Warner about the problems the agency was experiencing in China, and suggested that increased government subscriptions could help keep Reuters competitive in many overseas outposts.

> The point here to bear in mind is that where Reuters operates with a local deficit the position is marginal. If a British Embassy or Legation can allocate a couple of hundred pounds a year for delivery of the Reuter service this contribution to local costs may easily be the decisive factor when we have to consider whether or not we can keep an office going.[65]

In December 1948 Warner met with Chancellor. They agreed that any large subsidy would be too obvious, but that in certain cases help from the government such as 'an increased subscription on behalf of H.M. Embassy or reduced charges by Cable and Wireless' could be crucial. Chancellor said that he would appeal to the Foreign Office for help when necessary, and asked Warner to keep the arrangement highly confidential because of potential difficulties with the Reuters' board. In exchange for the government largess Chancellor promised close cooperation with the Foreign Office.

> Mr. Chancellor will be very glad to keep close contact with me on a personal basis, to discuss with me any criticisms or suggestions that we may have to make and to consider with me in each case ways and means of taking action.[66]

The arrangement between Warner and Chancellor set the pattern for the future. A few weeks later the subject of Reuters' representation in Latin America came up, and Warner stated plainly that higher payments by British missions would be 'the kind of concealed subsidy which Reuters could consider'.[67]

The Foreign Office's MI6 had close relations with a more specialised agency that the Kemsley newspaper group had created in 1945. Ian Fleming ran the

Foreign and Imperial News Service's eighty-eight foreign correspondents, and provided news copy to Kemsley's twenty-one British newspapers and some 600 overseas customers.[68] Most of the correspondents were seasoned journalists but some were actually MI6 agents who Kemsley had given journalistic 'cover'.[69]

After the war the Foreign Office continued to subsidise the Arab News Agency, Britanova agency and the India-based Globe Agency, which split into an Indian Globe and a Pakistani Star agency with the sub-continent's partition. *Picture Post* publisher Edward Hulton was the front man for the agencies, but company records clearly indicate the official provenance.[70] The FO's Ivone Kirkpatrick told Reuters' Cecil Fleetwood-May in August 1946 that Britanova would continue operating in Turkey 'for the time being' because the Foreign Office did not want to leave a news vacuum that would be filled by foreign services.[71] The Star agency quickly began to look at partnerships and news exchanges with agencies in other Moslem countries, presumably including ANA. Reuters' Cairo chief speculated that it was to get a tight hold on the Middle Eastern news market to pre-empt any nationalist news agencies.[72]

Although these news agencies were covertly funded as part of the British global news strategy, Reuters correspondents described the Britanova and Globe output as dull – rewritten British feature stories, diplomatic commentary and news of scientific discoveries.[73] The ANA had a more comprehensive, competitive operation with ninety-four staff members throughout the Arab world and the West, and service to 'virtually all daily papers within the Arab world and most weeklies'.[74] In early 1948 the covert news agencies were reorganised under the London-based Near and Far East News Group (NAFEN). Britanova's functions were apparently subsumed under NAFEN, while Globe became NAFEN (Asia) in 1952. All four specialised in news of interest to the Moslem world and kept up a news exchange with each other, Sharq al Adna radio, All-India Radio and several apparently unconnected agencies such as Indonesia's Antara agency.[75]

The British government covered the Middle Eastern airwaves as well. In addition, to the BBC Arabic service the MI6 also ran an ostensibly independent and very popular medium-wave radio station – Sharq al Adna, also known as the Near East Broadcasting Station. The intelligence services had set up the station in 1941 in Palestine, and moved it to Cyprus after the 1948 creation of Israel. It broadcast music, religious programming, news and commentary and was widely popular in the Arab world in the late 1940s and early 1950s.[76]

The BBC emerged from World War II with a greatly expanded audience and a good reputation for objectivity and truth-telling. The number of hours in the overseas services had been scaled back toward the end of the war, especially in the European language services, but they still comprised the largest international broadcasting system in the world.[77] In 1946 the BBC were broadcasting 714 hours a week in forty-three languages. In general, listeners tuned into foreign radio services when their local services were of poor quality, unreliable or untrustworthy; they also tuned in during crises.

Control was sometimes a problem. A July 1946 White Paper clearly spelled out the BBC overseas services' responsibility to consult with the government so as to produce programming in 'the national interest'. The government's overseas departments paid the bills, determined the languages and hours broadcast, and had the right to give 'advice'.[78] But they operated with the public service ethos and a sense of independence that differentiated them from either commercial broadcasters or straightforward propagandists. The BBC's Director-General William Haley fought tenaciously for BBC independence and objectivity, especially for home programming. The overseas departments were under the much different leadership of General Sir Ian Jacob, a career Army officer with no experience in journalism or broadcasting recommended by the Foreign Office.[79] Haley repeatedly confided to his diary worries about Jacob's background as a 'man under authority' and how that experience might short-change the BBC's independence.[80] Jacob himself saw his job as another type of national service.

> I realised that much of my experience in the Cabinet office, particularly in the last year or two when I had handled most of the business of a semi-military, semi-political nature and had worked closely with the Foreign Office, seemed to fit me for a duty where I should be directing the voice of this country in what was rapidly becoming the 'Cold War.' The out-and-out political warfare of the war might be giving place to a more measured form of broadcasting, but the task would still be of national importance.[81]

Despite this seeming clarity there were frequently disputes with the Foreign Office over policy and approach, especially toward the Soviet Union, Communism and nationalist movements.

The Foreign Office inherited some of the overseas MOI staff and handled much of the straightforward foreign propaganda in the post-war years, initially in conjunction with the COI. The Commonwealth Relations and Colonial offices operated at just a fraction of the FO's scale and scope until the mid-1950s.[82] The FO's Information Policy Department handled most of the open propaganda, leaving to the Information Services Department much of the mundane work with the COI.[83] And after January 1948 the IRD would handle anti-Communist propaganda.

The COI produced movies, published magazines, distributed photos, newspapers, magazines and books, and ran the successor to the British Official Wireless, which was renamed the London Press Service.[84] In early 1948 the LPS consisted of one main service, which was delivered in seven thematic transmissions, and several regional services.[85] Information officers at British missions furnished LPS stories to their contacts and used the overall service as raw material for embassy bulletins; LPS seldom handled breaking news.[86] The FO and COI also published and distributed 50,000 copies weekly inside the Soviet Union of the incongruously named *British Ally*, which had been set up in different circumstances in 1942.[87]

Conclusion

Two world wars and an economic slump had hurt British competitiveness in the global media, especially in the face of aggressive American expansion. After 1945 the government recognised the need to remain competitive, so continued to subsidise Reuters, maintained the BBC External Services and British Council at high levels and kept the wartime covert agencies in South Asia and the Near and Middle East. The Foreign Office absorbed many MOI and PWE personnel as they strengthened their system of information officers around the world; the wartime propaganda experience had given Britain a reputation for propaganda expertise that it would use to its benefit.

At home British journalists were conditioned after World War II to an almost reflexive deference to government-defined national security concerns, and accepted the continuing use of the D-Notice Committee and the Official Secrets Act without a murmur. They were less likely to accept the staff of propagandists, or public information officers that stayed on after the war as government public relations became institutionalised through offices like the COI. The press' readers for their part were less likely to accept as gospel the news they read each day, though levels of newspaper reading had shot up during the war and remained high afterward.

Notes

1. Stephens, *History of News*, pp. 65–9, 135–47, 163–6.
2. P. J. Cain and A. G. Hopkins, *British Imperialism: Innovation and Expansion, 1688–1914* (London: Longman, 1993), p. 21.
3. Donald Read, *The Power of News: The History of Reuters, 1849–1989* (Oxford: Oxford University Press, 1992).
4. Simon J. Potter, *News and the British World: The Emergence of an Imperial Press System, 1876–1922* (Oxford: Oxford University Press, 2003), pp. 14, 22.
5. Ibid, pp. 70, 152; P. M. Kennedy, 'Imperial cable communications and strategy, 1870–1914', *English Historical Review* 86 (1971).
6. Daniel Headrick, *Invisible Weapon: Telecommunications and International Politics, 1851–1945* (New York: Oxford University Press, 1991), pp. 140–9.
7. Read, *The Power of News*, pp. 127–30.
8. Gerard Mansell, *Let Truth Be Told: 50 Years of BBC External Broadcasting* (London: Weidenfeld and Nicolson, 1982), pp. 1–19, 21–39, 43–54.
9. Taylor, *British Propaganda in the Twentieth Century*, pp. 71–82
10. Read, *The Power of News*, pp. 172–83.
11. John Lawrenson and Lionel Barber, *The Price of Truth: The Story of the Reuters £££ Millions* (London: Mainstream Publishing, 1986), pp. 66–72, 88–90.
12. Headrick, *Invisible Weapon*, pp. 222–4.
13. Lashmar and Oliver, *Britain's Secret Propaganda War*, pp. xiv, 77–82.
14. Sanders and Taylor, *British Propaganda*, pp. 130–1 and 183–5; Taylor, *British Propaganda in the Twentieth Century*, pp. 35–46.

15. British Security Coordination, *British Security Coordination: The Secret History of British Intelligence in the Americas, 1940–1945* (New York: Fromm International, 1999), pp. 55–9, 123–32, 102–14; Nicholas Cull, *Selling War: The British Propaganda Campaign against American 'Neutrality' in World War II* (New York: Oxford University Press, 1995); Susan Brewer, *To Win the Peace: British Propaganda in the United States during World War II* (Ithaca: Cornell, 1997), pp. 11–54.
16. Robert Cole, *Britain and the War of Words in Neutral Europe, 1939–1945* (New York: St Martin Press, 1990).
17. Jean Seaton and James Curran, *Power without Responsibility: The Press and Broadcasting in Britain*, 6th edn (London: Routledge, 2003), pp. 24–37.
18. Qualter, *Opinion Control in the Democracies*, pp. 16–20.
19. Alasdair Palmer, 'The history of the D-Notice Committee', in Christopher Andrew and David Dilks (eds), *The Missing Dimension: Governments and Intelligence Communities in the Twentieth Century* (Urbana, IL: University of Illinois Press, 1984).
20. Departmental Committee on Section 2 of the Official Secrets Act 1911 [Franks Committee], *Report of the Committee*, vol. 1, Cmnd. 5104, (London, 1972); David Hooper, *Official Secrets: The Use and Abuse of the Official Secrets Act* (London: Secker and Warburg, 1987), pp. 11–15.
21. Phillip Knightley, *The First Casualty: From the Crimea to Vietnam: The War Correspondent as Hero, Propagandist, and Myth Maker* (New York: Harcourt Brace Jovanovich, 1975), pp. 80–135; Taylor and Saunders, *British Propaganda*, pp. 20–2.
22. Calder, *The People's War: Britain, 1939–45* (New York: Pantheon, 1969), p. 507; Ian McLaine, *Ministry of Morale: Home Front Morale and the Ministry of Information in World War II* (London: Allen and Unwin, 1979), pp. 240–4, 276.
23. 'Notes on the news', *Newspaper World*, 10 February 1945.
24. Tania Rose, *Aspects of Political Censorship, 1914–1918* (Hull: University of Hull Press, 1995), pp. 47–52, 107.
25. Curran and Seaton, *Power Without Responsibility*, pp.58–62; David Lewis, *Illusions of Grandeur: Mosley, Fascism and British Society, 1931–81* (Manchester: Manchester University Press, 1987), p. 233.
26. PRO FO371/39441 C8121/74/55, Frank Roberts Memo, 31 July 1944.
27. Mass Observation, *The Press and Its Readers* (London: Art & Technics, 1949), p. 92; *Royal Commission on the Press*, 1947–1949: Report, Cmd.7700 (London: HMSO, 1949), pp. 5–6.
28. Mass Observation, *The Press and Its Readers*, pp. 85–8.
29. Anne Chisholm and Michael Davie, *Beaverbrook: A Life* (London: Hutchinson, 1992), pp. 420–83.
30. Matthew Engel, *Tickle the Public: One Hundred Years of the Popular Press* (London: Victor Gollancz, 1996), pp. 145–201.
31. PRO FO800/494 PRS/46/40, Attlee to Bevin, 12 September 1946.
32. Mass Observation, *The Press and Its Readers*, p. 112.
33. David Hubback, *No Ordinary Press Baron: A Life of Walter Layton* (London: Weidenfeld and Nicolson, 1985), pp. 196–204.
34. Duff Hart-Davis, *The House the Berrys Built* (London: Hodder & Stoughton, 1990), pp. 64–149.
35. David Ayerst, *The Guardian: Biography of a Newspaper* (London: Collins, 1971), p. 573.
36. *Royal Commission on the Press*, p. 16.

37. *Royal Commission on the Press*, p. 18; Gordon Schaffer interview.
38. Richard Cockett, *David Astor and the Observer* (London: Andre Deutsch); William Clark, *From Three Worlds: Memoirs*, (London: Sidgwick and Jackson, 1986), pp. 114–45.
39. *White Paper on Broadcasting*, Cmd. 6852, 1946.
40. 'Newsreels must find a new policy', *Penguin Film Review*, 1949; 'Do you get bored during the newsreels?' *Daily Express*, 6 July 1949.
41. PRO FO1110/50 PR230, MacLaren Note.
42. Political and Economic Planning (for Arts Enquiry), *The Factual Film* (London: Oxford University Press, 1947).
43. PRO CAB134/545, Overseas Information Committee minutes, 17 April 1947; PRO T254/2, Economic Planning Board – Crisis Publicity, October 1947.
44. Newsreel Association Papers, Box 4, Newsreel Association of Great Britain and Northern Ireland, Meeting Minutes, 15 September 1949.
45. 'End of censorship', *Newspaper World*, 8 September 1945.
46. BBC WAC R28/5/1, 'D-Notice Committee' Meeting Minutes, 8 November 1945.
47. BBC WAC R28/5/1, A. P. Ryan to Haley, 5 October 1945.
48. Lord Francis-William, *Nothing So Strange* (New York: American Heritage Press, 1970), pp. 216–7.
49. Francis Williams, *Press, Parliament and People* (London: Heinemann, 1946), pp. 136–7.
50. PRO FO371/56788 N12332/140/G38, 'Circular to Members of Russia Committee, Committee on Policy Towards Russia, Annex 11: Scope of News Department Activities', 25 September 1946.
51. Richard J. Aldrich, *Hidden Hand: Britain, America and Cold War Secret Intelligence* (New York: Overlook Press, 2002), pp. 73–4, 79.
52. PRO CAB 128/5, Cabinet Minute 16 (46), 8 February 1946.
53. Marjorie Ogilvy-Webb, *The Government Explains: A Study of the Information Services* (London: Allen and Unwin, 1965), pp. 70–2.
54. 'Cost of govt. publicity "A gross extravagance" ', *Newspaper World*, 28 May 1949.
55. PRO CAB 102/609, David Garnett, *Official History of the Political Warfare Executive*, [n.d.].
56. *Royal Commission on the Press*, pp. 49–53.
57. UNESCO, *News Agencies: Their Structure and Operation* (Paris: UNESCO, 1953), p. 46.
58. *Royal Commission on the Press*, p. 52.
59. Reuters Archives, Chancellor to Bevin, 8 January 1946.
60. Read, *The Power of News*, pp. 246–56.
61. PRO FO953/118 P4324/21/950, 'Reuters News Agency', [n.d.].
62. PRO FO953/117–119.
63. PRO FO953/117 P2924, 'Reuters News Agency', compiled by R. S. Smith, 9 February 1948.
64. PRO FO953/118 P7720/21/950, Wardour to A. A. F. Haigh, 6 October 1948.
65. PRO FO953/119, Chancellor to Warner, 30 September 1948.
66. PRO FO953/119 P10539/21//950, Warner Memo, 30 December 1948.
67. PRO FO953/119 P10539/21/950, Warner Memo, January–February 1949.
68. Andrew Lycett, *Ian Fleming: The Man Behind James Bond* (Atlanta: Turner Publishing, 1995), pp. 159–219.
69. Ibid., pp. 169–70.

70. Lashmar and J. Oliver, *Britain's Secret Propaganda War*, pp. xiv, 77–82; Reuters Archives, Britanova File, Sporburgh to Chancellor, 6 December 1944, Chancellor to Herlihy, 6 December 1944; Reuters Archives, ANA File, Reel 108, Chancellor to Ridsdale, 21 January 1948.
71. Reuters Archives, Britanova File, Note for the General Manager by Mr Fleetwood-May, 19 August 1946.
72. Reuters Archives ANA File, Reel 108, Nicholson to Secretary (London), 28 March 1948.
73. Reuters Archives, Britanova File, Robert Biggio to Fleetwood-May, 4 September 1947, News Editor (Bombay) to Secretary (London), 24 March 1948.
74. UNESCO, *News Agencies*, p. 138.
75. Ibid., pp. 137–9.
76. Richard Beeston, 'My part in Britain's Secret War', *The Times,* 16 September 1994; Richard Norton-Taylor, 'BBC connived with MI6 to oust Nasser', *The Guardian,* 16 September 1994; PRO FO953/61 PME1499/1499/G, Ivone Kirkpatrick Memo, 30 September 1946.
77. Mansell, *Let Truth Be Told,* pp. 212–4.
78. *White Paper on Broadcasting,* Cmd. 6852.
79. Asa Briggs, *Governing the BBC,* (London: British Broadcasting Corporation, 1979), pp. 210–2; PRO FO953/4D, Ivone Kirkpatrick Memo, 8 April 1946.
80. Haley Papers, Haley Policy Diary, 13/35, 19 October 1946; Haley Diary, 13/7, Diary entries for 27 October 1951 and 29 September 1952.
81. Ian Jacob Papers, Draft Autobiography, p. 177.
82. Black, *Organising the Propaganda Instrument,* pp. 25–7, 30–1.
83. Ibid., pp. 18–19.
84. *Annual Report of the Central Office of Information for the Year 1947–48*, Cmd. 7567 (London: HMSO, 1949), p. 43.
85. Ibid., pp. 37–8.
86. Black, *Organising the Propaganda Instrument,* pp. 16–19; PRO INF12/23, 'Report on the production and uses of London press and regional services', 25 January 1949.
87. Quoted in 'The rise and fall of *Britansky Soyuznik*: a case study in Soviet response to British propaganda of the mid-1940s', *The Historical Journal* 41 (1998), p. 296.

2

Media, Propaganda, Consensus and the Soviet Union, 1941–8

As world war segued into an uneasy peace in 1945 the Soviet Union was the wild card in international politics. The outside world had tremendous difficulties in establishing even the most basic facts about life in the USSR. Yet this country had become a military titan and political superpower whose nature and intentions concerned much of the world, especially the victorious, precarious British Empire.

The British diplomatic elite initially believed they could peacefully coexist with the Stalinist state, despite serious doubts among the chiefs of staff. But British tactics designed to maintain status and to secure American support, coupled with ominous Soviet moves against British allies and interests, pushed already tense relations toward the breaking point within months of VE Day. Rough negotiations and steady disillusion followed. But despite Foreign Secretary Ernest Bevin's distrust of the USSR, he knew that a large segment of his Labour Party did not share this feeling. Also, the British government preserved some ambivalence, some faith in negotiations through to the end of 1947.[1]

From 1941 to 1945 British journalists largely viewed Soviet news through the prism, or journalistic frame, of the Anglo–Soviet alliance. This was conditioned by the fog of war, censorship and propaganda. It all led to more stories about their Soviet allies' virtues instead of their vices. After victory some news could still fit in the alliance frame, but more and more would not fit as Anglo–Soviet relations deteriorated and British leaders and journalists raised awkward questions about the future of those relations. This shift created a demand for stories dissecting and analysing the roots of the Soviets' behaviour. The Foreign Office monitored and coaxed the media toward a more critical line on the Soviet Union, but it was a negotiated and consensual process. By January 1948 the mainstream had shifted enough to speak of a Cold War consensus, one that assumed offensive Soviet intransigence and British defensive virtue.

During this transition Britain's propaganda apparatus was burnishing the country's image overseas, but was not yet receiving clear signal from the government about the new attitude toward the Soviets. By mid-1946 the government started partial, below-the-radar mobilisation of anti-Soviet propaganda. This gradually expanded through 1947 until Bevin finally abandoned hope of a negotiated settlement with the Soviets. Then the full power of the information state was turned toward exposing and attacking the USSR in every way possible.

The Rise and Fall in the British Media of the 'Grand Alliance'

Britain had been at war with Germany for nearly two years, fighting largely alone, when the Germans invaded the USSR on 22 June 1941. The British were ready for any ally and ignored any historical geopolitical grudges or differences in politics. Once it became apparent that the Soviets would not collapse, public enthusiasm and press interest in the USSR began to rise. The Ministry of Information sought to co-opt this enthusiasm through official boosting of the USSR that would both 'steal the thunder' of the British Communists and muzzle any anti-Soviet sentiments.[2] The Ministry encouraged the press and BBC to be more enthusiastic about the Russians, but it was pushing against an open door: the press was inclined to whitewash the Soviets.[3]

Most British journalists had very little first-hand information about the USSR in 1941 and tried several methods to fill the void. Many relied on MOI news releases and Soviet embassy publications, such as *Soviet War News*. All major news organisations tried to get their correspondents to Moscow for front-line reporting. For background many turned to Communist and pro-Communist sources of news within Britain. Four years of the Grand Alliance showed the communiqués to be unenlightening, the correspondents to be muzzled and the British Communists to be shameless cheerleaders for the USSR.[4] Reporters who would become hard-core anti-Communists after 1948 waxed uncritical over the USSR during the war – W. N. Ewer and A. J. Cummings, whose articles were 'glowingly pro-Soviet' stand out.[5]

Some newspapers went far beyond the officially sanctioned Russophilia and, in conjunction with the British Communists, mounted a campaign for a second front in Western Europe. Leading the way was Lord Beaverbrook's *Daily Express* and *Sunday Express*, with the Liberal *News Chronicle*, Conservative *Times*, and Labour *Daily Herald* following close behind.[6]

In mid-1944 the MOI became more ambivalent and some in the press grew more critical as the Soviets let the German's crush the Polish Home Army's revolt in Warsaw.[7] But at the end of 1944 the government was once again trying to discourage anti-Soviet news and views. Moscow-based PWE representative Tom Barman reported that in the winter of 1944–5, British Moscow Ambassador Clark Kerr met with several left-wing anti-Stalinist journalists in London and begged them to subordinate their views in the interest of winning the war.[8] The weekly *Tribune* had been one of the few left-wing publications to criticise the Soviet Union and did so when it was not fashionable. The *Newspaper World* trade weekly quoted *Tribune* at length and with approval: 'The Russian Press has been nagging for a long time, and up to now our own Press has played the part of a hen-pecked husband'.[9]

Some British diplomats were beginning to worry about the media's behaviour. From the Moscow Embassy Minister Frank Roberts urged a tougher, more pragmatic policy toward the Soviets. First, he wanted to 'educate' the British people, primarily to end the adulation of the USSR without provoking an equally emotional anti-Soviet reaction. In April 1945 he analysed British public opinion as 'divided into a dwindling but still important body of opinion ready to support the Soviet Union through thick and thin and a growing, but still somewhat inarticulate section, who are beginning to see a Prussian in every Russian'.[10] At the Potsdam Summit following the German defeat the allies hid the sharp difference that had emerged under a single anodyne communiqué claiming improved relations.[11] The victors' first post-Potsdam meeting came a few weeks later at the London Conference of Foreign Ministers. When the conference impasse became apparent the conventional wisdom in the British press looked for progress in the fact that disputes were now in the open; others were clear that the conference had 'failed calamitously'.[12]

Much of the news media was still providing glowing news reports and analyses of the Soviet Union to the dismay of British diplomats. Although more old-fashioned officials thought public ignorance made for better diplomacy, the Foreign Office in general felt that the public needed a 'realistic' picture of the USSR.[13] They felt that if the British knew the Soviets only through the rose-coloured haze of wartime propaganda they would not understand, and might not accept, the tough tactics anticipated in the post-war settlement negotiations. In addition, a public starry-eyed about the USSR would hurt the British negotiating position – the Soviets would be less willing to give in to a government they assumed did not have the backing of their press or people. It was a multi-faceted enterprise. Reporters in the field had to send back the right kind of stories, editors had to print them and the editorial (leader) writers had to put the proper spin on the information. The Foreign Office believed that if non-Communist British reporters in Moscow, liberated Eastern Europe, and occupied Germany could operate freely they would present a more realistic and critical picture of Soviet aims and behaviour. It did not necessarily work that way.

When Moscow correspondents were able to get critical news out, their papers were often unwilling to touch it. In spring 1945 *News Chronicle* correspondent Paul Winterton had written a scathing account of news reporting in the Soviet Union, but his own paper refused to print it.[14] Instead, his information found its way into the two newspaper trade journals, *World's Press News* and *Newspaper World*. Winterton blasted Soviet officials as incompetent and obstructive, and claimed that censorship was so pervasive that 'it resulted in a total eclipse of independent reporting, reducing correspondents in Moscow to mere "yes-men" or relayers of news'.

> it has been impossible for any foreign correspondent in Moscow to say a single word in the past three years which implied the slightest criticism of anything in Russia or disagreement with any aspect of Soviet policy.[15]

The Foreign Office was delighted with the story, but complained that it was only a drop in a very large bucket of information about the Soviet Union. Christopher Warner, who supervised both propaganda and Soviet relations, reacted emotionally to Winterton's news:

> At last! But alas! The general public do not read 'World's Press News' and the newspaper world must have known all this already. The British

public will remain in ignorance of the totally misleading nature of news
from Moscow, so long as the ordinary press maintain their conspiracy of
silence. Now that some papers have withdrawn their correspondents from
Moscow can they not be persuaded to speak out?[16]

Few did. Tight censorship of British reporters' dispatches continued in Moscow,
despite an occasional and brief loosening.[17]

In Eastern Europe liberation did not lead to open access for British reporters
or more critical coverage. The *Newspaper World* complained of the news dearth
and urged the British 'progressive press to lift the blackout on news within the
Russian sphere of interest'.[18] Few reporters got in, and when they did working conditions were nightmarish. Kemsley's Archibald Gibbon spent nearly a
year in Romania where 'severe censorship' eliminated from his dispatches any
critical information about the Soviets or their Romanian proxies and any positive information about their enemies. Then the Soviets blocked his exit for three
months.[19] Partly because of these experiences the British news media were reluc-
tant to send correspondents to Bulgaria, Hungary and Poland.[20] But stories on
negotiations about Eastern Europe offered opportunity for critical comment, one
taken by *Daily Herald* diplomatic correspondent, W. N. Ewer, who dismissed the
Communist-dominated Polish provisional government as an entity established by
'coup d'état'.[21] But gradually access to Eastern Europe improved and by March
1946 Western correspondents faced only a few political difficulties in Eastern
Europe.[22]

Freedom from censorship did not lead to a rush of news from obscure corners
of Eastern Europe, and what did come out was ambivalent. In November 1945 the
mass-market *News of the World* described the 'Chicago gangster-like atmosphere'
of murder, rape and robbery in Soviet-occupied Hungary, and emphasised that
the Russian authorities were trying to control it. But the newspaper did not
identify the culprits until the story's twenty-fifth paragraph, when the writer
noted that 'Red Army soldiers are by no means entirely responsible for this wave
of crime'.[23] Just before Christmas *Daily Express* correspondent Peter Smollett,
who had also been working as a Soviet agent, set out to debunk reports critical of
Red Army misbehaviour in Eastern Europe. He claimed he was able to travel freely
throughout Soviet occupied Europe and send uncensored dispatches home.[24]

Reporting Germany and Austria was even more complicated for British journalists. For much of 1945 British correspondents were barred from the Soviet
occupation zones, but not the Soviet sectors in Berlin and Vienna.[25] Although
reporters were well aware of Soviet mistreatment of Germans and Austrians –
including robbery, rape and murder – they either did not report the stories or
downplayed them. Some in the Foreign Office believed that the news media were
waiting for official prompting to report what they knew, especially in Austria:

> But after four years of misrepresenting the Russians as a chivalrous,
> civilised democratic people who can do no wrong, the newspapers find
> that they have by their own efforts (which were admittedly, to some extent,
> originally undertaken in what they felt to be the national interest) created

a public market and state of mind which they can now ill afford to jolt back to a state of reality. There is a further anxiety lest the publication of material discreditable to the Russians should result in the curtailment of facilities for the particular newspapers' correspondents in Russian-controlled territory; and the fear of being stigmatised by the Moscow press and radio as a kennel of Fascist dogs, etc., etc.[26]

Some press commentators agreed, but laid the blame on the government itself. Patriotism combined with logistical difficulties 'has led many editors to accept the guidance of Whitehall in news treatment. Inevitably, truth has given way to expediency'.[27] But critical coverage began to surface that autumn. The anti-Stalinist, left-wing weekly *Tribune* reported Soviet depredations in Vienna, including accusations that Red Army men raped some 100,000 Viennese women. Some readers harshly criticised it for its candour. They felt that even if those accounts were true they should not be printed – in the interest of allied unity.[28] On the right, *The Spectator* noted that facts on the Soviet kidnapping of Germans from the British zone were being published 'after considerable suppression'.[29] But the majority of the British reading public was getting another story. The liberal *News Chronicle* claimed there was no lawlessness in the Soviet zone, while the *News of the World* flat-out stated in a front-page story that accounts of Soviet cruelty to German women and children in Czechoslovakia, Poland and the Soviet zone of Germany were simply not true. 'It is time they were stopped – in the interests of peace'.[30]

Although the news media downplayed reports of Soviet misbehaviour, reports were making it back to Britain through personal channels. Ralph Parker, *The Times'* pliable Moscow correspondent, worried that the Soviets were doing nothing to counteract the bad impressions Red Army men were making on British soldiers they encountered in Central Europe. 'Our men going home will have some pretty lurid tales to tell'.[31] And they did. A sampling of public attitudes toward the Soviets in November 1945 showed growing levels of mistrust. Mainly, people were worried about the Soviets' obsession with secrecy and their recent diplomatic behaviour, and feared rising international tension. Some reported that their opinions of the Soviets had sunk with word-of-mouth reports from British soldiers of Red Army behaviour. As one respondent put it:

The boys that come home on leave seem to think pretty badly of them, and if anybody knows, they do. They say it's just frightful, the way they roam about, looting and raping, and murdering innocent people – they seem to think they're worse than the Germans.[32]

Iron Curtains and Newspaper Pages

In early 1946 Anglo-Soviet relations deteriorated at an alarming rate, and simmering Soviet-American disputes continued over the future control of atomic weapons. In January the Iranian government complained to the United Nations about Soviet encouragement of separatism. The Soviets countered with resolutions critical of British policy in Greece and Indonesia. Bevin and Soviet diplomat Andrei Vishinsky went head-to-head at the inaugural UN Security Council meeting in London, which made Anglo-Soviet differences clear to all. In rebutting the Soviet charges that British actions in Greece were a threat to world peace, Bevin sharply attacked the propaganda tactics of the Soviets and their allies.

> It has been the incessant propaganda of Moscow and the incessant
> propaganda of the Communist Party in every country in the world to
> attack the British people and the British Government as if there has been
> no friendship between us. That is the danger to the peace of the world. It
> sets us against one another, causes suspicion and misunderstanding, and
> makes one wonder what the motive is.[33]

Significantly, public approval for Bevin in Britain shot up after the Bevin-Vishinsky debate. In February 73 per cent of those polled in Britain thought Bevin was doing a 'good job' as foreign secretary, compared with only 47 per cent in December.[34] In February Stalin made a famous 'election speech' that was widely interpreted in the West as an abandonment of wartime alliance diplomacy and a return to messianic Marxist-Leninist revolutionary thinking.[35] And in March former Prime Minister Winston Churchill made his even more famous 'Iron Curtain' speech in Fulton, Missouri, calling for a strong Anglo-American stand against the malevolent Soviet threat.[36]

As diplomats clashed and tempers flared, public enthusiasm for the Soviets was gradually cooling in Britain. A Mass Observation survey in March 1946 showed that hostility toward the Soviets had grown, especially among the upper social classes. Much of this mistrust was fuelled not by reports of Soviet misbehaviour in Eastern Europe but by widely publicised disagreements over Iran and the future of the atomic bomb. One middle-class woman described the end of the wartime honeymoon this way: 'Well of course, I've said like everybody else how wonderful our dear allies were and all the rest of it – the regular war-time tune, but now I'm beginning to think again.'[37]

It was not yet clear if changes in news coverage were paralleling changing attitudes. In February 1946 a writer in the *Newspaper World* saw the British press at a crossroads. Pre-war coverage of both the USA and USSR had emphasised lurid human-interest stories – in the USSR propaganda-laced stories of purges, bloodshed, famine and despotism. 'No matter how accurate this news was, it was false in that it was presented with no corresponding background treatment, or with comparable news presenting achievements in the Soviet plan.' The needs of the wartime alliance led to different, more positive news about both countries. 'But what happens now? Are the old-style "human interest" standards and the propaganda-before-news prejudices putting us back where we were? I don't think these are merely academic questions in newspaper offices these days.'[38]

Within the Foreign Office a consensus was emerging that Britain not only had to get tougher with the Soviet Union, but also that the British news media needed to frame their news and views in a much more critical light to 'enlighten' the public as to the true nature of the USSR. They would need a firm push from the state to do so. From the Moscow embassy Frank Roberts sent a wide-ranging assessment of Soviet behaviour and prescription for British policy towards the USSR. Roberts believed that a combination of territorial insecurity, opportunism, and ideological messianism lay behind the Soviets' behaviour. They were, however, unlike the Nazis – Britain could coexist with them by following a policy of strength and patience.[39] For this new approach to work, the British public needed to be enlightened about the Soviet Union. Even the well-informed elite were dependent on either Soviet propaganda or anti-Soviet prejudices, 'which are equally dangerous counsellors'. Because of Soviet censorship and other obstacles to normal contacts 'the responsibility for educating the British public must rest with His Majesty's Government and the editors in London, to an extent which would be altogether abnormal in dealing with other countries'.[40]

One of the first chores was *The Times*, which had been very indulgent toward the Soviets. Much of *The Times*' attitude stemmed from the *realpolitik* of Editor Robin Barrington-Ward and his deputy, historian E. H. Carr. They reasoned that either Germany or Russia would dominate Eastern Europe. Germany had failed, and protesting against Russian domination would only antagonise the Soviets and possibly drive them toward rapprochement with Germany. Therefore, the USSR must have a free hand in their zone.[41] Diplomatic Correspondent Iverach McDonald and others were pushing for a less accommodating line toward the Soviets, but it was a 'lone and losing battle'. When Donald McLachlan was filling in for McDonald in March 1946 he wrote a pointed story, largely based on Foreign Office briefings, about Anglo-American-Soviet relations in Iran. But Barrington-Ward rejected it as the type of journalism 'that causes wars'.[42]

By early 1946 it was clear that *The Times* was not going to get back in step with the Foreign Office on its own. In January News Department Chief William Ridsdale urged Bevin to give Barrington-Ward a 'straight talk' about how his paper was hampering government policy in the UN and in Iran. Ridsdale also had arranged for the *Daily Herald's* W. N. Ewer to put out a 'counter-blast' ('he was very willing to do so') and was encouraging 'unofficial people of standing' to write to *The Times* protesting its policy.[43] The March 1946 meeting blindsided Barrington-Ward. Bevin verbally attacked the editor for his newspaper's 'spineless' and 'jellyfish' attitude, and demanded to know whether *The Times* supported him personally.[44] The attack backfired and Barrington-Ward left angry and even more set in his views, writing later that Bevin 'was a fool to try and attack (*The Times*) in this way'.[45] Even McDonald conceded that: 'It is hard to imagine a worse bungled affair'. Bevin, however, felt that Barrington-Ward had 'taken to heard [sic] these strictures'.[46]

Much of the criticism was aimed squarely at *The Times*' Moscow correspondent, Ralph Parker. FO Soviet expert Thomas Brimelow felt that *The Times*' prestige caused its 'perversions of essential facts' to introduce doubt to British public opinion and encourage further Soviet aggression. Brimelow felt that widespread misconceptions about the nature of the Soviet Union among the British public would limit Britain's diplomatic freedom of action.[47] From Moscow, Frank Roberts agreed. 'No doubt they think they are performing a public service by not losing their heads and publishing anti-Soviet stuff. But they should stick to the truth. Otherwise they do as much harm as the sensationalists hotting up opinion against this country.'[48]

The Foreign Office did not try another frontal attack, and instead waited out their opponents. Barrington-Ward dismissed Parker, E. H. Carr left to write history in July 1946 and Barrington-Ward's health deteriorated to the point where he had to take a leave of absence in late 1947 from which he never returned.[49] Parker did a brief stint with the *News Chronicle*, but eventually cast his lot with the Soviets, settled in Moscow and in 1949 wrote a scurrilous book accusing the British embassy of being full of spies.[50]

Others at the Foreign Office were re-examining their opinion of the Soviet Union, seeing it more as an ideologically driven expansionist power. Christopher Warner crystallised this new view in a watershed document, 'The Soviet campaign against this country and our response to it'. Warner recommended a far-ranging 'defensive-offensive' policy that would politically, economically and diplomatically counter Soviet actions. This would include a far-ranging propaganda campaign to expose the totalitarian nature of Communism and 'the myths which the Soviet government are trying to create in justification of their policy'.[51] To coordinate information and policy on the worldwide activities of the Soviets and local Communists, the Foreign Office set up an inter-departmental Russia Committee.[52] Most propaganda initiatives during the next few years would come from this committee.

Warner's memo went straight to the top, but when the Russia Committee submitted more detailed plans for carrying out the publicity campaign, Bevin balked: 'The more I study this the less I like it. I am quite sure that the putting over of positive results of British attitude [sic] will be a better corrective'.[53] The plan developed by information chief Ivone Kirkpatrick had been a far-ranging one that emphasised the need for public support from British politicians and press, the need for goodwill of journalists and publicists at home and abroad, and the necessity of 'invaluable' US support. This long-term operation would require cooperation of information officers overseas, official propaganda bureaucracies, independent trade unionists, the British Broadcasting Corporation and the Royal Institute of International Affairs (Chatham House). British journalists should be enlisted, but only 'very carefully and gradually'.[54]

In July a ministerial directive went out to publicise Soviet manufacturing of military equipment in their zone.[55] But when the information was officially released the British press initially did not cover it; and the TUC's own *Daily Herald* spiked its correspondent's story for fear that it didn't have official approval.[56] The *Daily Herald* spike highlighted for the Foreign Office a larger problem – the reluctance of many in the news media to cover stories critical of the Soviets. Also, the FO's Hankey noted that many of the British correspondents sent to

Eastern Europe were 'second rate' or even Communists or fellow travellers. The News Department's N. E. Nash explained the dilemma to the Russia Committee and traced the public's allegedly indulgent attitude toward the Soviets to the lack of news from Soviet-dominated areas. That stemmed not from Communist interference, but from newspapers' reliance on 'bald news agency reports' and unreliable foreign stringers, as well as the effects of a deep newsprint shortage and the newspapers misguided servility toward the British state.

> Some of the newspapers have not yet got out of the (wartime) habit of waiting for a ministerial lead before dealing firmly with matters of foreign policy. In the absence of such a lead, the provincial press in particular are inclined to think that by refraining from adverse comment on the course of Russian policy, they are best serving the public interest and are in fact displaying a sense of responsibility by refraining from outspoken comment.[57]

To remedy this, Northern Department Head Hankey wanted a discreet and indirect approach to editors to tell them that the government would like a steady stream of news from behind the Iron Curtain to educate the public – a direct and public government attack would 'much upset public opinion'.[58] Top officials also worked to distribute news indirectly about Soviet spying on the atomic bomb project to show how the Soviets mistrusted, abused and subverted their democratic allies even at the height of wartime cooperation. They used an official Canadian report on the case, issued in June 1946, to spur greater public scepticism towards the USSR. Even though the report was old news by September, articles appeared then in *The Times, The Spectator* and on the BBC after the Foreign Office had lent copies of the report to correspondents.[59] The government continued to push the spy story, negotiating with the Canadian government for an additional 2,000 copies of the report and considering using a planted parliamentary question to kick off a talk about the book on the BBC Home Service.[60]

The Foreign Office held off on a direct approach to media leaders as it appeared, by late August, that the news media was beginning to publish on their own initiative more news critical of the Soviets.[61] The Foreign Office thought that the regular flow of news from the upcoming Paris Peace Conference would continue the trend and do much of the anti-Soviet work for them. They were right. The press and the BBC covered the conference heavily. The BBC's star at the conference was ex-diplomat Harold Nicolson, who broadcast twice-weekly fifteen-minute interpretive talks on the conference for the Home Service. (These talks went out on the overseas service as well and reached a potential audience, home and abroad, of 20 million people.) At the beginning Nicolson worried that the conference would be boring and that he would not be able to 'tell the truth without enraging the Russians'.[62] He did, however, manage at the beginning to enrage the British delegation by placing some blame on the Americans and British while trying to give his listeners an idea of the Soviets' point of view.[63] Six weeks later, toward the end of the conference, Nicolson's broadcasts had grown much more pessimistic:

Watching their day-to-day conduct at the Paris Conference one is
sometimes forced to the conclusion that they have no hope of establishing
and even no desire to establish relations and confidence with the Western
Powers, and that they are using the Paris Conference merely as a platform
from which to spread distrust and insecurity among non-Communist
countries.[64]

Back in London the press was reporting more on the Soviets' anti-British
behaviour and propaganda, though they were not fully exploring the 'extent
and virulence' of the propaganda or the 'reign of terror and oppression' in
Eastern Europe. News reporting was steadily working in the government's favour,
thus mitigating the need for Attlee to approach editors. Nevertheless a few
proprietors – most notably the Conservative *Daily Telegraph* and the Kemsley
newspaper chain – were still believed to be holding back. Oliver Harvey went so
far as to describe it as 'a ban on anti-Soviet news and views' but hoped that the
effect of the ongoing Paris talks would alter the coverage.[65] The Russia Committee stepped up contacts for funnelling information to the Labour Party and the
TUC.[66] Anti-Communist writer George Orwell noted at that time that the tide
had turned against Russophilia in Britain, despite the protests of the 'minority
left-wing press'.[67] The results could also be seen in the Gallup public opinion polls – a full 61 per cent believed that the wartime Anglo-American-Soviet
alliance had disappeared.[68]

By early 1947 Bevin and the Labour government clearly had little hope of a satisfactory settlement with the Soviets, but hesitated to mobilise the government's
information machine for a full-scale propaganda offensive. Bevin was trying to
proceed simultaneously with military talks with the Americans, treaty negotiations with the French, and negotiations for the renewal of the Anglo-Soviet
Treaty with Moscow. A counter-propaganda campaign could upset the delicate
balance.[69] From Moscow Frank Roberts again urged a campaign to 'enlighten'
the British people, mainly by persuading the British press to cover the Soviets'
anti-British propaganda campaign.[70]

At the highest cabinet levels, however, things were moving ahead with the January 1947 creation of the Ministerial Committee on Subversive Activities.[71] That
committee's working party noted the tight restrictions on direct anti-Communist
propaganda, but thought there was room to manoeuvre both at home and abroad.
One official suggested setting up an apparatus for planting anti-Communist articles in the news media, especially the left-wing press. With any kind of propaganda, however, the best results would come if the state could 'hide as far as
possible the fact that the material was inspired'.[72]

By mid-1947 the Foreign Office decided to stick with the propaganda programmes already in place at least until the November Council of Foreign Ministers meeting. The Labour Party was still in danger of splitting over a too-
aggressive policy, and Bevin wanted to make one final attempt at compromise
with the Soviets.[73] Within Britain the news media and public opinion had already
developed a framework that interpreted Soviet behaviour in a negative light. 'To

a great extent therefore the Russians themselves could be trusted to look after the anti-Russian publicity'.[74]

But the dream of Anglo-Soviet amity died hard. The Beaverbrook press, however, had held out some hope for reconciliation, but it was on its last legs in January 1948. Beaverbrook leader writer George Malcolm Thomson summed up the situation with his tongue firmly in cheek before ending with a swipe at two reporters who had been cheerleaders for the USSR during the war:

> The Russians have not a friend left in Britain apart from the *Express*. (I do not of course count the *Worker*, and the lunatic fringe of the Socialist party). The liberals have all abandoned them.
>
> Alexander Werth still raises a thin pipe of praise in the *Guardian* (in other respects, a straight reactionary organ nowadays). But A. J. Cummings now ranks high as a Fascist Beast.[75]

Projecting the Cold War Overseas

The Foreign Office were also pushing for a more sceptical attitude in the media of the non-Communist world, but started slow. In January 1946 Bevin had hoped to counteract Soviet expansion in Southeast Europe with a 'steady stream of information about British life and culture'.[76] That didn't work. In May 1946 Bevin approved propaganda in Iran, though rejecting Kirkpatrick's proposal for a broader propaganda offensive.[77] The officials moved quickly in Iran, sending propaganda expert Lt Col. Geoffrey Wheeler from New Delhi to Tehran to head an expanded public relations bureau that would expose the 'true nature' of the pro-Soviet Tudeh Party.[78] A few weeks later Bevin authorised propaganda in Germany and Austria. The Russia Committee felt that the British should emphasise how the Soviets hurt the Germans through their policies on reparations and boundaries of occupation zones.[79]

The propaganda campaign in Iran had seemed to produce good results, and Kirkpatrick and other top officials quickly pushed for anti-Soviet propaganda throughout the Middle East. Public opinion there was moving against Britain; propaganda might help stem the flow.[80] As Kirkpatrick wrote:

> Our problems in the Middle East are not created by Russia. They existed before the war and would afflict us even if Russia disappeared from the scene. Nevertheless it is true that our difficulties are being deliberately aggravated by a savage Soviet campaign of anti-British propaganda . . . a reply must be made with all the means at our disposal.[81]

In mid-October Bevin gave the go-ahead for propaganda throughout the Middle East.[82] The Foreign Office moved relatively quickly, building on the Iranian propaganda operations and leaning on British companies in the area. The BBC had beefed up its Iranian services and plans were under way for an Iranian newspaper, provincial news service, and a Persian translation of Soviet defector Victor Kravchenko's sensational exposé *I Chose Freedom*. Iraqi newspapers were printing verbatim anti-Soviet news and views from the official London Press Service, and British companies based in Iraq, Syria and Lebanon were also co-operating with the Foreign Office to project a reformist British message to the local population.[83]

Meanwhile, British diplomats outside the Middle East were increasingly asking for information to rebut Communist propaganda attacks. They already received radio and press monitoring reports but wanted more.[84] This led the Foreign Office Research Department (FORD) to produce, in instalments, a handbook on Soviet affairs as background for counter-publicity.[85] The first production was an analysis that debunked article by article the much-ballyhooed 1936 Soviet constitution. Officials hoped that future coordination between FORD, the BBC and the COI could soon produce 'material of high enough quality for the BBC to use without exposing themselves to a smashing rejoinder from the Russian propaganda machine'.[86]

But the COI's leisurely working pace and what the Foreign Office saw as ideological slackness soon drove the diplomats to distraction. In 1947 a Cairo newspaper publisher wanted tough anti-Communist articles exposing life in the Eastern European satellite countries, but the COI productions failed the Foreign Office test by not emphasising enough the 'injustices and the intolerable conditions' there.[87] Additional material came from Britain's Cairo-based Middle East Information Division, which sent 'hot' anti-Communist articles to other British missions for distribution to local newspapers. These articles tried to make anti-Communism relevant to Arab readers, and occasionally tried to link Communism and Jews. One article, 'Russians' plan for the Middle East' blamed the Soviet Union and international Communism for Zionism, the creation of Israel, and Jewish immigration to the area.[88]

A directive drafted in late 1947 called upon British propagandists in the Middle East to discredit Soviet aims and local sympathisers, expose the falsehoods of Soviet propaganda, and vigorously counterattack Soviet propaganda attacks on Britain:

> It is essential that this exposure of the falsity of Soviet propaganda should be aggressive in its nature. Weak denials of the charges levelled against us in the Soviet press and radio will do no good. We must take the offensive and actively discredit the whole of the Soviet propaganda machine. Our tactics should be disruptive, not defensive.[89]

The British may have felt that they were making no progress, but a peak in the Soviet archives for that time show a much different evaluation from Moscow's perspective. Soviet propaganda chiefs characterised British propaganda as a 'truly grandiose organisation, far-flung and multi-form, penetrating to almost every corner of the globe'.[90]

The Soviet vision came closer to a British reality in January 1948 when months of preparation led Bevin to push for a full-fledged propaganda operation that would become the Information Research Department (IRD). The IRD's birth and growing pains have been well detailed in a number of recent publications. To sum up their conclusions: steadily deteriorating relations with the USSR and growing public support for a hard line against them meant that Bevin could openly pursue a tough anti-Soviet policy with the concomitant anti-Communist propaganda. The failure of the London Conference of Foreign Ministers in late 1947 was the justification and signal for the new policy. The department itself was shaped through the persistence of permanent officials such as Warner and the enthusiasm of junior minister Christopher Mayhew. Attlee gave a taste of the new approach in an early January address to the nation, and later in the month the cabinet approved both Bevin's Cold War strategy and anti-Communist propaganda.[91]

Conclusion

In slightly more than two years the British Labour government and news media profoundly changed the way they looked at the Soviet Union. In mid-1945 the Soviet Union was clearly still an ally and mainstream journalists did not go out of their way to seek news that would make the Soviets look bad. But a growing perception of Soviet intransigence and hostility towards Britain in late 1945 and through 1946 led the news media to seek explanations in stories of Soviet oppression, expansion and subversion. The government clearly encouraged this, with the Foreign Office leading the way by providing access to information that was bound to give an unflattering picture of the Soviets. When these tactics did not suffice direct leaks and subtle pressure were brought into play. Journalists themselves were not passive objects; with Germany safely defeated many began to take a dimmer view of the USSR in light of Soviet diplomatic behaviour and propaganda. By early 1948 the British news media had created a frame in which the Soviet Union was a brutal, untrustworthy adversary, which shaped the news that created the Cold War consensus. At that point the government created the IRD to spread this consensus overseas and reinforce it at home.

Notes

1. Victor Rothwell provides the more orthodox interpretation, while Kent's *British Imperial Strategy* gives a revisionist view that stresses the imperial and great power dynamics driving British policy in the Eastern Mediterranean. See, Victor Rothwell, *Britain and the Cold War, 1941–1947* (London: Jonathan Cape, 1982); John Kent, *British Imperial Strategy and the Origins of the Cold War, 1944–49* (Leicester: Leicester University Press, 1993).
2. McLaine, *Ministry of Morale*, pp. 186–216; P. M. H. Bell, *John Bull and the Bear: British Public Opinion, Foreign Policy and the Soviet Union, 1941–1945* (London: Edward Arnold, 1990), pp. 42–5.

3. Bell, *John Bull and the Bear*, pp. 185–6.
4. Richard Cockett, "'In wartime every objective reporter should be shot": the experience of British press correspondents in Moscow, 1941–5', *Journal of Contemporary History* 23 (1988); Knightley, *The First Casualty*, pp. 244–67; Douglas Hyde, *I Believed: The Autobiography of a British Communist* (London: Heinemann, 1950), pp. 115–6.
5. Bell, *John Bull and the Bear*, pp. 140–2, 151.
6. Ibid. pp. 52–3; Sîan Nicholas, *The Echo of War: Home Front Propaganda and the Wartime BBC, 1939–45* (Manchester: Manchester University Press, 1996), p. 165.
7. Bell, *John Bull and the Bear*, pp. 145–6.
8. Thomas Barman, *Diplomatic Correspondent* (London: Hamish Hamilton, 1968), p. 165.
9. 'Notes on the news: by man-in-the-street', *Newspaper World*, 10 February 1945.
10. PRO FO371/47882 N4919/165/G, Roberts to Warner, 25 April 1945.
11. Tony Shaw, 'The British popular press and the early Cold War', *History: Journal of the Historical Association* 83 (1998).
12. '5 Power talks: acute difficulties', *Sunday Express*, 23 September 1945; 'Soviet want to run a colony in N. Africa', Bill Greig, *Daily Mirror*, 19 September 1945; 'After failure', *The Spectator*, 5 October 1945.
13. Elisabeth Barker, *The British Between the Superpowers, 1945–50* (Toronto: University of Toronto Press, 1983), p. 17.
14. PRO FO371/47918 N6299/592/38, William Ridsdale minute, 10 June 1945.
15. 'Total eclipse! "Foreign correspondents in Moscow reduced to Yes-Men": Paul Winterton lashes out', *World's Press News*, 24 May 1945.
16. PRO FO371/47918 N6299/592/38, Warner minute, 6 June 1945.
17. PRO FO371/56864 N4343/2802, Roberts to Foreign Office, 30 March 1946.
18. 'Notes on news: by man-in-the-street', *Newspaper World*, 14 July 1945; 'Russians think foreign journalists are 'snoopers', says Winterton, *Newspaper World*, 7 July 1945.
19. 'Correspondent from Rumania tells of severe censorship', *Newspaper World*, 28 July 1945.
20. *Documents on British Policy Overseas*, 1st ser., vol. 1, brief no. 13 for UK delegation, 7 July 1945 (no. 83, Cal. i, FO934/6).; Also, see, *DBPO*, 1st ser., vol. 1, Foreign Office to Warsaw, 31 July 31 (no. 566, Cal. iii, N7796/436/55).
21. See Emile Burns, 'Editorial note', *World News and Views*, 26 May 1945.
22. 'Official censorship nearly non-existent in Eastern Europe', *Newspaper World*, 2 March 1946.
23. 'Gangster atmosphere behind the 'Iron Curtain' of Hungary', *News of the World*, 4 November 1945
24. 'Report to Britain – on the stories going around about the Red Army', Peter Smollett, *Daily Express*, 20 December 1945; 'Smolka "the spy": a letter from Vienna', Sarah Gainham, *Encounter*, December 1984.
25. 'Berlin barrier?' *Newspaper World*, 28 April 1945; 'Woman correspondent replies to Edward Hulton', Mea Allan, *Newspaper World*, 22 December 1945.
26. PRO FO371/46611 C5306/141/3, Curtis minute, *Newspaper World*, 3 September 1945.
27. 'James Bartlett on self-censorship by British newspapermen', 13 October 1945.
28. George Orwell, *The Collected Essays, Journalism and Letters of George Orwell*. vol. 4; Sonia Orwell and Ian Angus (eds) *In Front of Your Nose* (London: Penguin Books, 1970), pp. 53–7. This originally appeared as 'Through a glass, rosily' in *Tribune*, 23 November 1945.

29. 'Divided Europe', *The Spectator*, 28 September 1945.
30. 'M.P.s' denial of 'cruel Russians' story', *News of the World*, 14 October 1945; 'News', *World News and Views*, 20 October 1945; Emile Burns, 'Editorial notes', *World News and Views*, 6 October 1945.
31. PRO FO371/47918 N10955/592/38, Parker to Barrington-Ward, 15 August 1945.
32. Mass Observation, *Tom Harrisson Mass-Observation Archive: File Report Series* (Brighton: Harvester Press, 1983), File Report No. 2301, 'Attitudes to Russia', 7 November 1945.
33. 'Mr. Bevin's reply to Soviet charges', *The Times*, 2 February 1946.
34. George Gallup, *International Public Opinion Polls: Great Britain 1937–1975*, vol. 1, 1937–1964 (New York: Random House, 1976), pp. 121, 126.
35. Yergin, *Shattered Peace*, pp. 166–7.
36. Alan Foster, 'The British press and the coming of the Cold War,' in Anne Deighton (ed.), *Britain and the First Cold War* (Houndmills: Macmillan, 1990).
37. *The Tom Harrisson Mass-Observation Archive*, File Report No. 2301, 'Attitudes to Russia', 11 March 1946.
38. 'Outside Fleet Street', James Bartlett, *Newspaper World*, 9 February 1946.
39. John Zametica, 'Three letters to Bevin' in John Zametica (ed.), *British Officials and British Foreign Policy, 1945–50* (Leicester: Leicester University Press, 1990).
40. *DBPO*, 1st ser., vol. 6 (no. 83, N4157/97/38) Roberts to Bevin, 18 March 1946.
41. Donald McLachlan, *In the Chair: Barrington-Ward of 'The Times', 1927–1948* (London: Weidenfeld and Nicolson, 1971), pp. 221–2; Jonathan Haslam, '"We need a faith:" E. H. Carr, 1892–1982', *History Today*, August 1983.
42. McLachlan, *In the Chair*, pp. 250–51. Also, see Jonathan Haslam, *The Vices of Integrity: E. H. Carr, 1892–1982* (London: Verso, 1998), pp. 81–98.
43. PRO FO800/498 PRS/46/12, Ridsdale memo, 21 January 1946.
44. Iverach McDonald, *A Man of the Times: Talks and Travels in a Disrupted World* (London: Hamish Hamilton, 1976), pp. 114–15.
45. McLachlan, *In the Chair*, Appendix II, pp. 280–281.
46. McDonald, *A Man of the Times*, pp. 114–15; PRO FO800/498 PRS/46/25, Henderson to Ridsdale, 11 March 1946.
47. PRO FO371/56866 N3061/3041/38, Brimelow minute, 9 March 1946.
48. *The Times* Archives, Ralph Parker personnel file, Roberts to Ridsdale, 22 March 1946.
49. McDonald, *History of the Times*, pp. 145, 161–2.
50. *The Times* Archives, Unlabeled box, Parker File, McDonald to Sir Frank Lee, 25 June 1964.
51. *DBPO*, 1st ser., vol. 6 (no. 88) 'Memorandum by Mr. Warner: the Soviet campaign against this country and our response to it', 2 April 1946.
52. Ray Merrick, 'The Russia Committee of the British Foreign Office and the Cold War, 1946–7,' *Journal of Contemporary History* 20 (1985).
53. PRO FO930/488 P449/1/907, Undated Bevin minute; Zametica, 'Three letters to Bevin', p. 88.
54. PRO FO930/488 P449/1/907, Kirkpatrick memo ('The Soviet campaign against this country'), 22 May 1946.
55. PRO FO371/56886 N10141/5169/38G, Russia Committee minutes, 30 July 1946.
56. PRO FO371/56886 N10901/5169/38G, Russia Committee minutes, 20 August 1946; PRO FO371/56886 N11284/5169/38G, Russia Committee minutes, 28 Aug 1946.
57. PRO FO371/56788 N10965/140/38G, Nash memo, 1 August 1946, Hankey minute, 18 August 1946.

58. PRO FO371/56788 N10965/140/38G, Hankey minute, 5 August 1946, Hankey memo, 18 August 1946.
59. PRO FO371/56886 N11284/5169/38/G, Russia Committee minutes, 28 August 1946.
60. PRO FO371/56886 N14607/5169/38G, Russia Committee minutes, 7 November 1946.
61. PRO FO371/56788 N10966/140/38G, Warner minute, 21 August 1946.
62. Harold Nicolson, *Diaries and Letters, 1930–1964* (ed), Stanley Olson (London: Collins, 1980), Entries for 26 July 1946 and 27 July 1946.
63. See talks reproduced in *The Listener*, 22, 29 August 1946 and 5 September 1946.
64. 'We must burn no boats', Harold Nicolson, *The Listener*, 26 September 1946.
65. PRO FO371/56789 N12400/140/38G, Nash to Halford, 23 September 1946, Harvey minute, 25 September 1946.
66. PRO FO371/56886 N14607/51/69/38G, Russia Committee minutes, 7 November 1946.
67. Orwell, *In Front of Your Nose*, p. 222. This quotation originally appeared as 'London letter' in *Partisan Review*, Summer 1946.
68. Gallup, *The Gallup International Public Opinion Polls, Great Britain*, pp. 120, 137–9.
69. Barker, *The British Between the Superpowers*, pp. 70–4.
70. PRO FO371/66366 N3303/271/38, Roberts to Warner, 15 March 1947.
71. PRO CAB130/16, Minutes of an ad hoc meeting, 6 January 1947.
72. PRO CAB130/17, Cabinet Working Party on Subversive Movements Meeting minutes, 19 February 1947.
73. PRO FO371/66371 N9549/271/38G, Russia Committee minutes, 14 August 1947; NARA RG 59 DF741.61/7–247, Gallman to Secretary of State, 2 July 1947.
74. PRO FO371/66371 N9345/271/38G, Russia Committee minutes, 31 July 1947.
75. BBK Papers, H/129, Thomson to Beaverbrook, 16 January 1948.
76. PRO CAB128/5 5 (46), Cabinet minutes, 15 January 1946.
77. PRO FO930/488 P449/1/907, Bevin minute, 29 May 1946.
78. *DBPO*, 1st ser., vol. 7 (no. 56, Cal. i)
79. PRO FO371/56885 N9543/5169/38G, Russia Committee minutes, 16 July 1946.
80. PRO FO953/61 PME1499/1499/G, Kirkpatrick memo, 30 September 1946.
81. PRO FO371/56886 N13583/5169/38, Russia Committee minutes, 17 October 1946.
82. PRO FO371/56886 N1397/5169/38G, Russia Committee minutes, 24 October 1946.
83. PRO CAB158/1, [JIC (47) 39 (O)] Annex: British publicity in the Middle East, 9 May 1947.
84. PRO FO930/529, Routh [COI] to O. A. Scott, 30 November 1946.
85. PRO FO930/529, Scott to Routh, 23 December 1946.
86. PRO FO930/529, Scott minute, 7 December 1946.
87. PRO FO953/56 PME1849/96/965, Harrison to Lovell (COI), 21 November 1947, Harrison to S. H. Nelson (COI), 5 January 1948.
88. PRO FO953/56 PME2091/96/965, Maj. Gen. A. J. C. Pollock (Director Middle Eastern Information Department) to Howes (Information Services in Beirut), 8 December 1947.
89. PRO FO953/56 PME1475/96/975, 'Countermeasures against Soviet propaganda in the Middle East', November 1947.
90. Quoted in 'The rise and fall of *Britansky Soyuznik*', p. 296.
91. PRO CAB129/23, CP (48) 8, 'Future Foreign Publicity Policy', 4 January 1948.

3

Discipline and Consensus: The British News Media

Maintaining consensus in the twilight Cold War – not a time of war but not one of peace – was not an easy thing for British democracy. The government could use international tensions as a rationale to keep some troubling or sensitive facts out of the public eye, but not all. Communist publications could be disruptive and embarrassing, but the need to maintain political legitimacy meant that the government could not easily move to suppress them. The mainstream media had already shaped and adopted the consensus view about the iniquities of the Soviet Union and the necessity of Cold War vigilance, and from 1948 largely policed themselves. For those journalists who would not or could not conform to the new ways of thinking, writing and behaving, the career consequences could be steep.

(Self-)Policing the Boundaries of the Free Press

During the wartime Grand Alliance the boundaries of acceptable journalism, and acceptable journalists, had stretched to include sympathy or advocacy for the Soviet Union. With the Cold War chill after 1945 that boundary began to shift again, but this time away toward the right. By 1950 it had left many formerly acceptable journalists on the margins or on the other side of the East-West divide. This was a gradual and complicated process that relied a great deal on a general shift in thinking about the USSR among publishers, editors and producers. But ultimately, as the *Daily Telegraph*'s Malcolm Muggeridge argued in 1953, one had to choose sides.[1]

The Communists in Britain had their own range of publications that were obviously immune to this shift. In addition to the *Daily Worker*, they published *Labour Monthly, Labour Research, Communist Review, Bulletin, World News and Views* and *Challenge*. The Soviets and their British friends published *Soviet News, Soviet Monitor, Soviet Weekly, Russia Today* and the *Anglo-Soviet Journal*, as well as importing English-language publications from the USSR.[2] The East bloc embassies and friendship societies had a smaller, though similar range of publications.

Overseas, the Communist bloc was not making it any easier for correspondents with mainstream British publications to stay in the middle. They tightened visa requirements, expelled independent reporters en masse and hobbled the few who remained. By 1951 the *World's Press News* could list fourteen British, American and French journalists who had been expelled from Czechoslovakia alone.[3]

The shifts in Britain occurred at all levels – in the 'quality' papers *The Times* and *Manchester Guardian*, the 'popular' *Daily Express* and *Reynolds News*, the provincial *Yorkshire Post*, the weekly illustrated *Picture Post*, the BBC and Reuters.

The Times had largely abandoned its indulgence for the Soviet Union with the departure of Carr, Parker and Barrington-Ward, but problems still awaited several reporters. When *The Times* considered replacing Parker in Moscow with its Paris correspondent, Basil Davidson, some in the Foreign Office objected, writing that Davidson was 'a little pink'. Davidson's career on *The Times* ended in 1949 with a Foreign Office blackball. He was sent to Scandinavia but discovered that British diplomats there had been instructed not to talk frankly to him because of his views; he reasoned that he could not properly serve as *The Times* correspondent under those circumstances and resigned.[4]

The Foreign Office also disliked *The Times'* Vienna correspondent, M. C. Burn. He had cultivated Austrian Communists and Russians as sources and friends and later derided his colleagues in Vienna for having 'thrown such principles they had to the winds' and pumping out simplistic anti-Russian material. 'I had the impression that they had lost all power or even desire to analyse and were just letting things slide, doing automatically what they believed their office wanted the British public to (read)'.[5] Burn was criticised harshly for his reporting and at one point filed a libel suit against a British anti-Communist who had said at a public debate that Burn was being forced off *The Times* because of his 'dishonest' dispatches from Hungary.[6] *The Times* backed him up and he won. But he quit journalism and *The Times*, and began a second career as a novelist, poet and playwright.[7]

The *Manchester Guardian* had been indulgent toward the Soviets in the 1930s, but it was increasingly sceptical if not hostile after 1948. This spelled trouble for Russia expert and *Guardian* Moscow correspondent, Alexander Werth.[8] Despite tight censorship in Moscow Werth hoped that British readers could read between the lines of his stories. Apparently they did not. By early 1948 Werth was being accused of writing Communist propaganda. As *Guardian* editor, A. P. Wadsworth, pointed out to him, 'You have to remember that Western opinion has become a great deal more critical of Russian positions and propaganda nonsense'.[9] Werth argued that the Soviet Union was too important to neglect in favour of anti-Communist 'frenzy':

> Just because public sentiment in England to–day is worked up, as you say,
> to fever pitch is, surely, not a reason for newspapers to lose their heads too.
> Must one <u>follow</u> public sentiment all the time; is it not sometimes useful to
> judge things in a cool and detached way?[10]

Within a few months Werth transferred his base of operations to Eastern Europe, but again ran into problems. Wadsworth was complaining that he gave too rosy a picture of developments there.

After all, when one is describing a revolution which involves the suppression of most of the Western freedoms, the submergence of whole social classes, and the transformation of the law into an instrument of party dominance it is only fair to give as much emphasis to the black sides as to what the regime wants to be believed. If we do not we run the risk of conveying a false impression.[11]

With that said, Wadsworth sacked Werth.[12]

At other newspapers the changing political atmosphere was making life difficult for those sympathetic with Communism or the Soviet Union. At the Leeds-based *Yorkshire Post* cub reporter Peter Fryer and naval affairs contributor Commander Edgar Young were let go because their pro-Soviet activities conflicted with the Conservative orientation of the paper.[13] The 'Communistic tendencies' in the Co-Operative Press' *Reynolds News*, became an issue in spring 1948 when Defence Minister A. V. Alexander, a Co-Operative leader, accused the newspaper of pro-Soviet bias. In May the editor of *Reynolds News* and Alexander debated the Communist influences in the pages of the Sunday paper.[14] Alexander's attack may have succeeded in shifting *Reynolds News* away from its 'fellow-travelling' road, but one of his main targets, Assistant Editor Gordon Schaffer, was not forced out until 1953.[15]

The *Daily Express* and *Sunday Express* bucked the trend, for a while.[16] Owner Lord Beaverbrook had always favoured good relations with dictators – first Hitler then Stalin – in what long-time associate John Junor described as an admiration for naked power.[17] In Germany *Daily Express* correspondent Wilfred Burchett's strong left-wing opinions led him to increasingly favour the Soviet over the Anglo-American point of view.[18] Despite his opinions, during the height of the 1948–9 Berlin blockade the *Daily Express* had Burchett set up a 'Russian Window' feature in which he would analyse East bloc developments from Berlin. Editor Arthur Christiansen did not worry about his politics, telling Beaverbrook, 'He is, I think, a fellow-traveller, but nevertheless an able chap'.[19] The first instalment ran 20 October 1948. But Burchett's favourable reporting of Soviet life was soon raising eyebrows among other top managers. Beaverbrook's right-hand man, E. J. Robertson, had several talks with Christiansen about the 'Russian Window' material, especially one 'pure propaganda' piece about luxuries in Russian stores. Robertson assured Beaverbrook that Burchett's copy would be 'scrutinized more carefully' in the future.[20] Burchett continued writing for the *Express* as a free-lancer in Hungary.[21] When he reported on the trial of anti-Communist Cardinal Mindszenty Burchett challenged reports in the British press that Mindszenty had confessed under the influence of 'truth drugs'. Foreign Editor Charles Foley checked up on him, but accepted the report.[22] For his part, Burchett began to complain that the *Daily Express* was more interested in political trials than social revolutions and switched briefly to *The Times* before leaving mainstream journalism to report the Cold War from the Communist side.[23]

But sensationalism could trump consensus for Beaverbrook. In the early stages of the Korean War *Daily Express* editor, Arthur Christiansen, turned down a chance to buy dramatic pictures of South Koreans shooting prisoners because printing them would have given 'our enemies a chance to say we were playing the Communist game and doing the *Daily Worker*'s propaganda for them'.[24] The pictures later turned up in the *Daily Worker*. Beaverbook lamented the fact that the *Express* didn't have those 'real fine pictures'.[25] Anti-Communism could be sensational, and profitable, too. In early 1951 the *Daily Express* serialised ex-Communist Douglas Hyde's confession *I Believed* and sold up to 65,000 extra copies each day.[26]

At Reuters Eric Bourne had covered Berlin after the war, and the agency was so pleased with his work there that it planned to promote him to head the Moscow bureau in July 1947.[27] But British officials in Berlin said that Bourne was a 'member of the Communist Party and extremely pro-Russian'; FO News Department Head William Ridsdale passed on those suspicions to a thoroughly alarmed Christopher Chancellor.[28] Instead of sending Bourne to Moscow, Reuters sacked him.[29] The allegations followed Bourne to his next job as the Prague correspondent for the Kemsley International News Service, and his new supervisor, Ian Fleming, demanded an explanation.

> So far as I am concerned, you have already shown yourself an extremely competent and intelligent Correspondent with the possibility of a more responsible post on my staff in the future. But quite obviously Correspondents with communist sympathies (with all that they entail intellectually) can be of no more use to a group of Conservative newspapers than a Correspondent who is profoundly anti-Jewish, for instance, or one who thinks the world is flat, or is going to end at 5:20 next Wednesday evening.[30]

Bourne declared his loyalty to Britain and explained that he had been enthusiastic about the 1930s' Popular Front, which linked Communists to liberals and socialists, but that he had become increasingly disillusioned with Communism ever since the 1939 Hitler-Stalin pact. By 1948 Bourne said he was definitely not a Communist sympathiser. The explanation apparently satisfied Fleming, who said the letter 'rings perfectly true'; he also sent a copy to Ridsdale.[31] Bourne remained in Prague for Kemsley until the Czech Communists expelled him in 1950; he later worked for the *Daily Express* in Yugoslavia.[32]

Reuters faced more problems in 1950. In June its chief Berlin correspondent, John Peet, defected to the East Germans and held a press conference to denounce his career as a tool of the Anglo–American 'warmongers'. At the conference he assured his former colleagues that he was not under the influence of 'Russian money or Central Asiatic truth drugs', turned over the keys to the office safe, and then filed his last dispatch for Reuters – on his own defection. Reuters did not run it.[33] Back in London a quiet rumpus erupted over a case of 'journalistic sabotage' at the Fleet Street headquarters. Sometime soon after the June 1950 outbreak of the Korean War management at the Reuters news agency discovered a 'Communist cell' – a dozen Communist and sympathisers – among the editorial staff. Alterations made on a Cold War news story brought attention on

Sub-editor Frances Wheeler, who broke down and told management about the group's activities. Although 'cell member' Derek Jameson insisted that this case was the only incident of altering the news and that the group didn't do anything, all of those involved were gradually and quietly forced out. 'The blacklist had arrived. We began to be picked off one by one. I don't think anyone was actually fired. Nothing vulgar like that. It was simply made clear they would be better advised to take their services elsewhere'.[34]

Before the Communists and their friends had been cleared out, their leader Lawrence Kirwan forced management to qualify the famous Reuters objectivity by making a formal request to use a TASS dispatch on an official North Korean report about American and South Korean atrocities during their occupation of northern Korea. Manager Geoffrey Imeson summed up the dilemma:

> It puts us in a spot. We don't want to use it, but why not? What reason do we give for suppressing this official report unless we have a policy on such matter, i.e. frankly recognise that we cannot sit on the fence and must be anti-Communist. This is an example of what crops up once or twice a month. Point is that if an American authority reported on Korean atrocities we would use it.[35]

The Reuters 'cell' became common knowledge on Fleet Street. Malcolm Muggeridge lent his MI6 cachet to a talk with Reuters management in November – 'they asked me what I thought they should do about certain specific cases. I told them to the best of my ability'.[36] The Reuters case made even the Beaverbrook papers start to worry. In July *Sunday Express* editor, John Gordon, wrote to Beaverbrook.

> This business of political sabotage in journalism is much more prevalent than we are inclined to think. As you know, I have had instances of it here.
> There is no remedy except dismissal, and no real protection except never to employ anyone with any 'red' in his background, if you can discover it. But it is not always easy to discover.[37]

The BBC and the Problems of Objectivity

The BBC probably had fewer left-wingers on staff at the beginning of the Cold War because of a decade of MI5 vetting of new employees and MI5 tips that led to a close watch on any Communist employee.[38] If Communists worked impartially the BBC would take no action, though at least one was punished because his wife was a Communist.[39] Haley admitted that 'fellow travellers' could be trickier but he saw no means of controlling them other than through a 'witch-hunt', which he was not willing to do.[40]

When the government shifted to open anti-Communism in early 1948 the BBC followed, but not soon enough for some critics. Conservative leader Winston Churchill attacked the BBC's tolerance of Communists at a 25 February meeting on political broadcasting.[41] The simultaneous Communist coup in Czechoslovakia intensified that pressure. As Haley noted, the BBC was in 'the midst of the great Communist scare'. Churchill continued to complain about the 'Communist vipers' on the BBC staff, and Labour information kingpin Herbert Morrison began planning an investigation on Communism within the BBC.[42] Haley pre-empted this outside intervention by introducing a relatively mild anti-Communist measure to the Board of Governors, which considered it in March and April 1948. The governors agreed with Haley that no employee should be 'penalized for his political views' but if employees 'betrayed the Corporation's trust of impartiality' they would be sacked. The governors conceded that reporting of Communism and the British Communist Party had 'tended to get out of proportion' and that in the future the BBC would closely monitor the Communists' appearances and references to them.[43] Communists could broadcast on Marxist topics, but only in small doses, and should be avoided on most other topics when an objective voice is needed. Meanwhile, staff should carefully scrutinise all scripts on Russia.[44] But Morrison continued his pressure, demanding in April to know which staff member allowed a story on British Communist leader Harry Pollitt to air. Haley refused to say and complained in his diary that Morrison's action was 'witch hunting of the worst type'. Morrison made the same demand of Board Chairman Lord Simon of Wythenshawe who approached Haley 'in a dither'.

> I told him we had been through all this business of Cabinet Ministers demanding that people should be sacked during the war. It was quite unconstitutional and I hope the governors were not going to start such nonsense all over again.[45]

Nevertheless, the BBC cleaned house, at least in the overseas services. Malcolm Muggeridge noted that a friend in the BBC had told him in August 1949 that 'nearly all the Communists and fellow-travellers had now been weeded out of the European Service of the BBC'.[46] There was still the issue of outside guests on talks shows, which were believed to be quite important in building a public consensus on foreign policy. Frequent BBC contributor William Clark described it this way: the BBC would bring in a variety of respectable journalists – but not too wide a variety – to discuss world and national events in a non-confrontational way and in such a manner as to reach a broad consensus.[47] Acceptable and reliable contributors could stay within the BBC's bounds without damaging their sense of independence and integrity. As Third Programme World Affairs producer (and future Director General) C. J. Curran wrote about his guests: 'although they will accept a brief, they will not do so uncritically. The limit of what I can do is to use tactful suggestion'.[48] By the beginning of 1949 Curran had a stable of guests that included Donald MacLachlan, H. V. Hudson, Walter Taplin, Vernon Bartlett, Graham Hutton, and W. N. Ewer – all of whom were well within the Cold War consensus.[49]

Not all producers liked the idea of using the radio to build a political consensus. About the same time Curran was building his show, Cambridge historian and Third Programme talks producer Peter Laslett argued that the Third Programme had originally offered a stimulating range of opinion on foreign policies by dissidents such as A. J. P. Taylor and E. H. Carr.

> I realise that there is a possibility of embarrassing the Foreign Office if we go too far in this direction. But I feel that the Foreign Office is, or we take it to be, inordinately sensitive. In any case such an argument doesn't justify our robbing the Third Programme audience of one of its really important intellectual interests – the controversial discussion of British foreign policy.[50]

The Foreign Office was indeed sensitive about the guests the BBC brought on the air. Beginning in 1948 the Foreign Office regularly berated the BBC for allowing Soviet sympathisers to speak about the USSR's accomplishments – real or imagined. The BBC compounded the offence in their eyes by reprinting some of the talks in its prestigious weekly magazine *The Listener*. The steady hectoring and the worsening international relations led to fewer and fewer such guests.

Moscow Ambassador Maurice Peterson and Christopher Warner both complained to Jacob in early 1948 about a Home Programme talk by Olga Watts that gave a rosy, but they believed misleading, account of life in the USSR.[51] Peterson called it 'Communist-inspired drivel'.[52] Jacob forwarded the complaint to Barnes, the director of the spoken word, who apologised for the talk.

> The script was passed for inclusion in the programme with the important proviso that the producer should make it clear that Mrs. Watts was a privileged person in Moscow and was describing the life of a Commissar. Through an unfortunate error this qualification was omitted from the broadcast, which was then printed in the 'Listener'[53]

After complaints about a May 1950 Home Service talk that Haley thought 'lacked balance' fellow-travelling barrister D. N. Pritt appeared to deliver an effective justification for Soviet show trials and easily bested opposing guest Conservative MP Quintin Hogg. The exchange was then published in *The Listener* on 27 July 1950. Many listeners and the Foreign Office complained, but Haley merely noted that it would have been difficult to rig the debate beforehand. Pritt was not invited back.[54]

Scientist and Soviet sympathiser J. D. Bernal had praised Soviet construction methods in a Third Programme architectural show; the Foreign Office and others attacked him for his alleged factual inaccuracies and his politics. The FO's information chief Jack Nicholls went so far as to say that no Communist was capable of objectivity.[55] Apparently that affliction extended beyond Communists to include those who lacked enough enthusiasm for Cold War policy. *New Statesman* editor, Kingsley Martin, found in the summer of 1950 that BBC broadcasting offers were drying up after a successful run. He wondered why.

> My own theory is something like this. I think that without any formal ban being imposed, producers may be influenced against a broadcaster to

whom steady objection is raised, perhaps every time he speaks, from the Listeners Association or from some individuals in the American Embassy, the Foreign Office or from some religious body. That is only guess work, but it still seems to me likely to have some validity.[56]

In the midst of the wrangling over the acceptability of radio guests another dispute between the FO and the BBC came from a programme designed by staunch anti-Communists within the corporation to be utterly objective and to give elite British listeners an idea of Soviet propaganda distortions. The IRD repeatedly complained that *The Soviet View* and its unadorned quotations from the Soviet press was an example of 'false objectivity'. Third Programme head Harman Grisewood had first pitched the idea in March 1948, pointing out that British listeners had little idea of what sort of news the Soviet people were getting on events such as the recent Czech coup and Italian elections.[57] The BBC's strongly anti-Communist diplomatic correspondent, Tom Barman, was also behind the idea, and it is clear that the BBC envisioned this as helping the national cause in the Cold War.[58] Haley warned, however, that much of the Soviet domestic propaganda was 'just hard lying and we cannot at the same time say so'.[59]

Reactions to the 5 July 1948 inaugural broadcast were mixed. The FO's Ian Grey thought that it was so good that it should be put on the Home Programme on a weekly or fortnightly basis. But he was in a minority. The IRD's Colin MacLaren found *The Soviet View* programme 'too neutral' and discouraged the idea.[60] *The Economist* attacked it as 'objectivity run riot'. An indignant Grisewood defended the programme in a memo to Barnes: 'We are not seeking to promote "good understanding" by persuading the listener of the reasonableness of the other fellow's point of view. We are not seeking to expose the crudity of the Communist line. We are seeking to inform'.[61] Listener Research found that both 'Russophobes' and 'Russophiles' were both unhappy with the programme.[62]

The BBC added more disclaimers, paid closer attention to the announcers' tones, and vetoed any ideas of expanding it to the other services, but continued with it every five weeks in the Third Programme. The managers seemed to imply that the general audience would not understand the show's purpose, but that the elite Third Programme audience did.[63] Although some in the BBC made the case that the programme had an 'element of counter-propaganda in it' the IRD was not convinced. IRD specialist Hugh Lunghi criticised its failure to 'show up Soviet propaganda' and MacLaren cited it as an example of the BBC's 'false objectivity'.[64]

> The BBC argument, so far as it has been explained, is that to do anything other than to state the Soviet statement would be propaganda, which the programme claims not to be. This argument is quite invalid, because the programme is propaganda – Soviet propaganda, and very effective at that.[65]

The IRD made several approaches through Barman to try and modify the programme and even suggested ending it because of the danger of spreading Communism among British intellectuals, but met with little success.[66] In May 1950 the BBC reaffirmed its commitment to the programme, but also agreed on the need for more 'sign-posting' – at the beginning, end and four times during the thirty-minute programme – to avoid any confusion. By 1950 the programme quoted only news and views on internal Soviet affairs because the commentary on external affairs threatened to 'submerge (the programme) in a sea of boredom'.[67] The programme continued into the 1950s and by 1958 it, ironically, was actually using IRD material in its scripts.[68]

The shock of the June 1950 Communist North Korean invasion of anti-Communist South Korea spurred further soul-searching by the BBC and a harder anti-Communist line in all domestic services.[69] Haley resisted other pressures, such as Churchill's repeated demand for a total ban on Communists.[70] In late 1950 Talks Director Mary Somerville noted that her supervisors were planning to 'take the lid off' with a series or documentary critical of Communism.[71] At Haley's January 1951 briefing of top staff, he emphasised that the long-term issue was the ideological conflict; the more immediate issue was handling the heightened international tensions and rearmament pressures. For the Home and Third programmes the BBC would emphasise the moral, political and strategic aspects of the Cold War; for the Light Programme the BBC would condescend to discuss the Cold War's effect on everyday life.[72]

Within a few weeks the controller of Home Services proposed following up the new policy with a series of talks on two new books claiming to expose the malign inner workings of Communism – one on Communist methods in Czechoslovakia, the other Douglas Hyde's confessions of a British Communist, *I Believed*. Haley approved the controller's plans. His subordinates rejected calls from within the BBC to give the Communists a right of reply.[73] The show soon strayed from its stated intentions and became a general discussion between Denis Healey, the head of the Labour Party's International Department and a major conduit for IRD propaganda, and R. N. Carew-Hunt, an MI6 associate.[74] By that time there were serious misgivings about the programme within the BBC. Haley thought that it had veered too far from its original aims, and decided that 'fairness demands' that the BBC consider giving the British Communists a right of reply.[75] They didn't get it.

The BBC continued to keep a close eye on Cold War issues and, often favoured the government interest over the listeners and viewers.[76] In late 1954 and early 1955 the government sought to limit the BBC's freedom in reporting on the hydrogen bomb. Cabinet ministers, and the BBC director and chairman met to hash out the problem in February 1955. The government wanted control 'over the manner in which the effects of nuclear weapons were made known to the public. If these effects were presented too abruptly or in too alarming a fashion there was a real danger that people would adopt a defeatist attitude'. More seriously, they might not bother with home defence or civil defence. The government was less concerned with spot news than it was with special programmes or talks on the hydrogen bomb, for which it wanted close consultation between the BBC and the relevant ministries. Ian Jacob, now director-general, had no problems with these requirements.[77]

Censorship: Secrets, Technology and Policy

Government censorship marked the edges of acceptable public discourse. The-atre and film censorship had been long established and grudgingly accepted, not only for matters of taste and decency but also for politically explosive matters. Security censorship was ostensibly about protecting vital technical secrets and military operations, but after 1947 it became expansive – banning almost all de-tails of the British atomic bomb programme, keeping industrial and economic information out of trade journals, and planning for full-scale censorship in the event of war. Together they drew a line that most British journalists probably did not dream of crossing during the Cold War.

Cold War political film censorship tended to focus on Soviet- and Communist-bloc documentary and quasi-documentary feature imports. In 1951 cabinet min-isters and the Foreign Office had tried to ban, censor or delay the import licenses for East bloc documentary movies promoting the Soviet-style peace movement.[78] Although most of the pro-Communist films in the Cold War played to small au-diences, in 1952 a Soviet film *The Fall of Berlin* was slated for a major West End premier. Prime Minister Winston Churchill personally previewed the film, and suggested that the censorship board add an introductory disclaimer that the film represented only the Soviet view. The film went on to be a box-office success, leading some in the Foreign Office to worry about potential political repercus-sions and regret they had not pressed more vigorously for some sort of factual rebuttal.[79]

These foreign Communist films were nuisances for the government, but sometimes their mere exhibition could be embarrassing from a diplomatic perspective.[80] For example, in 1954 the British-Vietnam Friendship Society im-ported the pro-Communist, anti-French documentary *Fighting Vietnam* to show in London. The French government objected and the IRD and the BBFC pre-viewed the film and suggested cuts in the film and the commentary, most of which the distributor made.[81] This pleased the French, but British Communists and the NCNA (presumably the New China News Agency) were able to make sharp points about British political censorship, which led some officials to speculate on the downsides of censorship: '. . . limited political censorship in this country can have serious "boomerang" effects, and consequently we should always be chary of using it'.[82] Cinema newsreels were technically subject to censorship, but remained free as long as they toed the line.[83]

Security censorship through the collaborative D-Notice Committee was a dif-ferent matter. The rationale for the system was that Soviet intelligence could read British publications to assemble a mass of small, seemingly insignificant bits of information that would create a composite picture of British weapons and security. If the press didn't publish that kind of information the Soviets would have a tougher time gathering intelligence on Britain.[84] Innocuously worded D-Notices would keep potentially more damaging information out of the pa-pers. But as MI5 head Roger Hollis pointed out the system only worked with British journalists.[85] The Soviets had an eye on the D-Notice system through the *Daily Worker*, and American journalists often published details forbidden to their British colleagues. Only the British public remained ignorant.

Britain planned and built an atomic bomb with almost no press coverage or commentary thanks to the D-Notice system. The press was willing to go along with a nearly blanket ban, with the rare exception of *Daily Express* reporter Chapman Pincher. The atomic officials were the ones who repeatedly pushed for more openness and liberality, arguing that obsessive secrecy was interfering with recruitment and procurement and leading to unfounded press speculation. In May 1951 they complained to the JIC that extreme secrecy was 'unnecessary and futile, and is a hindrance to progress' but censorship remained in place.[86]

War fears in 1950 led the government to push the D-Notice committee to crack down on publication of economic and industrial information. Military planners worried that the Soviets could use that information to plan bombing and sabotage strategy. In the D-Notice Committee press representatives were persuaded, after a struggle, to go along with an 'advisory letter' that urged the press to bury details on everything from munitions plants to sewage plants. Further tightening the leash, MI5 urged some defence-related companies to cut off contact with the press, which they did.[87] The military representatives urged publishers to use 'utmost discretion' with aerial photographs, which could be used by the Soviets to determine bombing targets.[88] One critic on the D-Notice Committee cited the case of a factory visible in the background of a picture, which led to military rejection of *The Consulting Engineer's* plan to run an aerial photo of the not-so-strategic Spalding Flood Alleviation Channel.[89] In the Cold War thaw the D-Notice Committee relented and issued a more flexible 'advisory letter' in late 1954.[90]

The D-Notice Committee also was brought into the wartime censorship planning, which began during the 1948–9 Berlin blockade when the possibility of war with the Soviet Union seemed likely. After a quick review in August 1948 the cabinet's Defence (Transition) Committee decided to re-create press censorship and news distribution on a World War II model in the event of war with the Soviet Union.[91] The nucleus of the News and Press Censorship Bureau was attached to the COI under Capt. C. A. H. Brooking, who began planning for a 163-censor bureau.[92] The D-Notice Committee's Admiral Thomson was once again designated chief press censor.[93] In May 1949 the censorship committee brought the press, newsreels, and BBC into the process via the D Notice Committee.[94] The committee then asked the editors to not publicise the fact that planning for censorship had begun.[95]

As the committee denied information to the loyal British public, it gave it to the Communist enemy and presumably the Soviet Union by including the *Daily Worker* in standard D-Notice distribution.[96] The justification went like this: if the *Daily Worker* were cut off from the D-Notice system they would simply pick up D-Notices from other sources and make political problems out of their exclusion.[97] Besides, officials argued, the D-Notices themselves were written in a way that wouldn't give away secrets or the location of secrets.[98] War in Korea put a different spin on things. Admiral Thomson withheld three D-Notices from the

Daily Worker, whose editor then complained about the exclusion.[99] Eventually, cabinet ministers created a new series of D-notices – 'DX notices' – for atomic issues and other highly sensitive information that would not go to the *Daily Worker*. The Communists would still get the regular and 'innocuous' D-Notices.[100]

Another set of problems arose when foreign journalists started digging for news and publishing it overseas. American newspapers circulating in Britain often carried sensitive news, particularly about British military technology, and in 1948 the committee started exploring ways to plug the leaks.[101] American journalists continued to irritate British censors. In December 1954 the American trade magazine *Aviation Week* published details on new British air-to-air missiles, which were then picked up and reprinted by the London *Daily Express*. The information apparently came from an American visitor to Britain who gave *Aviation Week* the details when he had returned to the USA. The top level Joint Intelligence Committee explored setting up trans-Atlantic links so that American editors would know what to keep secret.[102] In another, still opaque incident apparently involving news in the Paris-based *Interavia* magazine the JIC argued that the leaks put the reputable press at a disadvantage and left the D-Notice system 'in imminent danger of collapse'. The Air Ministry representative wanted an investigation, complete with phone tapping and mail opening, and prosecution under the Official Secrets Act.[103] But the offending publication soon brought on a new London editor and the JIC decided to give him a chance. And that apparently did the trick.[104]

Although the D-Notice system had remained firm throughout the early 1950s, by the mid-1950s problems were cropping up. In 1956 the *Manchester Guardian* violated a D-Notice and a series of scandals and perceived abuses of the committee in the 1960s further eroded the trust between the services and the press. The committee, however, has continued to function, albeit in modified form.[105]

Sedition, Treason and the Communist Press

Despite the *Daily Worker*'s cooperation with the D-Notice Committee, British officials at the highest levels were deeply suspicious of the Communist newspaper and at several points considered suppressing it as they had during World War II. By early 1947 the Attlee government was considering contingency plans for once again banning the *Daily Worker*, this time in the event of war with the Soviet Union.[106] Four years later MI5 also suggested banning the newspaper, noting that British Communists wouldn't be capable of guerrilla warfare or sabotage in the event of war, but they could aggravate industrial disputes and depress morale.[107] But any suppression was academic until the June 1950 British involvement in the Korean War.[108]

British authorities first feared that Communists would call for sabotage or wildcat dock strikes to block arms shipments, part of a larger fear of left-wing labour militancy, and drafted legislation to punish incitement of interference through 'subversive or misleading propaganda'.[109] But the cabinet did not follow through as it became apparent that no sabotage conspiracy was in the works.[110] Another problem cropped up when *Daily Worker* reporter and British subject Alan Winnington showed up as a correspondent with the Communist North Korean army and began sending the *Worker* stories about Communist bravery and anti-Communist barbarism.[111] One riveting piece claimed US complicity in the South Korean police massacre of 7,000 political prisoners, who were killed before advancing North Koreans could free them.[112] British newspapers ignored the story, the Americans denounced it, British officials privately gave it some credence and archival evidence indicates that it was accurate, albeit exaggerated.[113]

In September the government announced that Winnington was 'laying himself open' to charges of treason despite private doubts about the law's fit for the Korean 'police action'.[114] The *Daily Worker* soon raised the stakes by publishing a collection of Winnington's stomach-turning dispatches in a heavily promoted pamphlet titled *I Saw the Truth in Korea*.[115] Shawcross took notice and came to the cabinet for advice: if he admitted to parliament that the *Daily Worker*'s coverage and Winnington's pamphlet were treasonous, as he believed them to be, he would have to take action. The only penalty for treason was death, which he believed to be excessive. More importantly, most juries would also think it excessive and refuse to send a journalist to the gallows. In World War II there had been special emergency legislation that would cover these activities, but now it was 'treason or nothing'.[116] Cabinet secretary Norman Brook shared that worry, writing: 'It seems clear that proceedings for treason are much too heavy a hammer for this particular nut.'[117]

The cabinet fretted, then agreed and opted for a policy of threatening ambiguity – to imply that Winnington's journalism was treasonous but stay vague about specific legal action.[118] But the *Daily Worker* was on the mind of Attlee's PR adviser, Philip Jordan, who favoured a hard line to galvanise the public behind the government's expensive rearmament policies. Shutting down the *Daily Worker* would not only focus public attention on the Communist threat but also eliminate an irritant.

> If the *Daily Worker* were suppressed, we could expect trouble from the *Daily Express* and bleats from the *Manchester Guardian* and the *News Chronicle*, but I think we could count on support from almost everywhere else that matters. If we prepared our case carefully and produced a list of treasonable and vile statements by the *Daily Worker* over the last six months, we should have the overwhelming majority behind us, in spite of anything the *New Statesman and Nation* might say to the contrary.
>
> No doubt mass meetings of protest would be organised, and halls would be filled by the usual crowds, but I am sure we need not worry about them.[119]

Attlee did not take his adviser's suggestion. The Communist journalists moved off centre stage until a more complicated figure, Labour Party activist Monica

Felton made a splash with a trip to North Korea and accusations of horrific American, South Korean and even British atrocities – on Radio Moscow, in the *Daily Worker*, and at a widely covered London press conference.[120] Parliamentary and public accusations of sedition, or even treason, once again forced the cabinet to consider ways to suppress this kind of discourse, and the behind-the-lines travel that fed it.[121] Government lawyers said no existing law would cover Felton's case.[122] The Labour cabinet briefly toyed with reinstituting World War II-style detention without trial, but instead seriously considered creating a new law for treason-like speech and writing – a proposed law of treachery – which would carry a two-year prison term. Truth would be no defence if it were proved that the intention was subversion.[123] The Conservatives who won the October 1951 elections shelved Labour's plans but kept Winnington in their sights, especially after he helped with North Korean propaganda in POW camps and at the Panmunjom truce talks.[124] They seized his passport when it came up for renewal in 1954, and offered him travel papers good for a one-way trip back to England. Winnington thought it would land him in prison or to the scaffold so he remained a stateless Englishman in Mao's China.[125]

Conclusion

Consensus created journalistic casualties as journalists who were Communists or merely seen as too indulgent of the Soviet Union in their work jumped or were pushed out of the mainstream media. This was largely driven by the news media's leaders themselves. But government threats, bluster and cooptation were important both in marking the outer boundaries of Cold War journalistic behaviour and discourse. Heightened security censorship and press self-censorship may have kept some facts from Soviet spies, but it kept more of them from the British public. This policy clearly reinforced cooperative press behaviour and limited public debate, especially on vital issues such as the atomic bomb development. As the American *Progressive* magazine noted years later in relation to nuclear secrecy, 'to know how is to ask why'.[126]

Notes

1. Quoted in Peter Coleman, *The Liberal Conspiracy: The Congress for Cultural Freedom and the Struggle for the Mind of Postwar Europe* (New York: Free Press, 1989), p. 38.
2. 'Wide freedom for Soviet publications in Britain', *World's Press News*, 15 September 1950.
3. 'Communists use slightest pretext to stop truth emerging from Prague', *World's Press News*, 11 May 1951.
4. PRO FO371/56886 N13981/3041/38, Hankey to Maurice Peterson, 5 November 1946; *The Times* Archives, Iverach McDonald Papers, Unlabelled Box, Iverach McDonald to A. P. Ryan, 18 February 1969.

5. *The Times* Archives, Deakin Papers, Burn to Deakin, 10 May 1948.
6. Pritt Papers, 1/21. Burn to Casey, 14 May 1949; McDonald, *The History of The Times*, vol. V, pp. 173–4.
7. *Who's Who, 1976–77*, entry for Michael Clive Burn.
8. Ayerst, *The Guardian*, pp. 582–6.
9. *Guardian* Archives B/W170A, Wadsworth to Werth, 30 March 1948.
10. *Guardian* Archives, B/W170A, Werth to Wadsworth, 7 April 1948.
11. *Guardian* Archives B/W170A, Wadsworth to Werth, 26 January 1949
12. Ibid.
13. 'Dismissal of Communist: 'Yorkshire Post' editor's account, *World's Press News*, 27 May 1948.
14. '"Communistic Tendencies" in Reynolds News' Inescapable', *World's Press News*, 27 May 1948.
15. Gordon Schaffer, *Baby in the Bathwater: Memories of a Political Journalist* (Sussex: The Book Guild, 1996), pp. 199-209.
16. Alan Foster, 'The Beaverbrook Press and appeasement: the second phase', *European History Quarterly* 21 (1991).
17. John Junor. Interview by Author. Tape recording. London. 27 November 1996.
18. Kelvin Rowley, 'Burchett and the Cold War in Europe', in Ben Kiernan (ed.), *Burchett Reporting the Other Side of the World, 1939–1983* (New York: Quartet Books, 1986).
19. BBK Papers, H/127, Christiansen to Beaverbrook, 14 October 1948.
20. BBK Papers, H/136, Robertson to Beaverbook, [January 1949].
21. Wilfred Burchett, *At the Barricades: Forty Years on the Cutting Edge of History* (New York: Times Books, 1981), pp. 130–1.
22. BBK Papers, H/136, Robertson to Beaverbrook, [January 1949], and 6 April 1949; Burchett, *At the Barricades*, pp. 141–3.
23. Burchett, *At the Barricades*.
24. BBK, H/141, Christiansen to Beaverbrook, 14 December 1950; 'THIS was done in your name!' *Daily Worker*, 29 November 1950.
25. BBK, H/144, Beaverbrook to Robertson, 18 December 1950.
26. BBK, H/148, Christiansen to Beaverbrook, 25 January 1951.
27. Reuters Archives, Eric Bourne File, Walton Cole to Eric Bourne, 24 June 1947.
28. PRO FO371/66417 N10540/1018/38, I.T.M. Pink to Roberts, 29 August 1947, Ridsdale Minute, 8 October 1947.
29. Reuters Archives, Eric Bourne File, Carter to Bourne, 28 November 1947, Bourne to H. B. Carter (Reuters secretary), 28 November 1947.
30. Reuters Archives, Eric Bourne File, Fleming to Bourne, 18 March 1948, Fleming to Bourne, 18 March 1948.
31. Reuters Archives, Bourne File, Bourne to Fleming, 30 March 1948, Fleming to Chancellor, 5 April 1948.
32. 'Four correspondents to leave Prague, *The Times*, 7 January 1950.
33. 'Reuter's chief Berlin correspondent denounces his career', *Newspaper World*, 15 June 1950; John Peet, *The Long Engagement: Memoirs of a Cold War Legend* (London: Fourth Estate, 1989), pp. 186–7.
34. Derek Jameson, *Touched by Angels* (London: Ebury Press, 1988), pp. 115–22. Also see *World's Press News*, 28 July 1950.
35. Reuters Archive, Lawrence Kirwan Personnel File, Imeson to Cole, [December 1950].
36. Muggeridge Papers (Hoover), Diary entry for 15 November 1950.

37. BBK, H/138 Gordon to Beaverbrook, 18 July 1950.
38. PRO CAB21/2745, Extract from GEN226/1st meeting, 13 April 1948.
39. Mark Hollingsworth and Richard Norton-Taylor, *Blacklist: The Inside Story of Political Vetting* (London: Hogarth Press, 1988), p. 102.
40. PRO CAB21/2745, David Stephens to Norman Brook (Communists in the BBC), 2 April 1948.
41. PRO CAB21/2745, Political Broadcasting: Draft minutes of 25 February 1948 meeting; Martin Gilbert, *Never Despair: Winston Churchill, 1945–1965* (London: Heinemann, 1988), p. 403.
42. Haley Papers, 13/34, Diary entry for 25 March 1948.
43. BBC WAC R1/16, Board minutes, 18 March 1948, 1, 15 and 29 April 1948.
44. BBC WAC R34/313/2 (G22/48), The Treatment of Communism and Communist Speakers: Note by the Director of the Spoken World.
45. Haley Papers, 13/34, Diary entry for 10 April 1948.
46. Muggeridge Papers, (Hoover), Diary entry for 14 August 1949.
47. Clark, *From Three Worlds*, pp. 117–9.
48. BBC WAC R51/651, Curran to H.T.D., 17 June 1948.
49. BBC WAC R51/651, Curran to A.H.T.D., 9 February 1949.
50. BBC WAC R51/651, Peter Laslett to Controller, Talks, 10 February 1949.
51. The talk was printed in *The Listener* on 5 February 1948.
52. PRO FO1110/16 PR10/10/913, Peterson to Warner, 17 February 1948.
53. PRO FO1110/16 PR10/10/913, Barnes to Warner, 10 March 1948.
54. BBC WAC RCONTI PRITT, Somerville to DSW, 8 September 1950; 'Are Communist political trials fair?' *The Listener*, 27 July 1950, pp. 114–15, 134–5; Letters to the Editor of The Listener, 3, 10, 17, 24 August 1950 and 2 November 1950; D. N. Pritt, *The Autobiography of D.N. Pritt, Part Two: Brasshats and Bureaucrats* (London: Lawrence and Wishart, 1966), pp. 156–8.
55. BBC WAC R34/530/1, #3, Jack Nicholls to G. W. Harrison, 2 November 1950, Warner to Jacob, 8 August 1950.
56. Francis Williams Papers, 8/9, Kingsley Martin to Francis Williams, 27 June 1951.
57. BBC WAC R28/254, Grisewood to Barnes, 11 March 1948.
58. BBC WAC R28/254, Barman to Foreign News Editor, 9 April 1948.
59. BBC WAC R28/254, Haley to Barnes, 25 June 1948.
60. PRO FO371/71630 N4485/1/38, Ian Gray Minute, 14 July 1948, MacLaren Minute, 15 July 1948.
61. BBC WAC R28/254, Grisewood to Barnes, 13 July 1948.
62. BBC WAC R/28/254, Christopher Holmes to Barnes, 21 December 1948.
63. BBC WAC R28/254, Editor (News) Postscript, 30 December 1948, Barnes to Haley, 30 December 1948.
64. PRO FO1110/224 PR2462/35/913, Lunghi Minute, 19 May 1949.
65. PRO FO1110/224 PR2462/35/913, MacLaren Minute, 13 July 1949.
66. PRO FO1110/224 PR2462/35/913, Barman to Matthews, 11 July 1949.
67. BBC WAC R28/254, (Hole) Editor, News to Haley, 22 January 1951.
68. PRO FO1110/1066 PR135/15, King Minute, 3 October 1958.
69. BBC WAC R34/313/3, Barnes to Strang, 14 September 1950; BBC WAC R34/530/1 'Note of D.G'.s and D.S.W.'s Interview with Sir Roger Makins and Mr. G. W. Harrison', 25 September 1950.
70. Haley Papers, 13/6, Diary entry for 10 September 1950.

71. BBC WAC R34/313/3, Somerville to D.S.W., Communists and Communist Speakers, [n.d.].
72. BBC WAC R34/878, 'Minutes of the Spoken Word meeting', 11 January 1951.
73. BBC WAC R34/878, 'Director of the Spoken Word meeting, 25 January 1951 and 8 February 1951. Also see BBC WAC R34/313/3, #1, Policy: Communism, File 2b, 1950–51, Stephens to John Green, 25 April 1951.
74. BBC WAC R34/313/3, #1, Policy: Communism, File 2b, 1950–51, Stephens to John Green, 25 April 1951.
75. Haley Papers, 13/6, Diary entry for 27 April 1951.
76. Anthony Adamthwaite, '"Nation shall speak peace unto nation": the BBC's response to peace and defence issues, 1945–58', *Contemporary Record* 7 (1993).
77. CAB21/3353, 'Note for the Record', 16 February 1955.
78. 'Not quite prepared for *Always Prepared*: Herbert Morrison and the film of the 1950 East Berlin Youth Rally', Bert Hogenkamp, *Contemporary British History* 12 (1998); PRO CAB129/45 CP (51) 56 'Propaganda film of the Berlin Youth Rally'; PRO FO1110/461 PR130/1, L. R. Hinson to J. H. Moore, 10 July 1951, Nicholls to G. L. Bond, 1 August 1951, Bond to Nicholls, 4 August 1951.
79. PRO FO1110/528 PR123/1, J. O. Roach Minute, 7 October 1952; H. A. F. Hohler Minute, [n.d.].
80. PRO FO11110/624 PR124/8, Manchip-White Minute, 5 April 1954.
81. PRO FO1110/624, Rennie Minute, 8 March 1954.
82. PRO FO1110/624, PR124/3 E. Bolland Minute, 16 March 1954.
83. Norman Fisher, Interview by Author. Tape recording. London. 30 October 1996.
84. BBC WAC R28/5/3, 'Security in Peacetime', 11 December 1953.
85. PRO CAB159/13 JIC (53) 13th meeting, 'Leakages of Information about Military Aviation', 30 January 1953.
86. Margaret Gowing, *Independence and Deterrence: Britain and Atomic Energy, 1945–1952*, vol. 2 (New York: St Martin's Press, 1972), pp. 117, 126–37; BBC WAC R34/272/1 D-Notice No. 25, 11 May 1948; PRO CAB176/30 J.I.C. 1140/51, Draft Paper for Ministerial Committee on Atomic Energy, 18 May 1951; PRO CAB159/14 J.I.C. 2194/52 E. Morgan (Controller of Atomic Energy) to Secretary, J.I.C., 24 September 1952.
87. PRO INF12/525, Note by D. C. Morland, Chairman of the Security of Economic Information Committee, 11 October 1951.
88. BBC WAC R34/272/2, Thomson to press members, 29 September 1951.
89. BBC WAC R28/5/4, 'Remarks made by Mr. Pendred at the meeting on the 17th May, 1954'.
90. BBC WAC R28/5/4, D-Notice Committee minutes, 17 May 1954; BBC WAC R34/272/3, Thomson to committee members, 20 October 1954.
91. PRO INF12/51, Defense (Transition) Committee (48) 17, Report by Publicity Sub-Committee, 27 August 1948; PRO INF12/51, A. T. Cornwall-Jones to Sir Robert Fraser, 2 September 1948 and 3 September 1948.
92. PRO INF12/51, Report of meeting between Capt. Brooking and BBC representatives, 8 June 1951.
93. PRO INF12/404, D. B. Woodburn to Admiralty, 22 March 1949.
94. PRO INF12/522, Peck to H. G. Barnes (BBC), September 1949: PRO CAB134/1138 PCC (49), 2nd Meeting, 5 May 1949.
95. PRO CAB134/1138 PCC (49) 2nd Meeting, 5 May 1949.

96. BBC WAC R28/5/3, Thomson to press members, 7 March 1951. Three D-Notices were withheld before 1950.
97. PRO CAB176/19 JIC 1246/48, 'A short aide memoire on "D" Notices to the press', 5 July 1948.
98. Ibid.
99. BBC WAC R28/5/3, Thomson to press members, 7 March 1951.
100. BBC WAC R28/5/3, D-Notice Committee minutes, 7 April 1952.
101. BBC WAC R28/5/2, D-Notice Committee minutes, 18 March 1948, 29 September 1948.
102. PRO CAB176/52 JIC 513/55, 'Leakage of information concerning a British guided weapon in the publication "Aviation Week" ', 21 February 1955.
103. PRO CAB159/13 JIC (53) 13th meeting, 'Leakages of information about military aviation', 30 January 1953.
104. PRO CAB159/14 JIC (53) 126th meeting, 'Leakages of information about military aviation', 8 December 1953.
105. Pauline Sadler, *National Security and the D-Notice System* (Ashgate: Aldershot, 2001), pp. 40–62.
106. PRO CAB 130/16 (GEN164/1), Minutes of an ad hoc ministerial meeting, 6 January 1947.
107. PRO CAB176/33 JIC/2641/51, 'Scale of Fifth Column activities to be expected in the event of war with the Soviet Union between the present date and the end of 1952', 28 November 1951.
108. For an in-depth account of the censorship problems during 1950–1, see John Jenks,'The enemy within: journalism, the state and the limits of dissent in Cold War Britain, 1950–51', *American Journalism* 18 (2001).
109. PRO CAB129/4 Cabinet memorandum CP (50) 183 'Overseas Operations (Security of Forces) Bill: memorandum by Home Secretary', 22 July 1950; PRO CAB128/18 Cabinet Minute CM 49 (50) 3, 24 July 1950.
110. PRO CAB128/18 Cabinet Minute 64 (50) 1, 16 October 1950; PRO CAB129/42 Cabinet memorandum CP (50) 229, 12 October 1950.
111. 'Man on the spot', *Daily Worker*, 15 July 1950.
112. 'Daily Worker Correspondent tells of butchery of 7,000', *Daily Worker*, 9 August 1950.
113. Jenks, 'Enemy within'.
114. PRO CAB129/42 Cabinet memorandum. CP (50) 207, 14 September 1950, and CAB128/18 Cabinet minute, 60 (50) 3, 18 September 1950; *Parliamentary Debates* 5th ser., vol. 478, col. 203, 19 September 1950; *Parliamentary Debates*, col. 278–9, 19 October 1950, and col. 299, 23 October 1950.
115. Alan Winnington, *I Saw the Truth in Korea* (London: People's Press Printing Society, 1950).
116. PRO CAB129/43, CP (50) 259 'Communist propaganda in connection with the Korean campaign: memorandum of the Attorney General'. 2 November 1950.
117. PRO CAB21/2248, Norman Brook to Attlee, 3 November 1950.
118. PRO CAB128/18 CM 76 (50) 7, Cabinet Minute, 20 November 1950.
119. PRO PREM8/1368, Jordan to Attlee, 13 January 1951.
120. Monica Felton, *That's Why I Went* (London: Lawrence and Wishart, 1953).
121. *Parliamentary Debates*, (Commons) 5th ser., vol. 489, cols. 1–4, 18 June 1951.
122. PRO LO2/909, 'Re: Monica Felton. Joint Opinion (Christmas Humphreys and John S. Bass), 19 June 1951. PRO PREM8/1525, Soskice to Attlee, 22 June 1951.

123. PRO CAB130/71 (GEN377/1), Minutes of meeting, 13 August 1951.

124. See Jenks, 'Consorting with the enemy'.

125. Alan Winnington, *Breakfast With Mao: Memoirs of a Foreign Correspondent* (London: Lawrence and Wishart, 1986), pp. 177–8.

126. 'The H-bomb secret', *Progressive*, November 1979.

4

The IRD: Inside the Knowledge Factory

The Information Research Department had overlapping functions. At its most basic it was an information factory, bringing in facts from around the world with which to create a variety of anti-Communist news and information products, products that would compete with those produced by the Soviets and their allies. The lack of reliable hard facts about the Communist world made the IRD's output potentially valuable to journalists, academics and other opinion leaders, especially since the Stalin-era Communists' own products were so blatantly propagandistic. As the engine of Britain's Cold War propaganda, the IRD drew upon the expertise of wartime propaganda and the knowledge from a network of experts to help create the raw material necessary to build a new commonsense view of the Soviet enemy. On another level the IRD supplied high-quality background information for top politicians and officials throughout the non-Communist world – it never engaged in mass propaganda. It consistently aimed the bulk of its propaganda to 'enlighten' people in the non-Communist world, particularly in areas susceptible to Communist takeover. Propaganda for the Soviet Union itself tried to present a clear picture of the outside world and stimulate 'fundamental criticism' of the Communist system. Propaganda for the satellites tried to 'keep hope alive'.[1]

The IRD in Bureaucratic Context

In the critical early years of the Cold War the Foreign Office was able to centralise and control the British government's overseas propaganda. Additional policy influence came from a plethora of ministerial and official committees. The Russia Committee was important early on for broad Cold War strategy, but was superseded by the Permanent Undersecretary's Committee by 1949.[2] The misnamed Colonial Information Policy Committee was set up in August 1948 to coordinate anti-Communist work in the Foreign, Commonwealth and Colonial offices.[3] Inner cabinet committees dealing with subversion, communism and information also helped coordinate policy, intelligence and propaganda. But not everyone accepted the status quo. The Chiefs of Staff had wanted more control over propaganda as part of tough political warfare against the Soviets and were not satisfied with the January 1948 creation of the IRD.[4] Foreign Secretary Ernest Bevin's power kept these interlopers at bay and put an end to talk about a revived PWE. He felt that 'black propaganda' in the East bloc was expensive, ineffective and futile in peacetime, though he indicated the FO was already involved in some.[5]

The Foreign Office's MI6 had inherited SOE's responsibilities and black propaganda channels, but Cabinet Secretary Norman Brook thought that MI6 chief Maj. Gen. Sir Stewart Menzies didn't 'know anything' about propaganda and didn't have anyone working for him who did.[6] Associate Malcolm Muggeridge, a wartime MI6 agent and post-war *Daily Telegraph* correspondent, leader writer and deputy editor, taught black propaganda and subversion courses for MI6 and took on other writing jobs for them.[7] In 1948 he apparently helped ex-Communist Douglas Hyde write propaganda, perhaps the explosive tell-all *I Believed*.[8] But MI6 used the Kemsley Foreign and Imperial News Service, and perhaps the *Daily Telegraph* and *Economist* as well, as cover for their agents.[9]

The IRD's oft-stated goal was to 'destroy the Soviet myth' of a peace-loving worker's paradise. The corollary, less frequently articulated, was that the IRD was trying to replace that myth with a new unquestioned, bedrock common-sense view of the USSR as aggressive, oppressive and expansionist – in a way just another myth. As far as can be determined the IRD hardly ever consciously spread falsehoods, though on occasion the department wilfully neglected to check the accuracy of highly dubious but effective pieces of information.

Research may have been the IRD's middle name, but as a 1955 report emphasised the research was conducted 'solely in order to provide propaganda material, and would otherwise probably not be initiated'.[10] The Foreign Office's Research Department – FORD – carried out the truly disinterested research. The IRD's obsessive secrecy was to keep its existence from the British parliament and public, and to minimise the links between the government and its covert propaganda. The September 1948 decision to put much of the IRD's budget on the 'secret vote', largely to help recruit specialists and provide cover for double-dipping journalists, reinforced this tendency toward stealth while freeing the IRD from parliamentary scrutiny and civil service rules.[11] By January 1950 the IRD was spending £25,000 of secret vote money on salaries and £75,000 for articles and other operations 'which could not possibly be acknowledged by HMG'.[12] Even though the Soviets knew about the IRD the department had to remain covert to keep tensions from escalating, Department Head John Peck said in 1951.[13]

The wartime SOE and PWE background of some of the early IRD leaders reinforced that sense of secrecy. Founding Director Ralph Murray had been a BBC journalist, then worked on PWE radio operations to the Balkans before taking on broader responsibilities for propaganda and political warfare, mainly in the Eastern Mediterranean.[14] His successor, John Peck (1951–3), had been Churchill's private secretary. John Rennie, head from 1954 to 1958 had done propaganda in the United States during the war and later, in the late 1960s and early 1970s, headed MI6.[15] The man in charge of channelling the propaganda, Editorial Adviser Lt Col Leslie Sheridan, had worked on Fleet Street before joining SOE where he created espionage and propaganda networks in neutral cities using journalists as cover; even in the IRD a colleague said Sheridan 'tended to go back to the era of dirty tricks'.[16] After the war he set himself up as a high-visibility public relations consultant while working for the IRD; his first client as a consultant was the exiled Spanish republican government.[17] In 1950 the ever-caustic Muggeridge summed him up in a sentence: 'rather a sad piece of debris, former news editor of *The Mirror*, now "publicity consultant," and black propaganda specialist for the Government, SOE in the war – the whole bag of tricks.'[18]

Some of the early FO staff such as Robert Conquest, Hugh Lunghi, Jack Brimmell and Cecil Parrott did have experience in the East bloc; others such as Peter Wilkinson and Norman Reddaway had experience in wartime special operations. Various British writers and émigré translators helped fill out the department. Reddaway said the rest of the Foreign Office was suspicious of the IRD. 'The establishment always thinks that if you have people doing odd things on the periphery then it will get them into trouble'.[19]

Despite any suspicions about 'private armies' the IRD was essentially a bureaucracy, and soon developed the required structure. By the mid-1950s IRD operated according to plan – an annual 'Basic Programme' devised at the beginning of each year – but the nine geographically organised research desks had to be flexible enough to adapt to changing circumstances. In 1955 the IRD desks had forty-three researchers and twenty-five support staff – translators, clerks and so on. Naturally, the Soviet and Eastern Europe desks were the largest, with thirty-eight researchers and support staff.[20] These London desks (plus one devoted to International Organisations) created most propaganda, but some parts of the world needed localised adaptations and special attention. In 1949 the IRD devolved some of the propaganda production, revision and distribution responsibilities to three key locations – Cairo (later Beirut), Singapore, and Caracas. For example, in late 1951 the Singapore office had in production or on the streets more than forty pamphlets and books in English, Chinese, Tamil and Malay, and had sent out print blocks for a cartoon version of George Orwell's *Animal Farm* to Southeast Asian newspapers.[21] But relations were not always smooth. In Beirut Leslie Glass argued that only London had enough staff or could check on the accuracy of all points and get clearance for propaganda. IRD Head, Peck, however, wrote that devolution gave a more authentic feel to the material.[22]

The Caracas-based Latin American operation was dominated by Emile Lecours, who eschewed the indirect approach. Instead he sent reams of propaganda articles including biting personal attacks and exposés he called 'type b operations' under pseudonyms directly to his newspaper contacts. For example, after he placed a story about arms purchases in Costa Rica for use against the Venezuelan government, prominent Communists were arrested in both countries. 'The way I see it is that in a battle such as is being fought it is essential to use weapons which damage or frighten the enemy, not those which please ourselves'.[23] At one point Lecours suggested setting up a news agency to handle the volume of IRD propaganda, which his superiors discouraged because he would be even further out of their control.[24] But his London superiors did admire his productivity. 'I have the impression that the average Latin American

can hardly open a newspaper without being confronted by an article by Raul Pichardo, Martin Martin or some other alter ego of Lecours'.[25]

The IRD eventually put the brakes on Lecours 'type B' operations despite the department's feeling that the articles had decisive and beneficial effects.[26] He had done at least eighty-eight of these 'type b' articles in 1952 alone, but his combination of energy, zeal and sloppiness could sometimes lead to trouble and Latin American resentment about interference – especially when the attacks appeared in the 'yellow press'.[27] London headquarters also tried to steer Lecours more toward the indirect approach that the IRD used elsewhere in the world to target opinion leaders rather than the media. 'If we can convert these people to active anti-Communism they will do our propaganda for us, and moreover, they will do it more effectively and more convincingly'.[28]

Much of the IRD's research was predictable and prosaic, trawling through the published record and broadcasts of the Communist world looking for evidence of brutality, venality, repression and incompetence, and seeking patterns and connections. For less obvious information the department relied on the intelligence-gathering ability of British diplomatic posts, especially in the Communist bloc and by 1950 an ever-increasing flood of material from American sources, which will be described in Chapter 6. The IRD had close connections with military intelligence, MI6, MI5 and shadowy private intelligence groups such as the Economic League. All provided information. In addition, the IRD quickly developed its own contacts with trade union leaders, academics and journalists who could provide information as well as spread propaganda.

Researchers at the various desks pored through a vast number of books, magazines, newspapers and hours of broadcasts provided by the BBC Monitoring Service. The Soviet desk alone slogged through thirty-two newspapers and forty-three periodicals, émigré publications, Soviet books, BBC Monitoring reports, pro-Soviet British publications, Chatham House publications and 'a vast amount' of American material.[29]

The IRD regularly canvassed British diplomatic posts for inside information that the Communists were less likely to publish, as well as gossip and local colour to spice up the propaganda. When news moved fast, as when riots broke out in East Germany and in Poland in 1953, the IRD pushed posts hard for quick information.[30] But a typical example was a 1951 fishing trip the IRD took looking for information on collectivisation, the food situation, labour, religion, and cultural affairs in Poland. The negative angle was obvious. Under the 'labour' category the IRD wanted material showing 'exploitation of workers, raising of norms, reduction in wages, use of women and youth in heavy industry, sabotage, strikes, absenteeism or passive resistance'. The propaganda department put in a special request for stories 'with a 'human angle' illustrating the harsh treatment meted out to the individual Pole'.[31] Five years later the IRD wanted similar news from Romania and information from restaurant menus, tour guidebooks and sight-seeing leaflets.[32] Chatty reports from East bloc posts like Prague delighted the IRD and its clients, especially in the BBC: 'This is exactly the kind of personal impression letter which is most useful for us, providing atmosphere and background in addition to the political developments which can be gathered from other sources'.[33] When travel restrictions in the Communist bloc loosened after Stalin's death the IRD started looking for tourists with reliable politics who would be willing and able to describe their experiences in articles or broadcasts.[34]

Raw material came from the intelligence agencies in the form of censorship intercepts, interrogation reports, Joint Intelligence Bureau reports and various 'secret material'.[35] In the early 1950s when information from Soviet and East bloc defectors was at a premium, the IRD worked closely with military intelligence in Germany, the site of most defections. This arrangement will be described in depth in Chapter 8. The department also relied on MI5 spies for inside information on real and suspected British Communists, their friends and others considered likely to be subversives. For example, MI5 gave IRD intelligence on British trade unions, student groups, peace activists and British involvement in any international groups linked to Communists.[36] The IRD then forwarded some of this to the Labour Party and Trades Union Congress to use for their own discipline and propaganda. But the relationship could get testy. When MI5 gave IRD photostats of an informer's reports, and requested that the originals be returned, the IRD's Overton remarked – 'What do the Security Service think we are: *The Daily Mirror?*'[37]

Although IRD veterans insisted that the truth was sacrosanct in their research and output, the records indicate otherwise. The department was sometimes willing to pass on unsubstantiated rumours or information that they knew was likely to be false. The IRD did not actually fabricate any disinformation – at least according to the documents available thus far. Cases from Asia, Europe and Britain do indicate, however, a propensity for speculation, rumour and wilful disregard of the facts if they got in the way of a good story.

In Southeast Asia the British were trying to heighten Thai suspicions toward Ho Chi Minh's Communist Vietminh movement in 1950. The embassy suggested putting, through 'the normal grey channels', information about Ho's long-standing plans to invade northeast Thailand. Ethnic Vietnamese in the area were undergoing paramilitary training and would help in the invasion. Despite objections that many of the allegations were probably untrue, and in any case they would heighten ethnic tension in the area, the IRD gave the go-ahead. As one official wrote:

> I think Bangkok's proposal is a reasonable one, and that we need not be unduly disturbed if the propaganda points are not 100 percent accurate. 100 percent accuracy is impossible to attain in those parts. The important thing is to turn the heat on against Ho . . . and make the Siamese public sit up and take notice'.[38]

When the United Press reported speculation that the East bloc countries might form a 'federation of peoples' democracies', the IRD's Watson wanted to use it –whether or not it was true. As he pointed out it was effective propaganda and there was no reason not to play up the story and speculation, even though he thought such a federation was unlikely. 'It is bound to have an unsettling effect in Transcurtania (the East bloc). The BBC should quote all material . . . in all Eastern European languages. Denial should be described as "repeated" and "yet another" '.[39]

Within Britain the IRD apparently had a hand in spreading speculation that the odd behaviour of Roman Catholic Cardinal Mindszenty during his 1949 Hungarian show trial was due to drugs. The suggestion started with the FO's Sir Orme Sargeant's doctor, a Hungarian refugee. Neither the Budapest embassy nor the Foreign Office had any evidence but 'I.R.D. are launching the suggestion'.[40] Others apparently were working the same angle. A similar story surfaced in the 7 February *Daily Mail*. According to one official, 'IRD could not claim credit for (it), directly at any rate. I have told Sir O. Sargent that various little bits are being put out by IRD the whole time: and the 'drug' theory is one of them'.[41]

Packaging Facts

As advertisers and marketing experts had long known, packaging, presentation and careful use of images and symbols were the keys to successful persuasion. The IRD recognised this and packaged its work in a wide variety of formats for different markets, and tried to strike just the proper tone with its choice of words and phrases. Although other historians have divided the IRD's work into Category A and Category B, the IRD propagandists seldom used those terms. There was instead a continuum, much of it supervised by the IRD's Editorial Section. The IRD packaged some material for high-level policy-makers; at the other end the department also pulled together human-interest snippets suitable for the popular press. In between there were more than a dozen different packaging formats, in addition to custom-written articles, books and plenty of ad hoc arrangements with individual clients. None of the IRD's regular publications was ever attributed to HMG, indirection and secrecy being the IRD's signature. And much like their World War I predecessors at Wellington House the IRD insisted that they 'addressed itself to the small number of people in every country who influence and form public opinion' and avoided mass propaganda.[42]

The earliest IRD format was the ten to twelve page briefing paper, well documented and written in a deliberately dry, understated style, and distributed to top government officials and to 'authorised clients' among politicians, labour leaders, and elite journalists.[43] They were not designed to be reproduced. By 1955 the basic papers continued to be a mainstay for narrow distribution to an elite 'who specialise in serious discussion'.[44] In the 1950s the IRD also used the monthly *Interpreter* for the elite market at home and abroad under the cover story that it was prepared for British Foreign Service officers and that the clients were getting to share in the secrets.[45] Like the basic papers, the *Interpreter* played it cool – 'adjectives should be avoided as far as possible and tendentious and propagandist adjectives are taboo'.[46] A sample from 1952 was twenty-nine pages of tightly written and systematically organised anti-Communist analysis, with an introduction that read almost like a quality newspaper leader.[47] By late 1954 the IRD were sending out 1,886 English-language copies and 1,452 in other languages.[48] More than 300 were for British consumption – on the left some went to the Labour Party, a handful of Labour MPs, the TUC and 'stalwarts' in individual unions such as the National Union of Teachers.[49] A large number of non-Communist governments' foreign ministries were getting the *Interpreter* by 1955.[50] An *Interpreter* spin-off, *Asian Analyst*, concentrated on Chinese developments, Soviet and Chinese foreign policies and the activities of Asian Communist parties. It came out in English and French, and was aimed at the Asian market.[51] A lighter version of the basic paper was packaged as *Basic Booklets* for readers with minimal knowledge of Communists and Communism. The IRD encouraged publishers and editors overseas to 'pirate' these books.

At the other end of the spectrum the IRD aimed its propaganda at less cerebral journalists through a *Digest* series begun in July 1948 that pulled together short items, preferably snappy, quotable, and fresh enough to appear as news.[52] The *Digest* grew to fill a niche, offering material that journalists wouldn't be able to get from the syndicated British press, the London Press Service, *The Economist* or other more easily available sources.[53] Soon, the IRD were publishing French, Spanish, Italian, and Greek versions of the *Digest*. A companion *Religious Digest* came out monthly in English and Italian.[54] The *Digest* mixed previously published and unpublished news and provided its own rough coding. Stories with specific attributions had obviously been published already. Vague attributions, such as 'a refugee recently returned from the Soviet zone', meant that the story was based on secret, unpublished sources. Attribution to 'diplomatic observers' or 'correspondents' meant it drew on both.[55] However, the primary source came to be the self-criticism articles that regularly ran in the Soviet-bloc press because they could be attributed to named sources.[56] By 1954 the reliance on self-criticism articles left the *Digest* with too many trivialities and not enough meaty stories. Even Sheridan admitted that it had become too 'niggling and nagging'.[57] More importantly, it was becoming less effective. As the Rome information office pointed out, the *Digest*'s 'trifling incidents' of industrial accidents, transport delays, shortages of water and consumer goods were likely to occur anywhere, especially in countries like Italy.[58]

The format followed function. The *Digest* was fragmentary and designed to be ripped apart, allowing each issue to be divided among several specialised correspondents – for example, one section would go to a newspaper's labour correspondent, another to its diplomatic correspondent.[59] Alternatively, the information officer could cut and paste it into his own daily embassy bulletin.[60] As Sheridan pointed out, the typed, double-spaced pages allowed easy editing by client journalists. 'The digest is the PA (Press Association) of the I.R.D. and should be factual, leaving each journalist to re-write or sub-edit if he wishes to do so to suit the needs of his own paper'.[61]

By the mid-1950s the IRD was producing an array of other publications for other functions. *International Organisations*, the IRD's update on Communist 'front' organisations, was aimed at the elite market of diplomats, politicians, bureaucrats and the more serious journalists and came out every month. *Quotations from the Soviet Press* was a reference compilation that came out every two months and was aimed at libraries and reference rooms. *Facts About...* books were designed as handy reference for editors, journalists and speakers, while *Speakers Notes* served as a regularly updated anti-Communist primer. Other regular but less well-circulated publications included: *Developments in China, Central Asian and Transcaucasian Press Summary, Developments in Outer Mongolia, Recent Events in the Soviet Union, News from Eastern Germany, Communist Propaganda and Developments in the Middle East, Scientific Material Translated from the Soviet Press* and *Trends in Communist Propaganda.*[62]

The IRD became most heavily and directly involved in journalism through their production and commissioning of news-feature articles and, later radio scripts for planting in newspapers, magazines and broadcast services. (IRD staff wrote some articles.) For this service they relied not only on Editorial Section staff writers but also on a stable of reliable London-based writers and a network of clients both overseas and in Britain, both of which will be described fully in Chapter 5. The system combined domestic and overseas propaganda and frequently led to such overlap and complexity that the IRD wound up buying overseas republication rights on articles they themselves had produced for the British press.[63]

Although there were plenty of variations over time and between countries, this is basically how the system worked: The IRD would identify a topic that they wanted covered, recruit a friendly writer through an intermediary, provide him or her with suitable background information and then buy and distribute the resulting piece of work. Originally Sheridan used his Fleet Street connections and publicity consultant cover to arrange many of these commissions from high-profile names, but a mid-1949 progress report clearly implied that Sheridan was not the only literary middleman the IRD was using.

> In this manner we have obtained articles from Harold Laski, Woodrow
> Wyatt, M.P.; Rhys Davies, M.P.; Oscar Hobson, Mr. Phillips Price, M.P.,
> and other lesser lights. Articles now coming forward through this
> machinery include ones by Lionel Elvin of Ruskin College: A. J. P. Taylor;
> and R. H. S. Crossman (yes, and quite a good one!).[64]

The report was apparently referring to Crossman's article, 'The Hitler-Stalin pact of 1939 – a reassessment', which turned out to be a big success for the IRD. It was published seventy-seven times in eleven countries. Not all IRD-sponsored 'big-name' articles had that kind of reception. More typical was Labour MP Woodrow Wyatt's 'Two imperialisms', which was republished twenty times in seven countries.[65]

Market saturation was always a possibility, and by May 1950 the IRD's Adam Watson thought they may have reached that point in some places. 'This strengthens the case of the use of the digest technique, syndication, passing of less written-up material to editors and speakers, etc'.[66] The embassy in Uruguay complained that some of the articles had become hackneyed, 'contaminated one fears by the very dullness of the creed they combat'.[67] By 1954 the production of IRD-written articles had settled at about twelve a month as the department seemed to be devoting more of their time and material to its ever-expanding number of regular publications.[68] The IRD had begun producing radio scripts during the Suez Crisis for the Voice of Britain radio station – formerly Sharq al Adna – and continued to do so for other Middle Eastern radio stations after the crisis had passed and the Voice of Britain shut down.[69] By the end of 1957 they were producing ten scripts a month, many of which were broadcast or printed as feature articles.[70]

In addition to its own publications and the commissioning of news articles, the IRD had jumped heavily into the book publication, translation and distribution business by the early 1950s.[71] Anti-Communist author Arthur Koestler had pointed out 'forcibly' to the IRD the need to create a popular, cheap and non-Communist left series of books that would have the dramatic and allegedly hegemonic effect that Victor Gollancz pro-Communist Left Book Club series had in the late 1930s.[72] The IRD sounded out several publishers, including Gollancz, before making an arrangement with the Batchworth Press, which would publish them in the Background Books series.[73] The IRD would suggest writers and themes and then guarantee a bulk purchase to erase any risk to the company.[74] By early 1951 the first IRD book – more a booklet – *What is Communism?* came off the presses and was followed quickly by Victor Feather's *Trade Unions – True or False?*, J. A. Hough's *Co-Operatives – True or False?*, and a collection of heavy-hitters (including Bertrand Russell, Leonard Schapiro and W. N. Ewer) gathered under the title *Why Communism Must Fail*. Although the books were originally published in Britain and many circulated there, the IRD encouraged all British posts to find local translators and publishers if they thought the book would have the right impact. The IRD sent out 3,169 copies of the first book, with most going to the Middle East and Asia.[75] The books were successful at home and overseas, an IRD veteran recalled: 'They were not too long, they were good clean handy format, and they sold well on the commercial market in addition to our buying 15,000 copies which we then distributed to Foreign Office posts around the world ...'[76]

After financial problems led to Batchworth's mid-1950s collapse the Background Books series moved to Phoenix House in 1955.[77] But even that could not guarantee publication for everything the IRD offered. When Sheridan pitched *Communist Distortions* in 1956 the publisher rejected it because of its unrelenting polemical tone in a climate of improving Anglo-Soviet relations.[78] But the IRD had other book publishing connections. Sheridan had registered the publisher Ampersand in 1946, and in 1958 told information officers that while the IRD did not own the company their relationship was 'very close'.[79] In 1955 the IRD started shipping Ampersand's new Bellman Books series to posts around the world, encouraging them to arrange for local translations, and newspaper and radio serialisations. Titles included Leonard Schapiro's *The Future of Russia*, Hugh Seton-Watson's *The Revolution of Our Time*, Denis Healey's *Neutralism* and Maurice Cranston's *Human Rights Today*.[80] Although the IRD considered these books to have special value in their efforts to expose Communism, it warned that some books criticised the 'free world' as well.[81] On another track the IRD was in contact with top-flight British academics to try to put together a rigorous and thorough sociological examination of Soviet society that would discredit the idea of the USSR as a 'superior civilisation'. Murray turned to St Anthony's College, and particularly to F. W. Deakin and the philosopher Isaiah Berlin.[82] Unfortunately, a great deal of the file relating to this has been withheld, so it is difficult to know what came of it. However, a 'sociological series' was on the IRD catalogue by 1954.[83]

Many of the most effective anti-Communist books had been produced independently. In these cases the IRD helped with distribution, foreign rights and translation. For example, the IRD was worried about Communist inroads in Burma and managed to get foreign rights for Victor Kravchenko's *I Chose Freedom*, Douglas Hyde's *I Believed*, Freda Utley's *Lost Illusion*, and Nora Murray's *I Spied for Stalin*, and had translated and distributed some of them by 1951.[84] Some of the independently produced books the IRD boosted included Richard Crossman's *God that Failed*, Czeslaw Milosz' *The Captive Mind* and Margarete Buber's *Under Two Dictators*.[85]

Although the IRD had a strong textual bias, the department did respond to opportunities for visual propaganda when they arose. British writer George Orwell had been an early backer of the IRD (and his supply to the department of a list of names proved to be explosive when revealed in the 1990s). His anti-totalitarian books *Animal Farm* and *1984* were widely distributed by both American and British propaganda agencies.[86] By December 1950 the department had acquired the foreign rights to turn *Animal Farm* into a seventy-eight-instalment cartoon strip with suggested text for local adaptation.[87] By July the strip was being published in India, Burma, Thailand, Venezuela and Eritrea; many others were planned.[88] *Animal Farm* was popular despite the fact that it was widely known to be a British official production and 'was broadly too occidental in treatment'.[89]

The success with *Animal Farm* inspired Sheridan and his artistic collaborators to consider spin-offs, one of which was an anti-Communist cartoon merger of Voltaire's *Candide* and Swift's *Gulliver's Travels* that Sheridan originally hoped to place in the *Daily Mirror*.[90] As Sheridan explained, the main character would be Guy Greenhorn, an ingenuous citizen of the allegorical land of Democrita who travels to Stalinovia under the wing of fellow traveller Dr Renegado. Greenhorn's misadventures – 'grim and comic' – would drive home the IRD's anti-Communist message. Of course, there would be sex appeal as well: 'During his travels in Stalinovia he meets a beautiful young native girl, who has already seen through the regime, or perhaps gradually comes to share his enlightenment on its defects, and he rescues her from death, and occasional "fate worse than" from amorous officials . . . '[91] The project disappeared from view, but a few years later the IRD cartoon strip 'Guy Gullible's Travels in Muscovia' had a successful run in Central American newspapers.[92]

Markets for Persuasion

During its first years the IRD tried to slant almost all of its propaganda toward the non-Communist left, which was viewed as the primary barrier to Communist domination of European progressive and working class movements and the best allies for a counter-offensive. This targeting meant that the general run of IRD propaganda made its anti-Communist case from a secular, social democratic point of view. Labour cabinet ministers thought Britain had a natural advantage based on their party's past, present and promise. But other propaganda markets quickly emerged. When the Soviet-backed peace movement tried to enlist clergymen and religious believers the IRD began to target them for anti-Communist propaganda with a more Christian tinge. At other places and times the IRD packaged propaganda to appeal to Moslems, Jews, Third World nationalists, secular Western scientists and Titoists, with varying degrees of success.

The original left-wing emphasis in propaganda did not always work. In many parts of the world Britain was allied with reactionary regimes. In such cases propaganda written to appeal to European social democrat regimes missed its mark badly. As one diplomat explained:

> The trouble here is that reasons of political expediency tie us to the reactionaries in the Middle East at the same time as we preach social progress. Unless we can change our policy, we cannot hope for our propaganda on this theme to be effective; while the charge that we go ahead socially at home and deliberately keep the Middle East back for purposes of our foreign policy is difficult to answer.[93]

Trying to appeal to the left could boomerang when religion was involved. When evidence surfaced of Soviet anti-Semitism some in the IRD sought to depict the USSR as a bigoted state. Adam Watson pointed out that Jews were influential in many non-Communist left-wing movements, and persuading them that the Soviets 'are not their friends' could help the anti-Communist cause. P. L. Carter emphasised that anti-Semitism had deep roots almost everywhere and the Communists could reap benefits by taking advantage of it.

> My disagreement with Mr. Watson seems to be fundamental: I should have said that the waverers are usually fairly anti-Jewish, or in other words that some degree of anti-Jewish feeling was almost universal in countries where the Jews are present in any numbers. This may be deplorable, but there are sound reasons for it – the soundness perhaps being that, as Dickens said, 'They do get on so'.
>
> However specifically the stuff is aimed at the Jews, it is bound to hit a lot of Gentiles as well; and I feel that they will say, if only to themselves:

'There's one thing to be said for these Communists; they keep the Jews in their place'.[94]

But the department decided it was worth the risk. In a 4 March 1949 letter to Middle Eastern posts the IRD mentioned the emphasis on Soviet anti-Semitism, but would understand if diplomats in Arab countries did not use the material. (In the Middle East the IRD had previously emphasised the tight connection between Zionism, Israel, and the Communist menace.)[95]

After the split between Stalin and Yugoslav leader Joseph Tito in 1948 there were bigger but more problematic opportunities for the IRD. At one level the British began supplying material for Tito's speeches and placing anti-Soviet material in the Yugoslav press.[96] There was also the possibility of spreading the dissension. In early 1950 the Russia Committee briefly considered encouraging nationalist Communism, or Titoism, in France to divide and confuse the staunchly Stalinist French Communist Party.[97] The ever-enthusiastic Christopher Mayhew predicted France might 'be more vigorous and a greater asset to the Atlantic Pact' were its Communist Party to reject the Kremlin and embrace nationalist Communism. The ambassador in Paris, Oliver Harvey, later objected strongly, arguing that 'were the French Communists ever to become Titoists, then they would indeed be a menace'. But the IRD continued to privately float the idea among diplomats.[98]

The targeting of the left also affected the language that the IRD used in its propaganda.[99] Much of this semiotic warfare aimed to make explicit and unflattering comparisons between the Soviet Union and the widely despised Nazi German regime. Throughout much of 1949 the IRD, the Russia Committee and the CIPC all brainstormed about new terms for the Soviet enemy and its allies, and tried to popularise them in speeches, press releases, and other media contacts. The brainstorming results emphasised predictable terms like Stalinist, Totalitarian, and Police State, as well as some designed to appeal to the more 'progressive' audiences, such as describing Soviet Communism as an 'out of date theory'. The best word, though, was Kremlin.

> This is thought to be the most useful single word for general audience in order to fix in people's minds the cruel, backward, tyrannical and centralising aspects of the Communist movement as it now exists in Russia. It is also applicable to Russia's foreign policy. A further advantage is that it may provide a useful peg for graphic propaganda.[100]

To hammer home the Nazi-Soviet comparison Murray favoured emphasising 'Communo-Fascism' while Warner preferred 'Red Fascism'.[101] Attlee urged diplomats, bureaucrats, and cabinet ministers to make use of the words and phrases.[102] But after six months, Murray reported that 'we have made precious little progress in obtaining any general acceptance of phrases or epithets. But I doubt if we can do more'.[103]

By the early 1950s the purity and the ardour of the IRD's wooing of the non-Communist left seemed to have waned somewhat, though the department insisted that the 'principal target remains the woolly minded left-wing intellectual and the not-too-woolly minded trade unionist'.[104] More and more other partners, outlets and approaches become acceptable. The right-wing Economic League in Britain, the Vichy-linked BEIPI in France and Franco's secret police in Spain all became clients or associates by the mid-1950s.[105] The department still had a degree of solidarity with the progressive world, however, as we can see when the IRD suspended some publications during a printers' strike rather than go to 'blackleg' printers.[106]

The IRD also tried to develop propaganda that would be appealing to other discrete markets, such as secular scientists, devout Moslems and pacifistically inclined Christian clerics. Most of these strategies were short-term responses to Soviet policy shifts. The British had long worried about the Soviet Union's appeal to scientists, partly because of the vulnerability of scientists involved in weapons research. In 1949 the IRD was already distributing to British scientists documentation demonstrating the limits on academic freedom and scientific inquiry in the USSR. The ascendancy of the quack geneticist Trofim Lysenko in Soviet science in the late 1940s gave the IRD a wonderful opportunity to discredit the USSR's reputation as a scientist's paradise and expand its propaganda to scientists in the rest of Europe. 'If some of these scientists, after receiving this evidence over a certain period, are then willing to write articles or make statements so much the better; and we can probably ensure that they reach a wide audience.'[107]

The IRD's propaganda aimed at the wavering clerics was more straightforward: the Soviets claimed to be for peace and most religious leaders favoured peace. The IRD wanted to expose Soviet hypocrisy on the issue as well as demonstrate the vicious persecution of Christians and other believers in the Communist world. Much of the original work consisted of digging up evidence of religious persecution from the Communist bloc press and British diplomatic posts.[108] In 1950 the department put together a monthly religious digest to supplement the regular distribution of religious material, initially to British clerics.[109] Much like the general *Digest*, the *Religious Digest* relied on the East bloc press for its articles, many of which were on persecution of Roman Catholics in Eastern Europe. By 1954 it had diversified somewhat with accounts of an atheism drive among Soviet youth, a Polish town's defence of a Catholic shrine, and a Hungarian attack on Jehovah's Witnesses as 'imperialist agents'.[110] The IRD hoped to eventually make the *Religious Digest* more ecumenical with articles that would appeal to Orthodox Christians, Muslims and Buddhists, but there is little evidence it did.

The IRD also developed propaganda on Soviet hostility toward Islam, but avoided using it in areas with anti-Moslem sentiment, such as India and Israel.[111] They did target Moslem leaders, slipping parts of the *Interpreter* to Egyptian clerics for their sermons.[112] By the early 1950s the IRD hoped to induce the Iraqi government to provide imams and mullahs with talking points for their sermons, and had begun a pilot programme to distribute covert propaganda at Shia holy places.[113] Information officers in the Moslem world often brought up the need for news about Soviet persecution of Moslems, but the IRD was never able to provide as much material as it wanted, especially from Moslem writers.[114]

Eventually, as Norman Reddaway recalled, the primary goal became generating negative information about the USSR, no matter where it came out. 'You know, this business of targeting is all very well, but what you want to do is get your information into the media.'[115]

Conclusion

The IRD's indefatigable research and myriad publications after 1948 undoubtedly filled a need – the generation of knowledge about the USSR and its allies – but clearly abused the ideals of disinterested inquiry in its production of facts, articles, scripts, journals and cartoons. None of their research would have been done if it were not for the propaganda requirement. Under Stalin the East bloc was virtually shut off from meaningful contact with individuals from the non-Communist world. Visits were few, meetings were choreographed, true interaction was almost non-existent and the information that was available about the East bloc in the West from Communists and their friends was seriously deficient – it suffered from its own propaganda myopia and distortion. Where could journalists, politicians, government officials, academics and other opinion leaders turn for straight information? Increasingly it was that small research department within the Foreign Office. The factual basis of most of the IRD's work made it appear to conform to Anglo-American norms of facticity and objectivity, and thus seem to be just another source of legitimate information with its basic papers, feature articles, digests and myriad other publications.

Notes

1. PRO FO1110/716 PR10111/34/G, 'Collation of intelligence: note by IRD', May 1955.
2. Aldrich, *Hidden Hand*, p. 128.
3. PRO FO1110/196 PR49/17/G, Murray to Halford, 28 March 1949.
4. Richard Aldrich, *Espionage, Security and Intelligence in Britain, 1945–1970*, (Manchester: Manchester University Press, 1998), pp. 181–4.
5. PRO CAB21/2745, Brook to Attlee, 10 May 1948, 14 May 1948, 'Anti-Communist propaganda' memo by Norman Brook, 12 March 1948.
6. PRO CAB21/2745, Brook to Bridges, 20 April 1948.
7. Muggeridge Papers (Wheaton), Research Notes: II. J. Propaganda, Itinerary for Propaganda Course No. 2, for 10 October–4 November, 1949 (Revised 12 October 1949), A. General Considerations Regarding Propaganda.
8. Muggeridge Papers (Wheaton), Diary entry for 7 December 1948; Muggeridge Papers (Hoover), Diary entry for 4 February 1950.

9. Lycett, *Ian Fleming*, pp. 169–70; Muggeridge Papers (Hoover), Entries for 12 January 1950, 14 September 1950, 4 October 1950.

10. PRO FO1110/716 PR10111/34/G, 'Collation of intelligence: note by IRD', May 1955.

11. Foreign Office Historians, *IRD: Origins and Establishment of the Foreign Office Information Research Department, 1946–48* (London: Foreign Office, 1995), p. 7.

12. PRO FO1110/328, 'Information Research Department's finances', 9 January 1949.

13. PRO FO1110/458 PR21/7/G, Western European Information Officers' Conference minutes, 12–14 September 1951.

14. David Garnett, *The Secret History of PWE: The Political Warfare Executive, 1939–1945* (London: St. Ermin's Press, 2002), pp. 86, 161, 312.

15. Aldrich, *Espionage, Security and Intelligence*, pp. 233–4.

16. Norman Reddaway, Interview by Author. Tape recording. London. 31 October 1996.

17. Lashmar and Oliver, *Britain's Secret Propaganda War*, pp. 12, 31–2; 'Personalities', *Newspaper World*, 25 May 1946; 'Hints on how to be a perfect Press Officer', *Newspaper World*, 18 May 1950.

18. Muggeridge Papers (Hoover), Diary entry, 13 November 1950.

19. Reddaway interview.

20. PRO FO1110/716 PR10111/34/G, 'Collation of intelligence: note by IRD', May 1955.

21. PRO FO1110/386 PR24/230, Rayner to Tull, 5 November 1951.

22. PRO FO1110/616 PRG104/49, Glass to Peck, 30 June 1953.

23. PRO FO1110/472 PR 15/30, Lecours to Peck, 28 July 1952.

24. PRO FO1110/472 PR15/101/G, Wilkinson to Tull, 11 December 1952, Peck to Wilkinson, 12 February 1953.

25. PRO FO1110/472 PR15/101/G, Nicholls to Taylor.

26. PRO FO1110/617 PRG105/4, Peck to Urquhart, 4 February 1953.

27. PRO FO1110/617 PRG105/4, Urquhart to Peck, 12 December 1952.

28. PRO FO1110/617 PRG105/35, Peck to Lecours, 4 May 1953.

29. PRO FO1110/716 PR10111/34/G, 'Collation of intelligence: note by IRD', May 1955.

30. PRO FO1110/614 PRG102/32, Nicholls to Kermode, 8 July 1953.

31. PRO PR27/49/51, Tull to Fordham, 24 July 1951.

32. PRO FO1110/909 PR1037/8, IRD to Chancery (Bucharest), 14 February 1956.

33. PRO FO1110/772 PR1012/65, Gregory MacDonald (BBC) to Overton, 8 August 1955.

34. PRO FO1110/641 PR1011/19/4/G, T.A.K. Elliot minute, January 1954.

35. PRO FO1110/716 PR10111/34/G, 'Collation of intelligence: note by IRD', May 1955.

36. PRO FO1110/275 PR2154/106/G, [Deleted] to IRD, 29 July 1949; PRO FO1110/325 PR56/45/G, 'Communism in the Colonies'. Although the names and organisations had been deleted in the archives, their address, Box No. 500 Parliament St. B.O. matches that of MI5 contained in less rigorously censored files. See, PRO INF12/525 Meeting minutes, 28 June 1951.

37. PRO FO1110/755 PR161/23/G, Overton minute, May 1955.

38. PRO FO1110/294 PR20/90/G, R. A. Hibbert minute, 1 August 1950; Minute 5 August 1950, and IRD to Bangkok Embassy, 10 August 1950.

39. PRO FO1110/23 PR1320/34/913, Watson minute, 27 October 1948.

40. PRO FO953/556 PE494/3/921, Talbot de Malahide minute, 5 February 1949.

41. PRO FO953/556 PE494/3/921, M. G. L. Joy minute, 7 February 1949.
42. PRO FO1110/716 PR10111/31/G, 'The use of Information Research Department material', May 1955.
43. PRO FO1110/532 PR101/2/G, Circular, 10 January 1953.
44. PRO FO1110/716 PR10111/31/G, 'The use of Information Research Department material. A note for the guidance of Information Officers and Chanceries', [n.d. Received June 1955].
45. PRO FO1110/731 PR114/5/G, Editorial Adviser (Sheridan) minute, 19 November 1954.
46. PRO FO1110/731 PR114/5/G, *The Interpreter* (signed by Peck), 29 July 1952.
47. PRO FO1110/516 PR 89/38/G, *The Interpreter*, June 1952.
48. PRO FO1110/731 PR114/5/G, Editorial Adviser (Sheridan) minute, 19 November 1954.
49. PRO FO1110/731 PR114/39/G, Rennie minute, 15 June 1955.
50. PRO FO1110/718 PR10111/68/G, 'IRD MATERIAL Passed to Ministries of Foreign Affairs and other Ministries by our Missions Abroad'.
51. PRO FO1110/716 PR10111/31/G, 'The use of Information Research Department material', May 1955.
52. PRO FO1110/87 PR590/590/913, Murray note, 23 July 1948.
53. PRO FO1110/730 PR113/40, Editorial Adviser (Sheridan) minute, 4 October 1955.
54. PRO FO1110/716 PR10111/31/G, 'The use of Information Research Department material. A note for the guidance of Information Officers and Chanceries', [n.d. Received June 1955].
55. PRO F01110/87 PR814/590/913, Murray to Tennant, 21 October 1948.
56. PRO FO1110/645 PR113/31, Mason minute, 30 December 1954.
57. Ibid.
58. PRO FO1110/645 PR113/31, Hebblethwaite to Rennie, 4 December 1954.
59. PRO FO1110/645 PR113/31, Editorial Adviser (Sheridan), 28 April 1955.
60. PRO FO1110/591 PRG53/1, Grant Purves to MacLaren, 22 January 1953.
61. PRO FO1110/645 PR113/31, Editorial Adviser (Sheridan), 28 April 1955.
62. PRO FO1110/636 PR10111/53, 'IRD output on June 30', [1954].
63. Quoted in Defty, *Britain, America and Anti-Communist Propaganda*, p. 91.
64. PRO FO1110/277 PR2891/112/G, 'Progress report: Information Research Department, 1st January to 31st July' (version addressed to Harold Caccia).
65. PRO FO1110/359 PR110/5/G, 'Report on the work of the Information Research Department, 1st August to 31st December, 1949'.
66. PRO FO1110/324 PR55/16/G, Watson minute, 1 May 1950.
67. PRO FO1110/588 PRG46/5/G, Chancery to IRD, 20 August 1953.
68. PRO FO1110/636 PR10111/53, 'IRD output on June 1', [1954].
69. PRO FO1110/979 PR1119/8, IRD to Chanceries, et al., 8 April 1957.
70. PRO FO1110/979 PR1119/8, IRD to Chanceries, et al., 11 December 1957.
71. PRO FO1110/54 PR942/265/913; PRO FO1110/373 PR8/27/51, IRD to Rangoon, 10 April 1951.
72. PRO FO1110/221 PR505/33/G, Murray note, 28 January 1949.
73. PRO FO1110/221 PR1373/33/G, Sheridan minute, 12 May 1949; PR1589/33/G, Murray to Mayhew, 10 April 1949.
74. Lashmar and Oliver, *Britain's Secret Propaganda War*, p. 100.
75. PRO FO1110/444 PR97/1/51G, IRD to British Missions, 13 April 1951, Sheridan minute, 31 January 1951.

76. Tucker interview.
77. Lashmar and Oliver, *Britain's Secret Propaganda War*, p. 101. From 1960 to 1971 Bodley Head published the series.
78. PRO FO1110/871 PR10111/32/G, Editorial adviser (Sheridan), 15 February 1956.
79. PRO FO1110/1072 PR144/5, Sheridan minute 29 July 1958; Lashmar and Oliver, *Britain's Secret Propaganda War*, p. 100.
80. PRO FO1110/738 PR121/299, IRD to Chanceries, et al., 18 August 1955.
81. Ibid.
82. PRO FO1110/446 PR104/1/51/G, Murray to Warner, et al., 19 February 1951.
83. PRO FO1110/636 PR10111/53, 'IRD output on June 1', [1954].
84. PRO FO1110/373 PR8/27/51, Barraclough (Rangoon) to IRD, 13 March 1951, Barraclough to IRD, 12 April 1951.
85. PRO FO1110/716 PR10111/31/G, 'Bibliography of Information Research Department material', May 1955.
86. The IRD paid 50 guineas for the Arabic rights for *Animal Farm*. PRO FO1110/319 PR48/82/G, Sheridan minute, 7 November 1950.
87. PRO FO1110/365 PR127/9, Sheridan to Peck, 4 December 1950, Circular letter, 11 December 1950.
88. PRO FO1110/392 PR32/89/G, '*Animal Farm*', 27 July 1951.
89. PRO FO1110/415 PR60/42/G, Meeting minutes, 20 June 1951.
90. PRO FO1110/392 PR 32/99, 'Strip cartoons', 13 August 1951.
91. PRO FO1110/392 PR32/89/G, '*Greenhorn's Travels – in Stalinovia*' attached to 27 July 1951 meeting minutes.
92. PRO FO1110/803 PR1049/1, Taylor (Costa Rica) to Grey, 7 July 1955.
93. PRO FO1110/227 PR2737/38/913, Beaumont minute, 20 October 1949.
94. PRO FO1110/225 PR472/38/913, Carter minute, 7 March 1949, Watson minute, March 1949, Carter minute, 11 March 1949.
95. PRO FO1110/225 PR286/38/G, Haigh to Murray, 2 February 1949.
96. PRO FO1110/608 PRG92/3, 'IRD articles published in the Yugoslav papers', 31 January 1953.
97. PRO FO371/86750 N1052/1/G, Russia Committee minutes, 5 January 1950.
98. PRO FO1110/364 PR123/1/G, Young minute, 8 June 1950.
99. PRO FO1110/191 PR740/14/G, Circular, 14 April 1949.
100. PRO FO1110/191 PR704/14/G, 'Memorandum on the use of words in publicity about Communism'.
101. PRO FO1110/191 PR704/14/G, Murray to Warner, 5 August 1940, Warner note, 7 August 1949.
102. PRO FO1110/191 PR704/14/G, Circular, 14 April 1949.
103. PRO FO1110/192 PR2122/14/G, Murray minute, 4 October 1949.
104. PRO FO1110/584 PRG43/18, Elliott to MacDermot, 8 June 1953.
105. FO1110/796 PR1041/11/G, Cortazzi minute, 9 December 1955; PRO FO1110/894 PR1017/19/G, Reilly (Paris) to Grey, 23 April 1956; PRO FO1110/1099 PR10100/24, 'The Economic League', 27 May 1958.
106. PRO FO1110/929 PR1085/9/G, Sheridan minute 3 May 1956. Security was also a factor.
107. PRO FO1110/265 PR502/82/G, Watson to Pilcher, Tennant and Bennet, 23 June 1949.
108. PRO FO1110/353 PR104/1, Sheridan to Ridsdale, [n.d.]; PRO FO1110/353 PR104/17/G, Circular, 11 September 1950.

109. PRO FO1110/382 PR20/87, Sheridan minute, 5 November 1951.
110. PRO FO1110/634, 'Digest: information about the churches and religion in the USSR, China and Eastern Europe and the Communist attitude toward religion', Number 30, 3 April 1954.
111. PRO FO1110/225 PR472/38/913, Speaight minute, 12 March 1949, Circular letter, 4 March 1949; PRO FO1110/364 PR123/1/G, Murray note, 7 June 1950.
112. PRO FO1110/731 PR11439/G, '*Interpreter* distribution and use'.
113. PRO FO1110/609 PRG93/8/G.
114. PRO FO1110/385 PR23/28/51/G, Peck to Middle East posts, 1 May 1951.
115. Reddaway interview.

5

IRD Distribution Patterns and Media Operations

The IRD depended on networks of information officers, information bureaucrats, clients, literary agents, feature syndicates, broadcasters and scoop-hungry journalists to discreetly get its propaganda to the desired markets. Almost nothing went to the reading and listening public directly from the IRD. It all filtered through something. At the most straightforward level the IRD material went through the other channels of the government information machinery. This preserved the IRD's anonymity while allowing it to operate with relatively low overhead costs. The IRD also developed contacts with journalists, news services, feature syndicates, book publishers and, of course, the BBC. In many ways the IRD's distribution system was a hybrid of past British operations. Like World War I's Wellington House the IRD discreetly gave high-level material to opinion leaders, and let them translate the message into the local political-cultural idiom. Like World War II's propaganda operations the IRD made extensive use of broadcasting and news services. Control of channels, transmitters and agencies was not enough however. As propaganda veteran Norman Reddaway explained to a field operative in 1957, the information had to appeal to those outside one's control:

> which means that we have to have publications or information or facilities that will make such individuals turn to us and value the connexion . . . In practice, we find that the results are distinctly encouraging, and that we have built up a pretty large and influential clientele of journalists, broadcasters and organisations who rely upon us for information and advice that they cannot get elsewhere. It is above all through such individuals in our confidence that the most effective work is done.[1]

Propaganda in and for London

Much of the IRD's work took place within a few miles of its Carlton House Terrace headquarters. The department worked closely with the rest of the powerful and extensive propaganda, spin and information system that the government had already built. Sometimes it was as simple as giving the Central Office of Information an article to send out, forwarding information to be included in News Department briefings or providing material for a minister's speech. The IRD's editorial section also worked closely with a stable of London-based writers and news agencies that produced anti-Communist propaganda for the overseas and home markets.

On a daily basis the IRD encouraged the COI to put an anti-Communist spin in the magazines and digests the COI produced for sale overseas and on the daily London Press Service transmissions – used by embassy information officers in their bulletins. The LPS transmitted non-IRD anti-Communist stories, IRD-inspired articles, IRD commentary (usually attributed to 'informed circles in London'), the dispatches of tame correspondents such as the *Daily Herald*'s W. N. Ewer and generic propaganda boosting Britain.[2] And although the LPS were not as fast as Reuters or Associated Press, they could get news, features and commentary around the world relatively quickly.[3] The IRD's overt twin, the Information Policy Department, was a frequent partner in propaganda, with information officers in the field handling both IPD and IRD propaganda.[4]

The IRD's mass marketing came in its development of publications such as *Digest* and *Interpreter* that were mailed to regular clients who had been cultivated over the years. These included labour leaders, politicians, academics, scientists, and journalists. The IRD needed to have consistently good information that could be found nowhere else. Ideally, the propaganda not only served to inform daily dispatches, but also wound up in newspaper clipping libraries where it would create a source 'which is drawn on year after year by writers who feel that what they say and what they quote is their own, and not put into their minds by some alien propagandists'.[5]

It's hard to gauge how much the recipients used the material. Many obviously considered the IRD as just one of many sources of information. In 1959, when the IRD was updating its mailing list, *The Times*' Iverach McDonald told the IRD he wanted to continue receiving the papers, digests and reports.

> You may have noticed that we seldom draw upon for immediate news but invariably they are of use when we are writing leaders and we regard them as a necessary part of our background material. If therefore, you can continue with them we shall be grateful.[6]

Journalist Frank Owens, then editor of the *Birmingham Mail*, liked the IRD's *Middle East Opinion* which had been 'most useful' as background for leaders.[7] Sovietologist Edward Crankshaw told the IRD that its material 'saves him untold hours of research'.[8]

The IRD editorial section worked with individual reporters and news syndicates in London to get more specifically tailored news into the media. There were three main techniques, and many secondary ones. The main techniques were:

- Commissioning an article to be planted directly overseas. Sometimes this was done with the writer's knowledge of the IRD's purpose, sometimes the arrangements were through a middleman. In that case the writer was unaware of his true patron or his article's goals and ultimate destination.
- Commissioning an article to be planted in a British publication to give it greater authenticity. The IRD would then buy the rights to republish

it overseas and offer what appeared to be a wholly independent piece of journalism, gratis, to foreign editors and news services.

• Buying the 'second (republication) rights' and distributing overseas hard-hitting anti-Soviet articles that had first appeared, without IRD involvement, in the British press. This took in a wide swath of the media, from sources as disparate as the *Tribune*, the *New Statesman and Nation* and the *Daily Telegraph*.[9]

To make this system work the IRD first needed writers. Sheridan and others regularly canvassed their contacts, such as Malcolm Muggeridge and George Orwell, to determine who would be good and discreet writers for them.[10] Muggeridge's suggestions may have been forgotten but Orwell's have had a longer half-life, generating, fifty years after his death, self-righteous and bitter controversy, largely because of the political struggle over his legacy.[11] Orwell hated Stalinism, distrusted propaganda agencies and loved the IRD's Celia Kirwin who visited him in March 1949 to discuss writing for the IRD. While Orwell was too sick to write he did suggest those who might, and those who shouldn't – even to the extent of providing a list of 'journalists and writers who in my opinion are crypto-Communists, fellow-travellers or inclined that way and should not be trusted as propagandists.'[12] Although some were the obvious usual suspects, such as 'Red Dean' Hewlett Johnson of Canterbury, others were not.[13] Although some 1990s commentators sensibly point out that most of those on the list probably would not have wanted to write anti-Communist propaganda for the IRD, the question remains to what extent Orwell's list became a blacklist once in the hands of the government.

The IRD's hardest working and most dependable client soon became *Daily Herald* diplomatic correspondent W. N. Ewer, who had been covering diplomacy and foreign affairs since his radical days in 1919.[14] In the late 1940s the by-then respectable Ewer wrote a weekly diplomatic commentary for LPS, appeared on innumerable BBC talk shows, and wrote prolifically for the COI and the IRD.[15] His work was popular among foreign editors.[16] In 1950 the Information Policy Department's G. W. Aldington noted: 'There are certainly better political writers than Ewer, but few of them would be as ready as he to take direction as to the lines on which he should write.'[17]

The *Daily Telegraph*'s industrial correspondent, Hugh Chevins – whom Muggeridge described as a 'former socialist and present anarchist, as far as he is anything' – wrote articles on commission for overseas distribution and was willing to take IRD information for the *Telegraph*. For example, on 11 November 1949, the IRD sent out his article about international trade unionism, 'International Labour', and got it published in fourteen newspapers in Turkey, Iran, Italy, Norway, Sweden, and the Netherlands.[18] Next Sheridan wanted him to write a quick 5,000-word piece for a pamphlet on the founding conference of the anti-Communist International Confederation of Free Trade Unions, while weaving in criticism of the Communist-dominated World Federation of Trade Unions 'as he has done in his articles'. Chevins was already covering the conference for the *Daily Telegraph* and would not need extensive briefing, Sheridan wrote, 'since he knows the IRD line well enough, and I have every reason to believe, subscribes to it'. Sheridan wanted the TUC to publish it in the UK, after which point the IRD could pick it up. At least he hoped the TUC would praise it for its 'authenticity'. Chevins agreed to do the job for fifty guineas.[19] Sheridan tried to appeal to Chevin's competitive instincts: he gave him a Polish government questionnaire that he said indicated that the Poles were readying an administrative purge:

> I cannot say that this is exclusive, but I do not know of anyone else who has been given it. It seems to me that it would make a most interesting 'Daily Telegraph' article – partly to illuminate the minds of readers in this country, and partly because, should it appear, it would, no doubt be quoted extensively abroad.[20]

Other writers came on a more ad hoc basis. In 1950 *The Chemical Age*'s reporter Peter Davies wanted to do an article on oppression in East Germany for the mass circulation weekly *Everybody's*. Wilkinson knew and trusted Davies, Sheridan liked the idea, and the IRD gave him a full briefing.[21] A year later an information officer in Burma remembered how effective an IRD placement in *Everybody's* was.[22] J. A. Hough, the British Cooperative Union's research officer, wrote articles like 'Cooperative Democracy and the new Peoples' Democracies' and pamphlets, such as 'Co-operation or Collectivisation'.[23] London-based freelancer Dennis Bardens was skilled in 'the kind of vulgarisation which makes his articles appeal to the popular press.' The department considered William Bluett a specialist on short simple articles primarily intended for the Middle East and Southeast Asia. Vienna-based correspondent G. E. R. Gedye worked for the *Daily Herald*, the *Manchester Guardian* and Radio Free Europe while contributing to the IRD.[24]

One of the most prolific and successful IRD writers in the early 1950s was the BBC's Walter Kolarz, a Czech refugee whom Denis Healey had introduced to the department in 1948. The IRD supplied much of the raw material for Kolarz' broadcasts on the European Services, and then regularly sent out the scripts to thirty to forty diplomatic posts to be published.[25] Kolarz also lent his name to books, pamphlets and news-feature articles that the IRD was able to place widely.[26] Kolarz wrote at least six books on Communism and the Soviet Union in the 1950s and early 1960s. American propaganda front groups, such as the Congress for Cultural Freedom's Forum World Features, later caught on to Kolarz' 'excellent BBC stuff' and distributed it worldwide.[27]

Other writers were committed and independent anti-Communists with dynamite raw material; they just needed the IRD's logistical help. For example, in the late 1940s the IRD worked with ex-Communist leader and current anti-Communist writer Ruth Fischer after her publication of *Stalin and German Communism*. Fischer had been the general secretary of the German Communist Party until 1926 when she was expelled as a 'Trotskyite'.[28] The IRD helped to publicise the book by arranging for BBC reviews and encouraging their American colleagues to put out a German translation and an abridged edition.[29] A few months later, when Fischer wanted to come to London, the IRD apparently arranged for the government to pay her way.[30] Fischer's agent was hoping to host a press conference in London and get Fischer on the BBC to talk about Stalin's plans for Germany.[31] Later the IRD hired her to write two anti-Communist pamphlets, a long one on Soviet control of Communist Parties outside its borders and a shorter one on Soviet aims in Germany.[32]

Although the IRD initially recruited famous British writers who had international cachet, an English name and a London dateline could sometimes be a liability when trying to peddle articles in the Middle East and Asia. As Murray noted, 'there is a natural "sales resistance" to *ex cathedra* statements on such a tricky subject as Communism by representatives of "imperialist" countries.'[33] Exchange controls and other logistical problems had made it difficult to commission foreign authors, but by late 1949 the IRD was making progress. For example, to publicise the founding of ICFTU the IRD commissioned articles from Munir Bayoud (Lebanese), Deven Sen (Indian) and Cecil P. Alexander ('Trinidad Negro').[34] The IRD was especially happy to get non-white allies. When leading black Caribbean politician Grantley Adams spoke against the Soviets the IRD were ecstatic. Watson wrote: 'Mr. Adams is the stuff for Africa. We must have more negroes putting out our publicity – and our IRD stuff.'[35]

Some in the IRD questioned the emphasis on big-name and special-appeal bylines, and preferred anonymous authors who let the propaganda, not the personality, lead their arguments. When press attaches were clamouring for 'big name' authors in 1950, the editorial section's Colin MacLaren itemised the problems these men and women presented:

> Generally speaking, the bigger the name, the greater the impediments. Big names are rarely amenable to precise briefing; they are busy and cannot do things when we want them; they are shy of official inspiration – however cunningly concealed; and if they are big writers, they are very difficult to please about copyright, payment and so forth. Nevertheless, big or big-ish names are always being added to the list.
>
> I think it is essential, however, that we should always be able to have articles written to an exact specification, and this can only be done in the Office, i.e. a certain number of articles sent out will always have to go out over a pseudonym and therefore over anything but a big name.[36]

Fake bylines like 'Arnold York', 'John Cardwell' and 'David Laidlaw' soon became common, and some of them soon developed fake biographies to accompany them.[37] For example, soon after IRD material began going to a Japanese news syndicate in 1951, the editors demanded biographies of the writers. The fictitious 'David Laidlaw' was described merely as a man who had travelled extensively in Eastern Europe and has written on conditions there and in the Soviet Union.[38] That didn't stop his material from doing well. In the last five months of 1949 eight 'David Laidlaw' articles showed up in eighty-one overseas publications. His article 'Red light on the dove of peace' appeared in fifteen publications in eight countries, including India, Belgium, Sweden, and Brazil.[39] In the field, information officers cobbled together articles from other products. In Venezuela the information staff produced articles from *Interpreter*, *Realidades* (the Spanish *Digest*) and other IRD publications and slapped on pen names such as 'John Hasker', 'William Benton', 'Harry Wooster'.[40]

By 1950 the IRD was ready to expand beyond individual British writers. Sheridan sometimes worked directly with newspaper management, as in 1950 when the IRD arranged for a simple story on Western nuclear strategy to appear in the Sunday mass-circulation newspaper *The People* so it could be picked up and distributed overseas. It apparently ran a few weeks after Sheridan's meeting.[41] In March 1950 the IRD were talking with the British-based syndication services running the *Daily Express* and the Kemsley Foreign and Imperial News Service to get better distribution overseas, especially in 'hideously difficult' countries like France.[42] Kemsley had a big operation and sold material to other news agencies and individual newspapers, adding up to appearances in approximately 600 overseas newspapers.[43] Despite ticklish problems about security and monitoring, the arrangement would give the IRD some major advantages: cut down on the information officers' work with suspicious editors, get a wider circulation with no Foreign Office link, and earn greater respect from editors who would have to pay for the IRD propaganda.[44] Sheridan and Murray had serious negotiations with Kemsley's foreign service head, Ian Fleming, but it is unclear from the still heavily expurgated documentary record if a news planting arrangement emerged from the talks. But other officials referred to 'our "K" syndication in late April 1950.[45]

By 1951 more journalists and publicists began to seek out the IRD for detailed, behind-the-scenes anti-Soviet material. Admiral Stephen King-Hall, publisher of the *National News-Letter* approached Warner about getting more reliable information about life in the Communist bloc. King-Hall told him he did not have the time to monitor the Communist press and radio, and wanted to know what information the Foreign Office had for his 80,000-circulation newsletter.[46] King-Hall's newsletter had had a very important role in the late 1930's struggle over appeasement, and was still influential in the post-war years. Murray described the *National News-Letter* as a successful combination of a chatty 'family circle' technique and the attraction of a Fleet Street newsletter or the confidential edition of the *Economist* aimed primarily at the professional and middle classes. Although that wasn't the IRD's target market, sending them information would get it into circulation.[47] The IRD put him on their list, giving him basic papers, reference books, BBC monitoring reports and other material.[48] By 1951 the *National News-Letter* was featuring hard-to-find details of Communist policy in its news pages and short, *Digest*-sized titbits based on Communist bloc press on Hungarian dance music, Romanian radio listening and family life in Czechoslovakia.[49] By late 1952 the IRD was sending out 'King-Hall pamphlets' and recommending them to information officers in the field.[50]

Ralph Poston, the editor of the prestigious Royal Institute of International Affairs' (Chatham House's) the *World Today* told Murray that relying too much on émigré material for information on Eastern Europe and the Soviet Union was too risky and that he would prefer IRD output. He wanted pre-written, unsigned

IRD stories on defections, Soviet science, collective farms and travel accounts that he could simply insert into the journal. The IRD decided it would be better to give him mainly raw material, plus a few articles ready for publication.[51]

Other relationships are harder to document. The IRD had good relations with *The Economist* and at least once promised to try to place articles, but it warned diplomats in the field that 'it is very difficult to induce an independent paper to carry articles in which it would not normally be interested.'[52] *The Economist* could be useful when it independently echoed the IRD line; the department had the rights to reprint its articles overseas.[53] *The Economist*'s confidential newsletter, *Foreign Report*, was a different matter. It promised secrets, analysis and stories that, perhaps, weren't 100 per cent sourced yet. Critics said it was 'too establishment' and *The Economist*'s historian has said that for a period 'it looked like a propaganda sheet for the CIA'.[54] Brian Crozier had been *Foreign Report* editor in the mid- and late 1950s, and was later quoted as claiming that on average 20 to 30 per cent of the *Foreign Report* originated with the IRD.[55]

The IRD liked committed anti-Communists and pliable tame journalists, but became nervous when more independent journalists started nosing around its proprietary information. This was especially the case for areas in which the IRD depended on the goodwill of the military and intelligence agencies, as was the case with Red Army defectors. The defectors had given tightly controlled interviews to the BBC's Overseas Services and to the IRD's tame reporters. That piqued the interest of a number of less pliable journalists who wanted part of the story. The *Daily Herald*'s Denis Martin and the *Picture Post* were both adamant about getting interviews with defectors, but both Intelligence Division and IRD worried about them compromising security and emphasising the wrong 'line' in their stories.[56] They set up a system in which unreliable reporters would be told to find the defectors in a refugee camp, while those who were reliable, or persistent, could apply for an interview if they agreed to let the IRD review their articles before publication.[57] No journalists could get an interview without IRD sponsorship.[58] Both the *Daily Herald* and *Picture Post* ended up with defector stories, though it is unclear how much cooperation the IRD gave them.[59]

Field Propaganda

The short jaunts to Fleet Street or the BBC's Bush House were obviously important for the IRD, but much of its world-wide influence came through the old-fashioned way of individual contacts in the field. The bulk of IRD and IPD material went out through regular information officers working at British embassies, consulates, and other posts. 'They act as IRD's agents in the field, make use of their contact to propagate IRD material, and advise IRD on local Communist activities.'[60] Four times a year these IOs inundated the IRD with facts, figures and claims about their operations getting IRD propaganda into the media. These reports reflect a kaleidoscope range of operations – in some countries the information officer merely sent out copies of the embassy bulletin, while in others he developed wide-ranging and intricate networks to distribute propaganda. Cold War listening posts such as Berlin and Vienna, strategic areas like the Middle East and countries like France and Italy received special attention.

Italy in the early Cold War had a large and powerful Communist movement, a weak and venal press and a well-funded and efficient British information service. The IRD made the country a priority, with information officers claiming some 312 individual contacts throughout the country. 'Outstanding publicity successes are usually the result of considerable personal persuasion of the editors concerned (by letter, 'phone, lunch, cocktails – or all these methods combined!).'[61] France was a more difficult market and the IRD often despaired of making any headway with the French press. In the late 1940s the IRD tried to set up several syndication services – one with a small-time French cooperative news agency, the other with a part-time *Observer* correspondent. Neither thrived.[62] By the late 1950s a former Paix et Liberté leader Rostini, then apparently on his own, offered an appealing partner in France after the relative failure of the IRD's own people to get IRD propaganda into circulation there.[63] Rostini sent repackaged IRD information out to some 20,000 recipients in France and its colonies – political parties, journalists, civic organisations, trade unions and other opinion leaders. Much of the material the IRD supplied him was not otherwise available in French, Rostini said.[64]

Japan was largely in the American sphere of interest but the British Information Officer H. Vere Redman had a constellation of contacts among academics, social workers, businessmen and freelancers – all of whom could be considered writers or publicists. Redman also set up a news syndicate in 1951, and in a three-month trial run World Information Service took a 20,000-word mix of IRD anti-Communist material and less polemical COI and second-rights articles every month. They were first offered to the Tokyo dailies, then to the provincial dailies. Success put the service on a permanent basis.[65]

We have about 200 people who are consciously working for us on what might be called an IRD programme even though very few even of these see it as part of a deliberately planned campaign. For the rest, there is the considerably larger group of those who serve IRD purposes somewhat incidentally in the course of making use of 'good articles, etc. of British origin'.[66]

The documentary record shows traces of IRD's use of regional links, connections and news agencies. There were persistent discussions on using India as a conduit for propaganda to East Africa and to Indonesia; this apparently would involve a close relationship with the covertly subsidised Globe News Agency and its sister agency, the Arab News Agency.[67] In the mid-1950s when the Indonesian national news agency Antara showed signs of expanding its activities into British-run Malaya, the IRD briefly considered guiding Malayan allies in setting up a pre-emptive agency, adding that 'such an agency might be a useful adjunct to our work in South-East Asia if it were sufficiently influential to extend its activities outside Malaya.'[68]

One of the more difficult areas for British propaganda was the Middle East. Nationalist resentment of the still considerable British presence was high, as was sales resistance to British propaganda. The British, of course, had the subsidised Arab News Agency and the Sharq al Adna radio station, but it felt a need to do more. In Egypt the IRD slipped propaganda to the Moslem religious establishment for sermons and discussed trying to work anti-Communist themes into lurid sex and detective pulp fiction, comedy acts, films and nightclubs; they went so far as to commission some fiction 'which all posts had asked for'. The plan was to produce them in English and have 'local hacks' render them into Arabic. Sheridan, however, had inspected the competing pulp fiction, and his associate J. V. Riley concluded that 'I.R.D. could not begin to compete at that level of pornography'.[69] By 1952 the Foreign Office was beginning to revive a thorough-going covert propaganda programme in the Middle East, aiming to split moderate nationalists from what the IRD referred to as extreme nationalists and Communists. Covert tactics were necessary because they were attacking nationalism as well as Communism, and because any severing of diplomatic relations would cut off more overt operations.[70]

> The object of the material produced by this organisation would be to denounce the activities of extreme nationalist groups and personalities, impugn their motives, show how they are prepared to sell themselves to the Communists or, in their ignorance, be fooled by the Communists, expose Communists attempts to penetrate nationalist movements and generally discredit extremist tactics.[71]

In other parts of the Arab world the British resorted to corruption, bribing Arab journalists to print their propaganda, as with a reporter for the Egyptian newspaper *Al Zaman*.[72] But even cash and black propaganda could only do so much. Peck pointed out that if an information officer had to pay an editor to take an article that meant that the readers would probably not pay any attention to it.[73] Despite suggestions that bribery might be useful in countries like Jordan where there were few newspapers, Peck favoured simply making the articles more attractive so they would sell themselves. Bribes could be limited to specific cases, or steered toward individual journalists for putting their bylines on IRD-written material.

> But the regular subvention of a newspaper is an expensive business and the alternative of paying ad hoc for the publication of selected articles may be a better way of doing it. It has been suggested that we might authorise each information officer to spend up to a maximum of say £100 a year in paying for the publication of anti-Communist articles but I am uncertain whether this is the best way of spending any money which might be available.[74]

The unusual situations in Berlin and Vienna, where the British, Americans, French and Soviets came together and jointly occupied the cities, created opportunities for the IRD to gather information and to spread propaganda. As the East bloc shut itself off from most Western contact in 1948–9, both Berlin and Vienna became important as 'listening posts' for developments in Eastern Europe. The Foreign Office exploited this to create anti-Communist propaganda that could credibly be passed off as hot news from deep behind the Iron Curtain.

In Berlin the IRD set up a 'special team' that operated on the borderline between propaganda and disinformation. This team would start with bare facts, embellish them with fabricated but plausible details and slip them to contacts in the German press – generally the Berlin socialist newspaper *Telegraf* located in the British sector. In September 1950, for example, the team took the basic fact that East German leader Walter Ulbricht returned early from a trip to the Balkans and added the rumour that he was accompanied by top Volkspolizei officials. On that base they concocted a story that Ulbricht and the officials were supposed to go to a top level defence conference, but the gathering was called off because the poor performance of Russian tanks in Korea necessitated the complete rethinking of Soviet strategy in Europe. Other stories were more mundane, yet effective. When a film about the Nazi era was banned without explanation in East Germany, the special team claimed the reason was the obvious similarities between the movie Gestapo and the real-life Volkspolizei.[75] It's not clear how many, if any, of these stories circulated outside of Germany. Later in the 1950s the IRD's Berlin-based Peter Seckelmann would give details of wiretaps and radio intercepts from the East Germans and Soviets to Berlin-based BBC Correspondent Charles Wheeler. Wheeler would then send the material, often gossip embarrassing to the Communist leadership, back to London for broadcasting on the BBC's German Service. In exchange, Wheeler would give the IRD any interesting titbits that he had picked up from his contact with East Germans.[76]

In West Germany proper the IRD used the more-or-less transparent agency British Features to sell its material to the German press, primarily within the British sector.[77] Later the IRD was paying for Bonn-based writer Robert Caro to specialise in moulding the department's propaganda into commercially viable articles. German editors told him they liked his stuff because it avoided the overheated anti-Communism.[78] By the mid-1950s Caro's articles were appearing in newspapers throughout Europe, including London's own august *Financial Times*.[79] IRD Chief John Rennie noted that Caro was also 'extremely useful for planting in neutral papers'.[80]

Vienna was more consistently productive for both journalists and the IRD. In early 1950 *Daily Herald* correspondent G. E. R. Gedye had pleaded with his editor not to cut his position because of the city's growing importance as a listening post; he obliquely added that the new High Commissioner Harold Caccia was 'dead keen on helping journalists to make Vienna the big news centre it should be.'[81] It did prove to be big. By May 1951 the British were planting information gleaned from their East bloc missions with Vienna-based British journalists. The IRD hoped to buy the second rights for those inspired British stories or use them in the *Digest*. The IRD even proposed a special review on

Eastern European conditions, prepared in London, for distribution in Vienna. The new system, they hoped, could snare French and Italian correspondents in Vienna, because placing IRD propaganda directly in French and Italian newspapers was becoming difficult.[82] That apparently did not materialise but the IRD continued to feed news – such as information on East bloc arms spending and budgets – to Vienna-based reporters. The correspondents appreciated the information and used it when they could. But the IRD's goal of creating an image of the East bloc as dreary, uniform, backward and oppressive hardly lent itself to exciting news. 'It is only when there is something of a story to write that the correspondents can weave in something of the background of life there.'[83]

The system paid off, however, in 1956 when Hungarians rose against their Soviet masters just a few hours away in Budapest. Then there was a story to write. In London the IRD made arrangements with Reuters' Sid Mason to funnel information from its Budapest embassy to Reuters, so long as Reuters put some other city in the dateline.[84] In Vienna the British took hot information from their embassy in Budapest and funnelled it to the reporters gathered in Vienna. Reddaway congratulated the IRD's man in Vienna. 'We cannot have too much of this and I would like to say how much we appreciate the enterprise and skill which the Vienna mission has shown in dealing with Iron Curtain news.'[85] In the months following the revolution British newspapers became more interested not only in Hungary, but also in the other satellite countries. The Vienna information officer, R. A. Burroughs, wanted to exploit that with lots of information – even though much of it was not used directly – to make sure that correspondents would have an 'informed background'.[86] Important correspondents represented the *New York Times*, *News Chronicle*, *The Times*, *Daily Telegraph* and Reuters. In a 1957 report, Burroughs said that if the IRD could anticipate events and produce short, prompt pieces, they could be successful. For example, a Reuters' article based on IRD material on the Rumanian elections showed up in thirty places around the world.[87]

The BBC and the Perils of Objectivity

The BBC External Service's wartime political warfare experience and the requirement to broadcast in the 'national interest' made it nearly the perfect vehicle for the IRD.[88] External Services Director General Sir Ian Jacob was figuratively and literally on the Foreign Office team – he sat on the Russia Committee. But although Jacob identified closely with military interests and enjoyed great autonomy within the BBC he was no stooge or puppet. He was a Whitehall insider with his own ideas on broadcasting and propaganda and the ability to fight for his organisation.[89]

At the top of the Foreign Office Bevin recognised the BBC's special value. The External Services generally went along with the government's wishes, he explained to cabinet colleagues, and the occasional differences were 'a small price to pay' for the BBC's widespread reputation for independence and objectivity. That reputation made its news and views far more credible and gave Britain a major propaganda advantage. Bevin's opinion helped the cabinet reject the possibility of putting the BBC under direct government control.[90] But a natural community of interest seemed to be emerging by early 1948. Jacob, Warner and Murray approved the new anti-Soviet approach in February, and broadcasting propaganda to Italy, France, Germany, and the Middle East quickly emerged as the IRD's immediate top priorities.[91] The relationship continued to evolve with Jacob suggesting in April 1948 that the head of the European Services, Tangye Lean, meet directly with Murray so that they could discuss propaganda projects as they were developing. Jacob felt that early collaboration would give 'far more value' than working separately.[92]

In October 1948, Jacob, Warner and Parliamentary Undersecretary Christopher Mayhew tried to forge closer bonds by encouraging direct contact between language service heads and British diplomats in the target countries. It was as much for BBC morale as it was for better broadcasting. As the Foreign Office explained:

we feel sure that nothing is better calculated to keep the BBC up to the mark and make them feel, as we are particularly anxious they should, that we are all working for the same end: to make our case and keep our end up with the audiences they address.[93]

The special responsibilities of broadcasting to Communist Eastern Europe led to a tight relationship. In early 1948 the Foreign Office had begun monitoring the Eastern European services as well as canvassing British diplomats in Eastern Europe on the BBC's effectiveness – they urged care in relying on Communist sources and suggested correcting potentially misleading information on the air.[94] In an October meeting, Jacob asked for FO comments and advice, after making the unusual admission that his broadcasters sometimes suffered from '"false objectivity", that is by giving the news "straight" they sometimes gave a false impression which should be corrected by the addition of a sentence or a commentary after the news putting it in its proper background.'[95] To that end in June 1948 the Soviet bloc missions began a special series of telegrams, known as ASIDE telegrams, for the BBC Overseas Services. By the end of the year about a dozen telegrams a week were providing information not available from East bloc-based correspondents, who may have been British but were 'either Communists, or cannot report really freely for fear of losing their visas.'

These telegrams provide both comment to offset the official Communist reports of important events in these countries, and news items of local interest which provide useful material for exposing the working of the Communist regimes. They also report press distortions of major aspects of His Majesty's Government policy.
    The B.B.C. European Services are finding these ASIDES very useful for correcting news of events behind the Iron Curtain given by official

Communist agencies, or, in the case of other agencies such as Reuters and Associated Press, by local string-men who are often forced by salient omissions to convey a very misleading impression.[96]

The BBC and other anti-Communist broadcasters were rattling the Soviets, who started jamming their signals in the late 1940s. The Russian Service was the first BBC operation to be jammed, in April 1949, and others followed.[97] The jamming kicked off a debate in the Foreign Office about broadcasting's utility. Some suggested that scarce money and manpower could be used elsewhere, but Hankey argued that continuing the broadcasts forced the Soviets to divert scarce resources into jamming, and proved that the British were getting to them.[98] The BBC later cooperated with the Americans, the Vatican and other broadcasters in increasingly elaborate schemes to get around the jamming. The Soviets and their allies did devote an extraordinary amount of money and energy to jamming, but were never 100 per cent effective. Some information was always getting through, and by the late 1950s even the Soviets privately admitted that listeners could easily bypass jamming in much of the country.[99] Also, a glitch in the Soviet command economy created a windfall for the Western broadcasters. In 1953 the Soviet Council of Ministers had ordered the radio industry to stop producing short-wave radio sets capable of picking up Western broadcasts. The message apparently never arrived and by 1958 there were nearly 20 million receivers capable of picking up Western stations in the USSR.[100]

By 1951 all IRD material was going to the BBC, primarily through Robert McCall, head of the Overseas Services, and Tangye Lean, controller of the European Services, while anti-Communist specialist Walter Kolarz met every week with IRD specialist Jack Brimmell and MacLaren.[101] The IRD continued, however, to butt heads with the BBC's Russian Service, especially commentator Anatol Goldberg. In 1953 the department believed that the service was too critical of the United States and not critical enough of the USSR. This could alienate the Americans and give the Soviets wrong ideas about Britain's priorities.[102] But a thorough review of the FO's power over the BBC was disheartening to the diplomats:

> The system it describes works perfectly – when it works perfectly. It also makes satisfactory provision for dealing with acts of unqualified lunacy by the BBC. But unfortunately it makes no provision at all for dealing with imperfection falling short of lunacy – except moral suasion and pressure, which may (and in the case of the Russian Service quite possibly will) prove ineffective.[103]

By 1955 the Russian Service was still a point of contention within the IRD, which thought it had become 'more satisfactory' on British policy and international relations in general but still disliked the lack of pointed criticism of the Soviet regime. Conquest and others pointed out that the criticism of the Soviet policy had all been from a Marxist point of view. 'This could perhaps be left to

Radio Belgrade.'[104] Others pointed out that criticism from outside would often be resented by the target audience, the Soviet intellectual – 'no matter how critical of it he might be in the family circle.'[105] Then there was the problem of the British public:

> My strongest criticism of the Russian Service is the occasional lapse into cosy sentimentality. I deplore this, not because it misrepresents public opinion in this country, but because it reflects it accurately. This I would distort and suppress til the cows come home.[106]

Conclusion

After nearly 10 years of operations the IRD was satisfied with the work they were doing. The report almost seems smug. It noted that on average seven IRD articles and two briefs were published somewhere in the world each day in 1957. At least 1,000 items from the *Digests* were reproduced and its books had been translated into Spanish, Chinese, Italian, French, Arabic, Malayan and Javanese.[107] To do this the IRD had managed to cultivate a range of contacts with which to get its message out. The LPS and the Information Officers took orders, the BBC's External Services legally had to 'consult' them, but journalists, opinion leaders and others who cooperated did so freely. The careful examination of the IRD's media operations also clearly shows that the British and overseas operations were inextricably linked and grew more so into the 1950s as the operation became more sophisticated and expansive.

Notes

1. PRO FO1110/991 PR103/16/G, Reddaway to Burroughs, 3 August 1957.
2. PRO FO1110/715 PR10111/15, F. C. Stacey Note, 8 March 1954; PRO FO1110/1100 PR10111/14/G, Reddaway marginal note, 'The London Press Service', 3 January 1958.
3. PRO FO1110/1100 PR10111/14/G, 'The London Press Service', 3 January 1958.
4. PRO FO1110/778 PR1018/86/G, Grey to R. Allen (Bonn), 7 June 1955.
5. PRO FO1110/293 PR19/8/G, Sheridan minute, 31 January 1950.
6. *The Times* Archives, McDonald Papers, Correspondence R, Unsorted Box, McDonald to Reddaway, 21 December, 1959.
7. PRO FO1110/980 PR10111/56/G, Owens to Reddaway, 30 October 1957.
8. PRO FO11110/991 PR103/16/G, Reddaway to Burroughs, 3 August 1957.
9. PRO FO1110/359 PR1110/5/G, 'Report on the work of the Information Research Department, 1st August to 31st December 1949'.
10. Muggeridge Papers (Hoover), Diary Entry for 17 October 1950.
11. Ian Murray, 'Orwell was recruited to fight Soviet propaganda', *The Times*, 11 July 1996; 'George Orwell's Cold War', *The Times*, 12 July 1996; Andrew Roberts,

'*Animal Farm*'s rich crop of humbug', *Sunday Times*, 14 July 1996. The controversy grew in 1998 when an expurgated version of the actual list was released. See
'Socialist icon who became Big Brother', *Daily Telegraph*, 22 June 1998.

12. PRO FO1110/189 PR113511/G Orwell to Kirwan, 6 April 1949.

13. George Orwell, *Our Job is to Make Life Worth Living, 1949–1950*. Vol. 20, in Peter
    Davison (ed.), *The Complete Works of George Orwell* (London: Secker and Warburg,
    1998), Appendix 9, pp. 240–59.

14. Nigel West and Oleg Tsarev, *The Crown Jewels: The British Secrets at the Heart of the
    KGB Archives* (London: HarperCollinsPublishers, 1998), pp. 30–2. During Ewer's
    youthful attachment to Communism in the 1920s he ran a spy ring for the Soviets
    that was unmasked in 1929. The government never prosecuted him or his spies in
    Scotland Yard, reportedly for fear of scandal. Ewer later turned toward the right
    wing of the Labour Party and became a close ally of Ernest Bevin in exposing the
    Soviet Union. It would be interesting to know how the spectre of public exposure
    of his spying affected his political conversion and his dedication to anti-Communist
    propaganda work. West and Tsarev consistently misspelled Ewer's surname as Euer.
    All other details match perfectly, however.

15. For Ewer's BBC appearances, see PRO FO371/86756 NS1052/60/G.

16. PRO FO1110/267 PR2324/84/913, Report, 10 August 1949.

17. PRO FO953/877 PG1173/3, Aldington minute, 7 June 1950.

18. PRO FO1110/359 PR110/5/G, 'Report on the work of the Information Research
    Department: 1st August to 31st December 1949'.

19. PRO FO1110/258 PR3648/69/G, Sheridan minutes 18, 22, 24 November 1949.

20. Chevins Papers, 1/16, Sheridan to Chevins, 3 July 1950.

21. PRO FO110/311 PR37/56, Sheridan minute, 21 September 1950, Wilkinson
    minute, 23 September 1950, Sheridan minute, 27 September 1950, and Stacey
    minute, 18 October 1950.

22. PRO FO1110/415, Rangoon IO to Rayner, 12 November 1951. The writer did not
    mention specifically Davies or the topic of the article.

23. PRO FO1110/360 PR111/5/G, MacLaren to Hough, 14 November 1950,
    MacLaren to Smith, 1 November 1950. Also see, PRO FO1110/359 PR110/5/G,
    'Report on the work of the Information Research Department: 1st August to 31st
    December 1949.'

24. PRO FO1110/652 PR104/10/G, Lewen to Bevan, 8 June 1954; *Manchester Guardian*
    Archives, B/G74, Gedye to Wadsworth.

25. PRO FO1110/741 PR131/22, Clare Harris minute, 14 February 1955, Ackland
    minute, 24 February 1955.

26. PRO FO1110/782 PR1022/41/G, 'Main features of IRD Work in Italy', 9 July 1955;
    PRO FO1110/608 PRG92/3, 'I.R.D. articles published in the Yugoslav papers', 31
    January 1953.

27. CCF Papers, Box 11, File 6 (Forum World Services), Note, 11 March 1958.

28. 'Ruth Fischer, 62, an ex-Red leader', *New York Times*, 16 March 1961.

29. PRO FO1110/55 PR1292/265/913, Murray to Lean, 9 December 1948, Lean to
    Murray, 17 December 1948, Watson minute, 23 December 1948, Murray minute,
    13 March 1949.

30. PRO FO1110/264 PR788/80/913, Sheridan Note, 28 February 1949.

31. PRO FO1110/264 PR788/80/913, Hellman (Fischer's agent) to Sheridan, 20 March
    1949.

32. PRO FO1110/264 PR1634/80/G, Sheridan to Hellman, 16 June 1949, Fischer to Sheridan, 21 June 1949.
33. PRO FO1110/359 PR110/5/G, Murray to Parliamentary Undersecretary, 15 February 1950.
34. PRO FO1110/359 PR110/5/G, 'Report on the work of the Information Research Department, 1st August to 31st December 1949'.
35. PRO FO1110/154 PR1058/1058/913, Watson minute, 8 November 1948.
36. PRO FO1110/359 PR110/2/G, MacLaren minute, 15 June 1950.
37. PRO FO1110/359 PR110/5/G, 'Annex A: Report on the work of the Information Research Department: 1st August to 31st December, 1949'.
38. PRO FO1110/451 PR110/1/51/G, Redman (UK Liaison Mission) to IRD, 20 February 1951, Murray to Redman, 15 March 1951.
39. PRO FO1110/359 PR110/5/G, 'Annex A: Report on the work of the Information Research Department: 1st August to 31st December 1949'.
40. PRO FO1110/589 PRG47/13, Boas to IRD, 27 June 1953.
41. PRO FO1110/358 PR109/1, Sheridan minute, 8 June 1950.
42. PRO FO1110/290 PR16/113/G, Murray to Marchant (Paris), 31 March 1950.
43. PRO FO1110/355 PR106/1, 'Kemsley Feature Articles Syndication Services'.
44. PRO FO1110/355 PR106/1, K. S. Butler minute, 3 April 1950.
45. PRO FO1110/358, R.L. Unknown notation, 28 April 1950.
46. PRO FO1110/344 PR85/10, King-Hall to Warner, 17 May 1950.
47. PRO FO1110/344 PR85/10, Murray to Pilcher and Marchant, 5 July 1950.
48. PRO FO1110/344 PR85/10, Murray to King-Hall, 19 June 1950, Murray to King-Hall, 14 July 1950.
49. 'Decadent dance tunes', National News-Letter, 1 February 1951; 'Father and son', National News-Letter, 15 March; 'Rumanians to be prosecuted for listening to the West', National News-Letter, 5 April 1951.
50. PRO FO1110/532 PR101/2/G, Circular, 10 January 1953.
51. PRO FO1110/422 PR68/51/51, Ralph Poston to Murray, 20 February 1951, Murray to Poston, 8 March 1951.
52. PRO FO1110/790 PR1093/7/G, Hopson to J. Y. MacKenzie (Baghdad)
53. PRO FO1110/652 PR104/10/G, Bevan to Lewen, 23 April 1954.
54. Ruth Dudley Edwards, The Pursuit of Reason: The Economist, 1843–1893 (London: Hamish Hamilton, 1993), pp. 900–1.
55. Lashmar and Oliver, Britain's Secret Propaganda War, p. 118.
56. PRO FO1110/377 PR12/26/51/G, Macdonald (Intelligence Division) to Wilkinson, 21 February 1951, Wilkinson to Macdonald, 14 March 1951, MacLaren minute, 4 April 1951.
57. PRO FO1110/377 PR12/26/51/G, Wilkinson to Macdonald, 14 March 1951.
58. PRO FO1110/377 PR12/46/51/G, Macdonald to Wilkinson, 5 April 1951 (with attachments).
59. PRO FO1110/377 PR12/60/51/G, Macdonald to Wilkinson, May 1951.
60. PRO FO1110/778 PR1018/86/G, Grey to R. Allen (Bonn), 7 June 1955.
61. PRO FO1110/668 PR1022/5, Hebblethwaite to Peck, 7 January 1954.
62. PRO FO1110/148 PR999, Tennant to Woolrych, 21 October 1948, Cloake Memorandum, 9 November 1948; PRO FO1110/229 PR3395/39/G Sheridan note, 15 November 1949.
63. PRO FO1110/1071 PR143/12/G, E.E. Tomkins to Reddaway, 22 December 1958.

64. PRO FO1110/1071 PR143/12/G, 'Report by Monsieur Rostini on the use of I.R.D. material by his organisation', [n.d.].
65. PRO FO1110/451 PR110/1/51/G, Redman to IRD, 20 February 1951, Murray to Redman, 15 March 1951.
66. PRO FO1110/669 PR1023/9, Redman to Bolland, 31 August 1954.
67. PRO FO1110/232 PR138/42/G, Cloake minute [April 1949]; PRO FO1110/395 PR36/28G, Tull minute, 2 November 1951, Tull to Rayner, 2 January 1952.
68. PRO FO1110/952 PR10106/40/G, Mayby to Rennie, 27 April 1956.
69. PRO FO1110/316 PR1, 'Anti-Communist propaganda in Egypt', 18 February 1950, 'Anti-Communist propaganda in Egypt', 20 March 1950, Murray to Warner, 8 June 1950, J. V. Riley minute, 20 June 1950.
70. PRO FO1110/508 PR67/83/G, 'Covert operations in the Middle East', 3 February 1953.
71. Ibid.
72. PRO PRG16/11, James Murray (Cairo) to Glass (Beirut), 19 June 1953.
73. PRO FO1110/616 PRG104/49/G, Peck to Glass, 16 July 1953.
74. PRO FO1110/616 PRG104/49/G, Peck to Glass (unexpurgated draft version), 16 July 1953.
75. PRO FO1110/311 PR37/78/G, 'Working report of Special Team from 15 September to 15 October 1950'.
76. Michael Nelson, *War of the Black Heavens: The Battles of Western Broadcasting in the Cold War* (Syracuse: Syracuse University Press, 1997), pp. 31–4.
77. PRO FO1110/311 PR37/16, 'List of IRD articles sold by British Features'.
78. PRO FO1110/664 PR1018/125, M.K. Caro note, 7 December 1954.
79. PRO FO1110/1005 PR1018/34, J.M. Fisher (BIS, Bonn) to Peter M. Foster (IRD), 27 May 1957.
80. PRO FO1110/1005 PR1018/51, Rennie to Murray, 18 July 1957.
81. Labour Party Archives, General Secretary's Papers, Box 8, Daily Herald (GS/DH), Gedye to Morgan Philips, 5 March 1950.
82. PRO FO1110/412 PR54/15/51/G, Wilkinson to Andrew Stark (Vienna), 25 May 1951.
83. PRO FO1110/764 PR103/61/G, Wallinger to Grey, 18 November 1955.
84. Reddaway interview.
85. PRO FO1110/991 PR103/16/G, Reddaway to Burroughs, 3 August 1957.
86. PRO FO1110/991 PR103/16/G, Burroughs to Reddaway, 28 June 1957.
87. PRO FO1110/991 PR103/9, 'IRD work in Vienna', 14 March 1957.
88. *Broadcasting White Paper*, (Cmd. 6852), 1946, p. 15.
89. Briggs, *Sound and Vision*, pp. 575–9
90. PRO CAB130/37 (GEN231/1st Meeting), Cabinet: Anti-Communist Propaganda, 11 May 1948, (GEN231/1) Anti-Communist Publicity: Memorandum by the Secretary of State for Foreign Affairs, 30 April 1948.
91. PRO FO1110/16 PR22, Murray minute, 17 February 1948, Woolrych minute, 26 February 1948, Murray minute, 1 March 1948.
92. PRO FO1110/16 PR266/10/913, Jacob to Warner, 26 April 1948.
93. PRO FO953/229A, Bowen to Eastern European Missions, 19 October 1948.
94. FCO Historians, *Notes: IRD*, p. 18.
95. PRO FO953/229A, Bowen to Eastern European Missions, 19 October 1948.
96. PRO FO1110/88 PR1268/590/913, Murray to Allen, 20 January 1949.
97. BBC WAC E2/119/1, 'Russian jamming', 23 May 1951.

98. PRO FO1110/223 PR2121/35/G, Watson minute, 8 August 1949, Hankey minute, 23 August 1949.

99. Nelson, *War of the Black Heavens*, pp. 22–3, 92.

100. Ibid.

101. PRO FO1110/393 PR33/32/51, MacLaren minute, 7 April 1951.

102. PRO FO1110/624 PR131/5/G, Mason minute, 16 December 1953.

103. PRO FO1110/625 PR131/1/G, Nicholls minute, attached to 'Relationship between the BBC Overseas Services and the Foreign Office', 14 December 1953.

104. PRO FO1110/741 PR 131/49/G, Conquest minute, 25 November 1955.

105. PRO FO1110/741 PR131/49/G, Storey minute, R. H. Mason minute, 20 June 1955.

106. PRO FO1110/741 PR131/49/G, R. H. Mason, 20 June 1955.

107. PRO FO1110/1100 PR10111/6/G, IRD to Information Officers, 27 January 1958.

6

Friends and Allies

The IRD was not a unilateral organisation. Everywhere they sought like-minded partners, allies and collaborators. This cooperative approach carried several benefits. British propaganda could influence the allied organisations or countries' own propaganda, which boosted the power and reach of the British point of view while making it appear pervasive and widely accepted. The British allies frequently provided information otherwise unavailable to the IRD. Finally, these allies supplied a cover in areas and with audiences where even covert British propaganda would be suspect and distrusted.

From almost the beginning the IRD began to develop a relationship with the new hegemon on the block, the United States. It was a complex evolving relationship in which the British were both teachers and supplicants to the less experienced but wealthier and more powerful Americans. By the mid-1950s maintaining good relations with the USA was one of the most important IRD goals. The IRD had developed close relationship with other governments – NATO members, Commonwealth partners and independent countries. But other governments were less than partners and more like clients, taking British propaganda but generating little return traffic of their own.

Americans: The Special Relationship

The most important partner was the United States government and, by extension, its own constellation of quasi-private fronts and private collaborators.[1] While the Americans obviously had more money and power than the British, the British brought enough experience, contacts and other resources to make it a roughly equal partnership, at least in the early years. The partnership allowed the British to infiltrate their techniques and messages into the better-financed American effort, and to restrain what they believed to be dangerous American moves. The Americans gained access to the contacts and assets acquired by Britain in two centuries as a world power, and had the chance to learn from the subtler and more indirect British propaganda experts.

The Anglo–American propaganda partnership covered much of the world with their shared vision but with different angles, tones, and voices. Throughout, the general trend was toward a greater reliance on covert, non-attributable and non-governmental propaganda, whether through front groups, booster organisations, or indirect methods. This clearly mirrored British propaganda and helped steer the overall development of Western propaganda and in some ways helped shape the modern American propaganda machine. In many ways this propaganda relationship resembled the tight Anglo-American relationship in intelligence. In both intelligence and propaganda the USA and UK had complementary strengths and interests that led to long-running cooperation.

The importance of the American partnership – even at the prosaic level of information exchange – was clearly spelled out in a 1954 memo for Foreign Secretary Sir Anthony Eden.

> The prestige which we derive from the distribution of our material is not to be underestimated, because there is no other power in the free world except the United States which produce this kind of thing on any serious or systematic scale. But the main advantage which Her Majesty's Government derive from the distribution of documents to a long list of American organizations is the effect which we are able to exercise on the enormous American publicity and propaganda output. For this there is plenty of evidence. Indeed, perhaps the most important aspect of the work altogether is the extent to which our ideas on how propaganda should be conducted, and even the points and themes which we want stressed, can be injected by this means into the much larger American operation. For the fact is that the operations carried out by the United States are on such a scale that influencing them in the ways we think desirable has become second in importance only to our own operations in the field.[2]

By that time the Americans had built and deployed a large and sometimes chaotic propaganda operation. Although there were innumerable feuding bureaucracies, mini-empires, state-private partnerships and independent propagandists most Anglo-American propaganda work centred on the United States Information Agency and the Central Intelligence Agency. Overt propaganda started under State Department auspices as the United States International Information and Educational Exchange but after political twists and turns it emerged in August 1953 as the United States Information Agency, an agency answering to the president that controlled official publications, overseas libraries, exchange programmes, embassy-based information officers and the Voice of America. The Central Intelligence Agency took covert propaganda after the State Department refused it. The Office of Policy Coordination ran most covert operations; after 1951 the International Organizations Division handled front groups and their propaganda. The CIA's Frank Wisner described the agency's propaganda assets as a 'mighty Wurlitzer' that could play any tune in multi-part harmony. Big elements included the Congress for Cultural Freedom, the European Movement, Radio Free Europe and Radio Liberation.

The British had worked closely with Americans on propaganda since 1940, to win the war against Germany and to bolster their waning power. There was a partial disengagement in 1945–7 as the new Labour government and the Americans followed different paths on emotional issues such as foreign aid, colonialism, Palestine, and – above all – relations with the Soviets. But the personal bonds formed during wartime joint psychological warfare operations against Germany endured. In mid-1947, for example, American journalist and propagandist C. D. Jackson used his influence with Richard Crossman, by then a Labour MP, to try to arrange 'frank discussions' for a congressional fact-finding mission to Europe investigating propaganda's importance.

> In spite of the war-time association, we are still babes in the woods compared to you and, worse than that, Congress and the Senate is just as ignorant of problems and techniques today as it was during the war when once a year OWI's back was to the wall in the Appropriations Committee hearings.[3]

The crystallisation of Cold War views made cooperation, once again, much easier. Within days of Britain's official turn toward confrontation the British embassy in Washington was informing the State Department about the developments and suggesting exchanges of material and ideas.[4] The consultations began soon on the basis of shared anti-Communist aims.[5] Christopher Warner travelled to Washington in early 1948 to work out the details of anti-Communist cooperation; an exchange of basic papers soon followed.[6] Later in the year Washington and London gave their diplomats in the field the go-ahead for Anglo-American cooperation.[7] Cooperation at that stage was generally sedate – a chat over up-coming projects or a casual swapping of finished propaganda and information guidance messages, an arrangement that did not impress the State Department.[8] For their part the British were not impressed with what they had seen of American Cold War propaganda, but hoped for access to American raw material and for a restraining hand on American field operators who were in danger of 'spoiling the market' for anti-Communist propaganda through over-zealousness and indiscretion.[9]

The propaganda alliance intensified in 1950 as a rising fear of Soviet power led to strategic reassessments, renewed American emphasis on propaganda, and increased personal liaison and high level meetings. At the beginning of the year IRD propaganda expert Adam Watson went to Washington where he quickly laid out the British programme and ideas about propaganda for the Americans. Propaganda had to be quick, accurate, factual, and appear as indigenous as possible. This was especially true in Asia where Europeans were widely distrusted. 'Native, if necessary obscure and small publishing houses, unsuspected of foreign contacts' could best handle distribution of propaganda books and periodicals. The British were beginning to have these in 'all ranges.'[10] Watson was a hit, especially among the American propagandists who considered British techniques to be superior to their own.[11]

The Americans unveiled their high-spending and aggressive 'Campaign of Truth' in April. The following month Ed Barrett, the US assistant secretary of state for public affairs met with Warner to talk white and grey propaganda cooperation. (Barrett didn't handle covert 'black' operations.) They discussed differences in approach, emphasis and targeting, plans for new operations, and avenues for further cooperation, as well as the need for greater field-level cooperation in critical areas, further exchange of propaganda material and research and VOA-BBC collaboration to circumvent Communist-bloc jamming.[12] More importantly, the British tried to convince the Americans that indirect, grey propaganda worked better than overt propaganda delivered in saturation doses, and found them open to suggestion.[13]

The British and Americans began more closely coordinating their work after the Barrett-Warner meetings.[14] This gathering and later meetings helped expose the British grey propaganda methods to the Americans, who were frustrated with the diminishing returns from overt propaganda and were looking for alternatives. Barrett later mentioned to a colleague that he had been learning a great deal about British grey methods and suggested 'we should give serious consideration to doing more in this field.'[15] By the end of 1951 Barrett could look back on the success of grey and covert operations 'that we have found to pay off so importantly.'[16]

Sometimes there was a not-so-hidden agenda with the IRD's liaison in Washington, as when the British sent Washington a report on Communism in Britain's African colonies in the hope it would blunt the Americans' vestigial anti-colonialism.[17] At other times the British merely wanted an opportunity to restrain the Americans from undertaking 'unreasonable activities'.[18] But there were times when partnership in propaganda promised much deeper Anglo–American cooperation. For instance, in 1951 and 1952 the IRD's Latin American representative Emile Lecours had gathered a great deal of information from unhappy Guatemalan army officers, men who would lead a CIA-backed coup in 1954. The IRD sent it to the Americans, who were judged to have the means and the responsibility to take action against what Lecours and others saw as a pro-Communist government in Guatemala.[19]

There were, of course, parts of the world where the British and Americans held each other at arm's length. In the Far East the Americans avoided a tie up because of the British 'colonial' legacy and sharp differences over China, while in India the British sought to emphasise the Commonwealth bond and avoid cooperation with the Americans.[20] When the Americans protested the Hong Kong colonial administration's decision to pull the plug on a VOA transmission relay, the British stood firm. Watson pointed out that Hong Kong was under the gun and had to do whatever necessary to 'preserve the security of the colony against Chinese Communist attack.'[21] When the British proposed joint Cairo-based propaganda for the Middle East the Americans declined the offer, privately claiming it to be 'an effort . . . to get us to pull some British chestnuts out of the fire' after sharp budget cuts.[22]

When it came to broadcast cooperation the British held good cards. Its residual empire – islands, bases and agreements with former colonies and satraps around the world – meant it controlled many key broadcasting sites. But the British were wary of American efforts to involve them with the CIA-funded Radio Free Europe, largely because the British disliked the American requirement that the British side be run through a refugee front group.[23] Once again the Anglo–American wartime personal connections came up. Murray told Adam Watson to give RFE-backer C. D. Jackson his respects if he ran into him 'and remind him of eating octopus at Paul's black market restaurant in Algiers in 1943.'[24] Eventually the British decided to funnel IRD material to the RFE, help it recruit staff among Eastern European exiles, and critique its broadcasts. In early 1952 Sir Robert Bruce Lockhart and BBC supervisor Gregory Macdonald toured the RFE's Munich headquarters and praised the station's energy and competence.[25]

The post-1950 spirit of Anglo-American cooperation may have helped the VOA to increase its reliance on the British Reuters news service. The VOA had relied on Reuters and the INS for the bulk of its news after the Associated Press and United Press blackballed it for its propaganda taint in 1946. The dependence on Reuters deepened in 1950–1, prompted by the dearth of Eastern European news and the VOA's desire to become more 'local' to its listeners behind the Iron Curtain. Reuters started providing a special and secret service for the VOA of news items considered too minor for the regular global service.[26]

The Americans covered their bets with the British with propaganda within Britain. This became especially important with the rise of anti-American feeling, in part generated by news of hysterical American witch-hunting personified by US Senator Joseph McCarthy, and the emergence of organised British left-wing Labour dissent under Aneurin Bevan. Much of it was done through front groups, and will be described below. But the US Embassy was also a prolific generator of overt propaganda and an undercover supplier of planted articles and convenient facts for friendly journalists.[27] The USIS helped the *News Chronicle*'s A. J. Cummings when he needed facts to attack anti-Americanism and planted articles ridiculing East Germany and the Soviet suppression of 'Western style dance music' with the Kemsley newspaper chain.[28] When the mass-circulation magazine *Illustrated* proposed a story on the McCarthy witch hunt the embassy tried to discourage it, then asked Jack Nicholls at the Foreign Office to pressure the magazine. He said he would 'do what he could to prevent the article.'[29] The British monitored anti-Americanism and relied on its own private partners to combat it, such as former Attlee spokesman Francis Williams who was behind an anti-anti-American push by the English Speaking Union and the British-American Association.[30]

With the Republicans taking over the White House in 1953, the embassy wanted to emphasise Britain's anti-Communist militancy. The Foreign Office sent the Americans an evaluation of their own ideas about political warfare in response to changes in American leadership.[31] The report emphasised a long-term objective of regime change in Moscow, and short-term objectives of rallying the waverers, informing the ignorant and bracing everyone against a settlement with the Soviet regime. The FO emphasised 'eventual liberation' for the East bloc, and the need to spread doubts and shake the faith among the Soviet elites.[32]

The Americans' 1953 review of their own propaganda operations raised the status of propaganda, reorganised the bureaucracy, emphasised the need for local and indirect propaganda, praised the value of allied cooperation, but recognised its limits 'even in the case of a close ally such as the United Kingdom.'[33] The inimitable C. D. Jackson did not let those limitations confine his enthusiastic predictions of Anglo–American convergence on formerly divergent questions and techniques – at least in his letters to the British:

> The day is well past when the United States automatically assumes that every native with a tommy gun in his hands is an 18-carat patriot on his way to becoming a local George Washington. Similarly, the day is well past when every Britisher automatically accepts the finality of Kipling's law of 'lesser breeds without the law'.[34]

The British doubted this new sweet reasonableness would last, or take very deep roots among American representatives in the field.[35] But propaganda co-operation did continue on a broad front, with the British hoping to moderate the Americans while exploiting their massive publicity machine. By 1954 the British were swapping information promiscuously with the State Department, the USIA, the CIA, the CIA radio fronts, research universities like Harvard and Columbia, émigré organisations, some foreign language press, individuals and 'really private organisations' such as the World Jewish Congress and the Union of Christian Churches. The British relied on ten official US publication sources and twenty non-official ones. The Foreign Office supplied twenty-nine separate categories of publications to the Americans, ranging from the IRD's front pub-lications such as *Background Books* to Communist news monitoring reports. All propaganda provided to the Americans had a multiplier effect through Wash-ington's own state-private partnerships. For example, by 1956 the IRD regularly sent to official Washington contacts 112 copies of the *Interpreter* and fifty-seven copies of the *Asian Analyst*, which 'then percolate through to those numerous private individuals who are in contact with the administration in this field and work either with or for them in some capacity.' The Americans also provided significant raw knowledge on the USSR that the British did not have access to, and social scientific information that would be useful in planning for psycholog-ical warfare.[36]

The British Foreign Office liked its independence and its special propaganda relationship with the Americans, and fought hard to limit any perceived chal-lenges to it, such as the 1950–1 American proposal to expand NATO propa-ganda. The American idea was to use NATO as a 'counter-Cominform' to better organise propaganda as Cold War tensions ratcheted up in late 1950. Some Americans had come to realise the limits of US propaganda in an increasingly anti-American Europe and wanted to use NATO as a 'cover' for largely American anti-Communist propaganda, while others were looking for new opportunities for empire-building. The British-led resistance to American pressure was based on three fundamental beliefs: any emphasis on NATO operations would foul up the cosy Anglo–American propaganda cooperation, continental allies without 'propaganda machines' would interfere with these efforts, and dominance by American 'hard-sell' propagandists would only alienate many Europeans. An-other unstated but obvious, reason was that it would take much propaganda out of the Foreign Office's control.[37]

After a great deal of bureaucratic and diplomatic struggle in 1950–1 a compromise emerged based on a fairly small NATO publicity office, which would funnel IRD propaganda, and a network of privatised booster groups operating in close cooperation with their national governments and the NATO command.[38] In early 1952 NATO's first secretary-general, British General Hastings 'Pug' Ismay, encouraged the British Society for International Understanding, an elite non-governmental group, to start building an international pro-NATO network. The society started with an Atlantic Community conference at Oxford in September 1952, followed by a conference in Copenhagen the following year, which led to the establishment of the international Atlantic Treaty Association. The organisers recognised that NATO itself operated under tight limits, but that their association could run exchange programmes, publishing ventures, media campaigns, and popular education programmes at all levels.[39] The British Atlantic Committee took shape in 1953 and became an umbrella for existing societies and 'ginger groups' for better international relations, such as the English Speaking Union, the United Nations Association and the Labour Party-backed Friends of the Atlantic Union.[40] The BAC had impeccable establishment credentials, with the Foreign Office's endorsement and former Moscow ambassador Sir David Kelly at its head.[41] Official and limited NATO propaganda continued, but the private entities now handled most publicity work.[42]

British relations to other governments did not compare to the Anglo–American partnership, and were essentially one-way streets. The British provided propaganda for information and redistribution and did not really expect much back. The March 1948 signing of the Brussels Pact opened opportunities to provide IRD material to the French, Dutch and Belgian governments; the formation of NATO the following year expanded those possibilities. The IRD gave basic papers and high-level material to the governments, and field operatives continued to distribute other propaganda in the host countries without the governments' knowledge. Soon afterward the IRD modelled its relationships with the new Commonwealth countries of India, Pakistan and Ceylon on what they had with the Brussels Pact. Much of the Indian propaganda went to the top, all the way to Prime Minister Jawaharlal Nehru.[43] By 1955 the Old Commonwealth governments were handling IRD propaganda on their own.[44] Other contacts came on an ad hoc basis, as when the embassy in Syria reported that the Syrian Prime Minister was asking them for material on Communism. They provided the basic papers 'Foundations of Stalinism', the 'Practice of Stalinism' and some information specifically on Communism and Islam.[45]

The State-Private Network

The British government had a clear legacy of state-private partnerships in propaganda work in both war and peace. Some of the partnerships were obvious and flowed logically from the fact that the ruling Labour government was pushing democratic socialism in opposition to Communism at home and abroad. Who better than Labour Britain to appeal to them? The cabinet envisioned the Labour Party and the Trades Union Congress as allies in this battle from the very beginning. Other partnerships sprang up with key players in British civil society – religious groups, professional associations and civic societies – while additional ones evolved more slowly as specific needs arose and as additional groups, often American-financed, emerged in the 1950s.

The most useful ally for the IRD in its wooing of the left was the governing Labour Party's central office at Transport House, with its networks of activists and publications at home, and connection with other socialists abroad. International Secretary Denis Healey worked closely with the Foreign Office laundering propaganda, providing tips and coordinating strategies. Early on Healey introduced the department to anti-Communist socialists in France, Italy, Scandinavia and the Netherlands and put their names on the IRD distribution lists.[46] He helped exiled Eastern European socialists such as Czech Walter Kolarz find work, often at the BBC or the IRD.[47] When the IRD needed Labour Party material to keep the Burmese socialists on the right track, they looked to Healey to provide it.[48] He later offered the IRD the party's *Talking Points* and a leaflet on the Soviet peace movement, suggesting that they might want to use them abroad. The IRD's Watson praised the material, but later pointed out that they were marred by factual errors.[49] IRD Head Ralph Murray was not thrilled by the party's efforts as of early 1949, writing: 'At present all they do is forward a certain amount of our material spasmodically and they occasionally let us have some material which can be sent out to e.g. Burma.'[50]

The IRD helped out the Labour Party on domestic issues. When Labour Party activists needed facts to make a better case for UN intervention in the Korean War the IRD provided the background detail and edited an article on Communist aggression for the party's weekly guide for party activists, *Talking Points*.[51] The following year it provided similar services to rebut a *Daily Worker* article on rearmament.[52] In 1951 the Labour Party's left-wing under Aneurin Bevan broke ranks, and the Conservatives regained power in the general election, but the IRD kept good relations and a prolific flow of propaganda to the Labour Party's International Office and Healey's successor, Saul Rose. When party officials were in a rush to get information on Communist union machinations in the colonies and commonwealth, they turned to the IRD.[53]

Despite Labour domination in the post-war years the IRD did not neglect the opposition – Murray had developed contacts with the Conservative Party Central Office but the IRD did not send it any propaganda. With Conservative victory in October 1951 the IRD aimed to re-establish the by-then dormant link – 'what we want above all is a liaison on the working level similar to our connexion with Mr. Denis Healey.'[54]

The IRD's partnership with the anti-Communist members of the trade union movement evolved over the years with its primary focus shifting from funnelling information to foreign trade unionists to attacking Communists within Britain. At an April 1948 meeting the Minster of Labour George Isaacs brought up with TUC General Secretary Vincent Tewson the idea of using the trade union international to help with government propaganda. Tewson told the minister he was quite sure that the general council would help and asked for regular information for use in the *Labour* periodical, other news services and among British delegations to international trade union gatherings.[55] The most ambitious early project, and the biggest failure, was to use TUC cover to disseminate IRD propaganda within Britain and to trade unionists around the world. Early in 1948 Mayhew had started subsidising and supplying propaganda to the TUC newsletter *Freedom First* with hopes of expanding internationally, but the newsletter was sloppily run and became peripherally involved in a corruption scandal that finished its propaganda effectiveness.[56] Mayhew pursued a TUC international publication, but Tewson did not like the idea and the IRD's Murray grew discouraged with the trade unionists' abilities.[57]

Another opportunity to use trade union connections for global propaganda arose when the non-Communist unions in the World Federation of Trade Unions split in December 1949 to create the International Confederation of Free Trade Unions (ICFTU). Healey vouched for the ICFTU's head of publications, Edward Thompson, who had been in wartime intelligence, became secretary of the International Socialist Conference and was 'thoroughly reliable.'[58] Of special interest was the ICFTU's publication *Spotlight*, which focused on conditions in the Communist bloc and was taking raw material from not only the IRD, but also the US State Department, the AFL and the BBC Monitoring Service.[59] But even those allies did not enjoy the IRD's full trust. When the IRD and MI5 gave the TUC and ICFTU information, apparently from an informer, about a WFTU training session in Hungary they expurgated detailed information 'which neither the TUC nor the ICFTU have any need to know.'[60]

During the mid-1950s the British government saw Communist leadership of strategically important unions, such as the 250,000-member Electrical Trades Union, as a potential threat to national security. In the event of war they could be expected to foment industrial disputes.[61] However, the ETU's Communist leaders had grown comfortable and corrupt in their posts with no coherent policy other than keeping their jobs, which they did through union election fraud. They certainly weren't interested in revolution. But the IRD apparently saw them and the Communist leadership of the Fire Brigades Union as potential Fifth Columnists. The IRD asked the *Daily Mail* to publish damaging information about the fire brigade leadership, which led to a lawsuit, and more information developed by the *Mail*'s 'ferocious ferrets' was slipped to the ever-cooperative Hugh Chevins at the *Telegraph* who 'lived on these stories for quite some time.'[62] IRD ally Woodrow Wyatt eventually published his warning of Moscow domination of British unions, *The Peril in Our Midst*, through Phoenix House, the publisher of the IRD's Background Books series.[63]

The IRD also developed direct partnerships with foreign socialist political parties and trade union officials through information officers and labour attachés. For example, the information officer in Helsinki regularly gave Swedish and Finnish translations of IRD material to the trade unions.[64] In Brazil the labour attaché worked closely with trade union leaders and the cooperative movement, resulting in IRD propaganda being published in Brazilian union publications.[65]

In addition to the obvious and helpful links with the main political parties and the trade unions, the IRD developed good relations with church hierarchies, peace groups and the independent groups that made up much of Britain's 'civil society' in the early post-war years. These relationships had mutual benefit – most of these leaders were suspicious, at best, of the Soviets and Britain's home-grown Communists and welcomed the IRD's information, which confirmed their suspicions and gave them the factual knowledge they needed in their own propaganda. In addition, there were a number of shadowy groups that were pre-dominantly obsessed with Communism, and sometimes served as fronts for other interests. With both types of organisations the IRD preferred to maintain ties with individuals within the group, giving the IRD more security and flexibility.

Churches and clerics would seem to be natural adversaries of atheistic Communism, but the IRD felt that they needed inside information to be stalwart and to make the best case against the Soviets to their flocks. The Church of England was involved early on. Its leader, the Archbishop of Canterbury, was invited to serve on the Russia Committee. The Reverend H. M. Waddams led the church's Council on Foreign Relations and had discreet connections with the IRD and other Foreign Office departments.[66] The Foreign Office sent material to the church's headquarters at Lambeth Palace, including a blacklist of organisations that churchmen should be discouraged from joining.[67] Although much of the IRD's work with the Church of England was to fortify the Cold War consensus within Britain, the propagandists were surely aware that the legacy of empire and centuries of missionary work meant that the church also had a global reach to clerics and congregations around the world.

In 1950 the IRD intensified their combing of East bloc missions for evidence of anti-religious attitudes and actions and began sending the results out to posts, including the Vatican, and British allies such as Waddams and the Roman Catholic *Tablet* magazine's J. D. Woodruff.[68] The following year the department put together the *Religious Digest*. As Sheridan explained, the *Religious Digest* was not for Waddams, who was involved in the production, but for 'his colleagues who are less well informed, and who have not the time to do the research which Mr. Waddams undertakes.'[69] In 1954 the IRD expanded their spread in the Vatican and began offering material to the Catholic International Organisations office, which then would distribute it to missions around the world.[70]

Student and youth groups composed another Cold War arena as Soviet-friendly leaders took over the major World Federation of Democratic Youth and the International Union of Students. The FO's Cultural Relations Department, with some help from MI5 and MI6, identified leaders and subsidised a new youth congress and permanent organisation – the International Youth Congress and the World Assembly of Youth, respectively – and promoted non-Communist leadership in the British National Union of Students.[71] Later the Foreign Office could rely on NUS leaders such as Stanley Jenkins to ask awkward questions at IUS gatherings.[72] For example, Jenkins used IRD data on the East bloc for a speech at the second IUS Congress in Prague, with an explosive impact on the hostile audience.[73] The IRD was pleased: 'Jenkins' first-class performance in Prague shows that our very discreet handling and briefing has borne excellent fruit.'[74] After non-Communist groups split from the IUS the Foreign Office helped subsidise some of their efforts.[75]

Other IRD partners were independent and quasi-independent anti-Communist activists who took money, information and direction from a wide variety of sources. Within Britain the department preferred institutions like unions and churches; they were willing to work with these groups. Elsewhere it was open season. The grand-daddy of anti-Communist publicists was the well-funded Economic League, which had been attacking Communists – as well as socialist and trade union activists – since industrialists and intelligence agents founded the organisation in the militant winter of 1919–20.[76] It had money, information and a bad reputation among the leftists whom the IRD was trying to 'enlighten' about Communism. The League's budget had more than quadrupled from 1945 to 1953, by which time it was spending £165,683 and employing 200 people, including seventeen researchers and press liaison officers, and producing more than a half dozen regular publications, including numbers such as *Communism at Work* and *Subversive News Bulletin.*[77] By mid-1950 some in the IRD were sending papers to the Economic League, which alarmed Department Head Ralph Murray because of the potential impact on the British non-Communist left.[78] But over the years the IRD gravitated toward cooperation with the league's Home Research Department director, John Baker White.[79] In 1954, for example, Baker White sent IRD boss John Rennie a background report on British dockworkers' activities.[80] By 1958 the IRD was 'discreetly in close touch' with Baker White in his work on British Communist activities. 'He is both a good source and a good outlet.'[81]

Other groups had lighter pockets and even spottier reputations, yet managed some cautious IRD patronage nonetheless. Ex-leftist C. A. Smith helped found Common Cause in 1948 to fight British Communism and gathered an odd coalition around him: right-wing aristocrats such as the Duchess of Atholl (founder of the British League for European Freedom), the Countess of Listowel (editor of *East Europe and Soviet Russia*), industrialists, anti-Communist Catholics and right-wing labour activists.[82] The British Common Cause had links with a parallel American Common Cause Inc., which was in turn linked to a host of covert and quasi-covert anti-Communist groups.[83] The IRD was wary of Smith and the group, though it was in contact with him and had offered to send him material.[84] Department Head J. H. Peck described him as 'a fanatic who sometimes comes dangerously near to advocating witch hunts and also appears to be vain and indiscreet.'[85] But Common Cause soon fell apart and its trades union members helped found a new group, Industrial Research and Information Services, Ltd. (IRIS) to fight Communist and far-left influence in unions.[86] Groups such as Common Cause could be frustrating to the mandarins at the Foreign Office, as Anthony Nutting wrote in 1953:

I'm getting both tired and confused by the ever-increasing proliferation of international voluntary societies. And I doubt very much that they do any serious good. It's always the same story – a bunch of enthusiasm from some well-meaning but not very stable do-gooders and then a gradual run-down, leading to collapse.[87]

The American-backed front organisations, described above, had much better funding and greater durability, and provided the British with more opportunities for collaboration. The IRD and MI6 frequently worked with the CIA-sponsored Congress for Cultural Freedom, influenced its local branch the British Society for Cultural Freedom and helped finance the CCF's London-based showcase intellectual journal *Encounter*. The journal was born when the CCF and MI6 were looking for something to challenge Kingsley Martin's *New Statesman and Nation*. Christopher Monty Woodhouse had been handling 'deep cover work' for the IRD and negotiated for the British. The IRD got a promise of consultation and agreed to pay for the salaries of British co-editor Stephen Spender and a secretary and buy copies of the new magazine *Encounter* in bulk for distribution overseas. The IRD paid publisher Secker and Warburg, which paid the British Society for Cultural Freedom, which paid Stephen Spender's salary at *Encounter*; the CIA picked up the rest of the bills. The IRD wanted *Encounter* to influence Asians and continental Europeans – the CIA thought it was needed to influence Britons as well.[88]

At the same time the CCF was emerging in the late 1940s, American pressure led the French government to launch the Paix et Liberté movement to counter the Soviet-backed peace movement. CIA money kept it going. Paix et Liberté specialised in clever, creative satires of the USSR and French Communists pointing out Communist hypocrisy.[89] The group's leader, Jean-Paul David, had international ambitions and several foreign affiliates, and by 1951 wanted one in Britain. The Foreign Office thought propaganda in Britain went best through existing organisations, and worried about creating an artificial and militant anti-Communist group. But they wanted to support Paix in France and elsewhere so suggested several potential partners to David and even the possibility of a small 'front organisation' that would work both with Paix and the IRD. After more than a year of false starts, David settled upon Common Cause as an ideal partner.[90] The IRD was probably grateful when the partnership did not pan out.[91]

CIA, IRD, MI6 and private money created a new professional category of anti-Communist writers, researchers, organisers and publicists. The early career of John Clews provides an interesting example. He came to the IRD's attention as a student leader in 1950 when he wrote to East bloc British missions asking ingenuous questions; the IRD was suspicious – he could be a good channel, he 'could be a Communist' and initially put him off.[92] Later Clews helped link the IRD to the BSCF, and funnel IRD material to the group, first as the BCSF's national organiser and then as its general secretary.[93] He also attended Communist-front group meetings to gather intelligence, and reported to the CCF's Paris office on the activities of his BCSF successor, Jasper Ridley.[94] By 1954 he was joint editor of Lady Listowell's *Soviet Orbit*, formerly *East Europe and Soviet Russia*, and the chairman, pro-tem, of the Committee of Student Affairs of the British League for European Freedom, a hard-core anti-Communist group linked to MI6 and exile groups. He also kept his options open, checking out jobs with Radio Free Europe and the OEEC and (freelance) work for the USIS, and was also writing for other anti-Communist publications such as *BEIPI*, *Ost-Probleme*, *Problems of Communism* and, of course, for the CCF itself.[95] His inspired work also appeared in the mainstream British press, as when he used material provided by the CCF via Diana Josselson to write articles that appeared in the *Birmingham Post*, *London Evening News* and *Coventry Evening Telegraph*. He noted that the Coventry piece was then picked up and circulated world wide by the COI.[96]

Conclusion

The Foreign Office was able to develop a close relationship with the burgeoning American propaganda machine in the years after 1948, supplying it with their propaganda, advising it on strategy and tactics and using the flood of information the Americans generated in their own propaganda efforts. The Foreign Office used the partnership to restrain from the inside what they saw as irresponsible American behaviour, and to piggyback on the Americans extensive and well-funded operations. Outside challenges either to the partnership or British autonomy, as posed by NATO propaganda plans, were stoutly resisted. At the same time the IRD used and expanded a state-private network to launder propaganda, gather information and fortify their friends.

Notes

1. For the state-private network, see Scott Lucas, *Freedom's War: The American Crusade against the Soviet Union* (New York: New York University Press, 1999), pp. 93–106.
2. PRO FO1110/684 PR1045/79, Makins to Eden, 31 July 1954.
3. Jackson Papers, Box 54, Crossman, R.H.S. (3) file, C. D. Jackson to Crossman, 13 August 1947.
4. PRO FO1110/1 PR7/1/G, Warner to Balfour, 16 February 1948.
5. PRO FO1110/24 PR41, Talbot minute, 16 March 1948.
6. PRO FO1110/128, Warner memo, 6 October 1948.
7. PRO FO1110/128 PR1034/865/G, Secret circular, 29 November 1948.
8. NARA RG 59 DF511.41/2-950, Annex A: Cooperation with British and other Information Services, 30 December 1949.
9. PRO FO1110/236 PR4076/46/913, Warner to Hoyer-Millar, 31 December 1949.
10. NARA RG 59 DF 611.41/1-1650, 'Meeting with Mr. Adam Watson, representative of the Information Research Department of the Foreign Office, United Kingdom', 16 January 1950.
11. PRO FO1110/305 PR30/31, Hoyer-Millar to Warner, 12 February 1950.
12. PRO FO953/629 P1013/33, Meeting minutes, 20 May 1950.

13. Defty, *Britain, America and Anti-Communist Propaganda*, p. 146.
14. NARA RG 59 Office Files of Assistant Secretary Edward W. Barrett, 1950–51, Bureau of Public Affairs, Lot File 52 D432, Box 5, Barrett Overseas Trips, 1950–51 file, 'Rough notes on European trip', [n.d.].
15. NARA RG 59 Office Files of Assistant Secretary Edward W. Barrett, 1950–51, Bureau of Public Affairs, Lot File 52 D 432, Box 5, MacKnight file, Barrett to MacKnight, 3 June 1951.
16. NARA RG 59 Office Files of Assistant Secretary Edward W. Barrett, 1950–51, Bureau of Public Affairs, Lot File 52 D432, Box 5, Undersecretary 1951 file, 'Psychological offensive in the so-called Cold War', 13 November 1951.
17. PRO FO1110/394 PR34/6, Washington Embassy to FO, 15 January 1951.
18. PRO FO1110/418 PR63/5/51, Watson to Murray, 2 February 1951.
19. PRO FO1110/452 PR111/60/G, Tull to Watson, 24 March 1952; PRO FO1110/452 PR111/11/G, Meeting minutes, 10 July 1951.
20. NARA RG 59 Lot 53 D 47, Box 15, Cooperation with British file, Henderson to State Department, 27 May 1950; NARA RG 59. Lot 53 D 47, Box 15, Cooperation with British file, Stone to Connors, 14 June 1950, Connors to Stone, 16 June 1950.
21. NARA RG 59 DF 611.41/1-2751, Memorandum of conversation (Watson, Connors, et al.), 27 January 1951.
22. NARA RG 59 Box 3436 DF740.5, Barrett to Hopkins, 10 August 1951, Southworth to Barrett, 27 April 1951; DF 611.41/7-2051, Memorandum of conversation (Watson and Schwinn), 20 July 1951.
23. PRO FO1110/374; PRO FO1110/393 PR33/64G, Burrows to Reilly, 25 July 1951.
24. PRO FO1110/374 PR15/51/G, Murray to Watson, 21 February 1951.
25. PRO FO1110/518 PR94/8/G, Lockhart to IRD, 18 February 1952, Peck minute, 5 March 1952.
26. Reuters Archives, Reel #194, VOA file, New York Manager (D. Kimpton Rogers) to London Secretary, 7 December 1950.
27. NARA RG59 Lot 52 D 3654, Box 47, EUR-Regional Bureau Europe file, 'The United States Information Service in the United Kingdom: a comprehensive service of books, press, films, radio educational exchange', [n.d.]; Defty supplies a detailed accounting of overt activities in Defty, *Britain, America and Anti-Communist Propaganda*, pp. 209–10.
28. NARA RG 59 DF 511.41/9-353, UIS London to USIA, 8 September 1953.
29. NARA RG 59 DF 611.41/12-625, Evans to Schwinn, 6 December 1952.
30. PRO FO1110/423. PR68/127/G, M. A. Hamilton minute, 26 October 1951.
31. PRO FO1110/587 PRG45/110/G, Nicholls to Watson, 27 June 1953
32. PRO FO1110/587 PRG45/110/G, 'The strategy of political warfare', 25 June 1953.
33. *National Security Council Documents, 4th Supplement*, Reel 5, 'State Department report on implementation of the Jackson Report'.
34. PRO FO953/1528 PG14517/18, C. D. Jackson to J. W. Nicholls, 31 March 1954.
35. PRO FO953/1528 PG14517/17, Nicholls to Watson, 20 May 1954.
36. PRO FO1110/684 PR1045/79, Makins to Eden, 31 July 1954; PRO PR1045/7/G, Marshall to Cortazzi, 12 January 1956.
37. John Jenks, *Hot News/Cold War: The British State, Propaganda and the News Media, 1948–53* (Ph.D. dissertation, University of California-Berkeley, 2000), pp. 238–49.
38. Ibid.
39. Flynt Papers. Box 21, NATO – First International Study Conference, Oxford, England, 1952, 'Draft recommendations for Oxford conference, 30 July 1952'.

40. Flynt Papers, Box 3, Atlantic Committee (American, British, French, German) file, 'The British Atlantic Committee'.
41. Sir David Kelly, 'In defence of NATO', *Sunday Times*, 21 June 1953.
42. Ismay Papers, CM (54)115, Secretary General's Report for 1954, 9 December 1954.
43. PRO FO1110/929 PR1085/6/G, 'Note of a discussion between G. S. Bozman, Cosley-White and N. D. Middleton', 27 March 1956.
44. PRO FO1110/840 PR10108/30, G. S. Bozman minute, 19/20 December 1955.
45. PRO FO1110/345 PR86/19, Fletcher to Murray, 20 September 1950.
46. PRO FO1110/15 PR1211/1/913/G, Healey to Watson, 8 December 1948.
47. PRO FO1110/15 PR869/913/G, Healey to Watson, 2 November 1948, Watson to Healey, 25 November 1948.
48. PRO FO1110/6 PR220/1/913/G, Mayhew to Healey, 1 June 1948, Mennell to Mayhew, 3 June 1948.
49. PRO FO1110/15 PR1272/1/913, Watson minute, 21 December 1948, Watson to Healey, 3 January 1949.
50. PRO FO 1110/213 PR110, Murray minute, 10 March 1949.
51. Labour Party Archives, Labour Party International Department, Korean War – documents and correspondence, 1950–1.
52. Lashmar and Oliver, *Britain's Secret Propaganda War*, p. 109.
53. PRO FO1110/703 PR10100/8, T. A. K. Elliot minute, 6 January 1954, Mennell minute, 12 January 1954.
54. PRO FO1110/521 PR103/2/G, Sheridan minute, 4 January 1952, Wilkinson minute, 5 January 1952.
55. PRO CAB21/2745, Letter from Minister of Labour, 19 April 1948.
56. PRO FO953/142 P4967/1319/950/G, Mayhew to Bevin, 11 May 1948; PRO FO1110/380 PR18/38/51, Tull minute, 3 May 1951.
57. PRO FO1110/213 PR110, Murray minute, 10 March 1949, Sheridan minute, 31 December 1949.
58. PRO FO1110/380 PR18/3/51/G, Healey to Peck, 8 December 1950.
59. PRO FO1110/380 PR18/9/51, Sheridan minute, 8 December 1950, F. C. Mason minute, 22 January 1951.
60. PRO FO1110/755 PR161/23/G, (MI5) Box 500 to IRD, 10 March 1955, 12 May 1955.
61. PRO CAB176/33 JIC2641/51, MI5/MI6 report, 'The scale of Fifth Column activities to be expected in the event of war with the Soviet Union between the present date and the end of 1952', 28 November 1951.
62. Reddaway interview.
63. Lashmar, *Britain's Secret Propaganda War*, pp. 105–12; Glyn Powell, 'Turning off the power: the Electrical Trades Union and the anti-Communist crusade 1957–61', *Contemporary British History* 18 (2004), pp. 3–6.
64. PRO FO1110/690 PR1056/1, Information Officer (Helsinki) to IRD, 10 February 1954.
65. PRO FO1110/340 PR77/3/G, MacLaren minute, 4 April 1950.
66. PRO FO1110/382 PR20/11/51, Church affairs, 30 January 1951.
67. Dianne Kirby, *The Anglican Church in the Period of the Cold War: 1945–65* (Ph.D. dissertation, University of Hull, 1990), pp. 527–30.
68. PRO FO1110/353 PR104/17/G, Sheridan minute, 26 April 1950, Circular, 11 September 1950.
69. PRO FO1110/382 PR20/87, Sheridan minute, 5 November 1951.

70. PRO FO1110/691 PR1057/25, Chancery (Vatican) to IRD, 28 June 1954.
71. Aldrich, *Hidden Hand*, pp. 122–8.
72. PRO FO1110/321 PR51/3, Mayhew to Warner, 24 January 1950.
73. Joël Kotek, *Students in the Cold War* (London: Macmillan, 1996), pp. 162–4.
74. PRO FO1110/322 PR52/83/G, Wilkinson to Malcolm, 11 September 1950.
75. PRO FO1110/756 PR171/53/G, Assistance for the International Students' Conference. [1953]; PR141/53/G, A. W. Jackson to R. S. Mason, 7 June 1953.
76. Arthur McIvor, ' "A crusade for capitalism": The Economic League, 1919–39', *Journal of Contemporary History* 23 (1988).
77. Federation of British Industry Archive, MSS.200/F/5/S3/4 'Points of policy and organisation' (dated May 1954), and MSS.200/F/3/D3/9/32.
78. PRO FO1110/361 PR113/9, Murray minute, 6 October 1950.
79. Ibid.
80. PRO FO1100/704 PR10100/193, John Baker White to Rennie, 2 November 1954.
81. PRO FO1110/1099 PR10100/24, 'The Economic League', 27 May 1958.
82. Wilford, *The CIA, the British Left, and the Cold War*, pp. 67–70.
83. Dorrill, *MI6*, pp. 436–7.
84. PRO FO1110/547 PR143/9, 'Information Research Department's dealings with "Common Cause", 27 February 1953; PRO FO1110/704 PR10100/134/G, Manchip-White note, 12 July 1954.
85. PRO FO1110/547 PR143/9, Paix et Liberté and Common Cause, 1 March 1953.
86. Hugh Wilford, *The CIA, the British Left, and the Cold War: Calling the Tune?* (London: Frank Cass, 2003), p. 70.
87. PRO FO1110/547 PR143/9, Nutting minute, 3 March 1953.
88. Defty, *Britain, America and Anti-Communist Propaganda*, p. 210.
89. Irwin Wall, *The United States and the Making of Postwar France* (Cambridge: Cambridge University Press, 1991), pp. 150–1.
90. PRO FO1110/547 PR143/9, Paix et Liberté, 18 February 1953.
91. PRO FO1110/547 PR143/9, Paix et Liberté and Common Cause, 1 March 1953.
92. PRO FO1110/322 PR52/63/G, Paton minute, 6 June 1950.
93. Frances Stonor Saunders, *The Cultural Cold War: The CIA and the World of Arts and Letters* (New York: New Press, 1999), p. 111.
94. Wilford, *The CIA, the British Left and the Cold War*, pp. 197–8, 208–9.
95. CCF Papers, Box 78, File 8, Clews to Josselson, 15 February 1954, Clews to Josselson, 26 August 1954, Clews to Josselson, 6 June 1955, Clews to Josselson, 16 June 1956; Dorril, *MI6*, pp. 425–49.
96. CCF Papers, Box 78, File 8, Clews to Josselson, 16 June 1956.

7

Making Peace a Fighting Word

Peace became a fighting word in the late 1940s. Pro–Soviet partisans fought for peace and built peace fronts, while anti–Soviet forces accused them of peace mongering and tried to counter-attack against the Soviet-backed peace offensive. Behind these verbal contortions there was a real political and propaganda struggle over the nature of East–West relations and the very meaning of the word peace in a polarised and militarised Cold War Europe.

The struggle had some meaning within Britain, but the government saw it primarily as a diplomatic problem, not a domestic one. The British saw the Partisans of Peace as threatening NATO in Europe, the Commonwealth in Asia and innumerable British interests elsewhere. In the British counterattack the comparatively weak British partisans group became a convenient target. The British partisans themselves posed little threat, but their ability to project an exaggerated image overseas did. It would hearten Britain's enemies, discourage its allies and convince the allies of the state's weakness and society's divisions. The attack on them was mainly to inspire worried anti-Communists overseas and to demonstrate anti-Communist bona fides to the Americans.[1]

There was an ambiguous preface for the peace battle of the late 1940s and early 1950s. The massive destruction and death of World War II, and the arrival of the atomic bomb, gave strong incentives to avoid further wars. Within the British Labour Party pacifist feelings were still strong, though not nearly as powerful as in the 1930s. But at the same time there was a widespread belief that some things – such as Nazism or other forms of totalitarianism – were worse than war. 'Appeasement' had become a dirty word, and 'peace' would soon become soiled as well.

By 1948 Communists tried to manipulate peace sentiment – and the widespread fears of nuclear war – through public calls for peace and a series of ostensibly independent peace congresses and organisations. The Communist-backed Peace Partisans – later renamed the World Peace Council – fought for peace in ways that were favourable to Soviet state interests, such as focusing on the American reliance on nuclear weapons.[2] For Communist activists the reasoning went something like this: fighting for peace meant supporting the Communist bloc, since the American and British 'imperialists' would inevitably seek war if not stopped.[3]

The Soviets claimed their peace mobilisation was a defensive move in the face of growing Western military strength and cohesion, while privately recognising its ability to carry the offensive into Western domestic and alliance politics.[4] Britain, the US, and other NATO powers clearly saw it as a threat. To them the

Peace Partisans were nothing more than tools in a Kremlin–directed international conspiracy to weaken and divide the West in the face of superior Soviet military strength.[5]

The Soviets' graceless push for hegemony in the peace movement damaged the credibility of all peace groups. That, combined with Western counter-propaganda and action, left the word peace battered, bruised, and debased well into the 1950s. In Britain there had always been doubts about the patriotism of peace activists, but the blatant use of peace appeals by the Soviets and anti-Communist rebuttals led to widespread distrust – on the right, left, and centre – of any peace advocacy.[6]

Communists and Peace: From Wroclaw to Paris

Communists had a chequered record on peace since 1917, and largely took their cues from Soviet diplomatic needs.[7] Sometimes, of course, these needs coincided with and were able to articulate and organise public opinion far beyond the party faithful. But not always. When the Soviet Union was tacitly allied with Nazi Germany in 1939–41 the British Communists called for a negotiated end to the war and a 'people's peace'.[8] When the USSR was dragged into the struggle Communists everywhere immediately embraced an uncompromising pro-war position. Western Communists applauded the atom bombing of Hiroshima and Nagasaki, denouncing moral criticism of the bombings as a 'psychological perversion'.[9] But by 1948 the Cold War had replaced the wartime Grand Alliance and Communists were against the atomic bomb and for peace. The following year the Soviets would begin awarding the Stalin Peace Prize.[10]

The first steps of the international peace movement came at the August 1948 'World Conference of Intellectuals' in Wroclaw, Poland. To some non-Communist Westerners the Polish-sponsored event seemed to be an authentic opportunity for East-West dialogue and a possible way to ease a very tense world situation. As Ritchie Calder, journalist and peace activist, wrote in the liberal *News Chronicle*, 'Wroclaw is six hours away by air. The Russians will be there. It is worth trying.'[11]

The British Foreign Office, however, never had any doubts that the congress would be merely a louder version of the typical Soviet 'front' operation and had prepared for Wroclaw with that in mind.[12] Before the conference Foreign Office propagandists briefed one of the British delegates – Herman Ould, secretary of the writers group PEN – on Communist tactics. They were disappointed when Ould did nothing with the information.[13] But support came from an unexpected source – iconoclastic left-wing historian A. J. P. Taylor. Taylor went to Wroclaw with an open mind, but he was soon repelled by the one-sided and violent attacks on the West. Speaking with the backing of other disgruntled British delegates, Taylor ridiculed the pro-Soviet distortions of the congress and urged delegates to be critical of all Great Powers – including the Soviet Union.[14] Taylor's remarks made a splash in the Western media, to the delight of Foreign Office propagandists, but they did not try to enlist him in their campaign against the peace movement. His reputation for independence made him an effective critic, but also made him an unreliable vessel for Foreign Office propaganda.[15] Instead, they searched for other, more pliable figures to 'play the part of an A. J. P. Taylor' and infiltrate other Communist front gatherings.[16]

The Wroclaw congress left a bad aftertaste with many non-Communists. Mainstream press coverage was negative and some influential people who had been willing to cooperate with Communists were alienated from them. When British Communists tried to set up a British peace committee, a few of the Wroclaw veterans balked. *New Statesman and Nation* Editor Kingsley Martin told them that in the past he had favoured 'popular fronts' of all left-wing forces, but that it was clear that Communists now wanted 'stooges' instead of allies. Martin predicted that if he associated with them he would lose credibility as a peace advocate, and thus refused to sign on to the new British Cultural Committee for Peace, which later became the British Peace Committee.[17] IRD Head Ralph Murray noticed this new group and groused that 'those muddle-headed people' might embarrass the government.[18] Little did he know.

By late 1948 the peace movement had become a top priority for the Soviets and their friends, spurred on by the spectre of growing Western strength and cohesion.[19] In widely publicised statements later in the year Stalin and Molotov both made the struggle for peace the most important job for the world's Communists.[20] The firmly pro-Soviet Women's International Democratic Federation began planning in December for a major congress and two months later joined with the Wroclaw liaison committee in calling for an April 1949 congress in Paris.[21] At the Kremlin the Soviet Politburo met on 8 March and ordered a worldwide campaign in support of the congress, budgeting up to $100,000.[22]

After toying with ideas of Taylor-esque infiltration and disruptive pranks the IRD eventually decided that the congress would be hopelessly rigged and that it would be more effective to attack the gathering from outside as a total fraud.[23] (They may have helped British delegate Harvey Moore raise awkward points at the congress.)[24] To discredit the congress the Foreign Office funnelled material to their allies at home and abroad to portray the congress as unrepresentative and invalid. British diplomatic correspondents were encouraged to ask probing questions about delegate selection and conference procedures. A critical analysis of Communist tactics, using the Wroclaw conference as a case study, went out to all diplomatic posts and friendly journalists, politicians and trade union leaders.[25] Propagandists in the IRD must have been pleased by the British media's response. The *Manchester Guardian* questioned whether the peace congress delegates really spoke for the people they claimed to represent.[26] The BBC composed several home news bulletins from a speech by junior minister Christopher Mayhew, who denounced the movement as a 'Fifth Column' and 'Partisans of the Red Army.'[27] The mainstream press criticised the Communist domination and hypocrisy of the congress, especially the widely reported ovation for the Chinese Communist capture of Nanking, and mocked the congress's Picasso 'dove of peace' logo.[28]

Media Structures and Peace Discourse

The IRD did not try to re-appropriate the language of peace from the Soviets but rather tried to show that the Soviets' pacifistic claims were fraudulent. That would discredit the Soviets' tame peace movement in the process. In addition, playing with peace advocacy at a time when Western governments were painfully rearming could be dangerous.

> We cannot well use the slogans of peace ourselves for two reasons: we could not do so nearly as effectively as the Russians; and with different conditions prevailing in the West, there would be a danger that people might actually demand unilateral disarmament. The truth – that it is necessary to build up Western military strength at a cost – is not always expedient to proclaim and is in any case a rather weak defence against the strong emotive cards held by the Kremlin. We cannot encourage the illusions of the masses about peace, but we may at least disillusion them about the USSR and show that the Kremlin's claim to be the leader of the forces of peace is false.[29]

In general, the official and unofficial British discourse against the Peace Partisans constantly emphasised the deceptive and subversive nature of an organisation that urged the West to disarm at the same time it applauded Soviet bloc rearmament. This theme became even more important after the outbreak of the Korean War in June 1950 when anti-Communists could point to the blatant hypocrisy of the Peace Partisans, who were calling for peace in Europe while supporting North Korean aggression in Asia.[30] Speeches, pamphlets and leaflets from Labour politicians and their allies – many of which were well reported in the press – brought out that hypocrisy and made clear comparisons between contemporary Soviet behaviour and Nazi German action in the 1930s.[31] The Labour Party pamphlet 'End the Veto on Peace' accused the Soviets of sabotaging peace and criticised the British peace supporters. 'Like Chamberlain in 1938, they try to sell appeasement under cover of a war scare.'[32] They pointedly reminded people that the Communists had also been pro-peace in 1939–41, when Britain alone withstood the Nazi German onslaught. Since then, NATO had become the vessel of 'collective security' and the Soviet Union became the insatiable aggressor that understood only force.[33]

Fleet Street's imagery was that of sabotage, the Fifth Column betrayal, and the militarised confidence game: Communists were out to trick the West into lowering its guard. They relied on woolly minded dupes, dishonest fellow travellers and cleverly disguised Communists to spread doubts about Western rearmament and build up fear of atomic weapons. Several key images emerged again and again – the Partisan movement as a Trojan horse (or Trojan dove) carrying Soviet aggression, the Partisans as wolves in sheep's clothing and Western pacifists as deluded sheep. The Archbishop of York improved the cliché and played off the Russian connection, by urging BBC listeners to recognise 'the bear under the sheep's clothing.'[34] At its most sinister, the Partisan movement appeared as an infrastructure for future subversion and sabotage – a Fifth Column being impudently mobilised under British noses.[35] And just in case any readers or listeners missed the point, the press placed the word peace in inverted commas, described the Partisans as a 'so-called' peace movement, or just emphasised that it was the 'Moscow brand.'[36] Artist Pablo Picasso, who created the Partisans' 'dove of peace' trademark, served as a symbol in the British news media of the befuddled fellow traveller.[37] His dove was another deception. Repeatedly, journalists pointed out that it was actually a trumpeter pigeon – or as the *Daily Express* quipped, 'just a fellow-travelling pigeon with an artificial olive-branch.'[38]

Although this sort of imagery was important in influencing public discourse in Britain and overseas, control of the actual news events could be even more important. If the Partisans could not organise congresses, rallies or other media events, there would be little for the world's press to report. If these events were disrupted, the disruptions could become more important news than the congress itself. In 1950 the British government had a chance to use their political and police muscle as well as its propaganda.

The Stockholm Petition

Public fears about war and atomic weapons had been increasing ever since the news of the Soviets' first atomic test emerged in September 1949. The US push to develop the hydrogen bomb, announced in January 1950, heightened public worry. The Peace Partisans capitalised on this mood by launching in March the Stockholm Petition for international nuclear disarmament, which called for a ban on nuclear weapons and widespread international atomic inspection. It also urged that the first country to use atomic weapons be branded a war criminal. The full text reads:

> We demand the total banning of the atomic weapon, the arm of terror and the mass extermination of populations.
> We demand the establishment of strict international control to ensure the implementation of the ban.
> We consider that any Government which first uses the atomic weapon against any country whatsoever would be committing a crime against humanity and should be dealt with as a war criminal.
> We call on all men of good will to sign this appeal.[39]

This landed squarely on the USA because of its heavy dependence on nuclear weapons.[40] In the second half of the year, the European and American arms build-up coupled with the outbreak of the Korean War and its threatened escalation made world war seem a real possibility. In that tense season, peace advocacy became increasingly linked with Communism. The respectable National Peace Council, representing some fifty non-Communist peace groups, was feeling the heat. Under pressure from Peace Partisans for a joint 'peace campaign' the council's leaders asked the government for guidance. Foreign Secretary Ernest Bevin personally described to them the cynical Soviet use of the Partisans and urged them to avoid any contact. They did.[41] Nevertheless, the NPC and its affiliates repeatedly had to deny accusations that they were under Communist domination.[42]

That July the British Peace Council kicked off its petition drive with mass meetings, speeches, and a Trafalgar Square rally capped by a speech by Soviet writer Ilya Ehrenburg. The events attracted a great deal of press attention, most of it negative.[43] To counter the peace council's weekend of media spectacle, the Labour Party countered with a well-reported speech by left-wing cabinet member Aneurin Bevan attacking the Peace Partisans. Bevan told Durham County coal miners that Stalin had betrayed peace, as well as the Russian Revolution, and the international working class.

> I say to the Communists: Don't hold your peace conferences in London. We don't need them.
>
> Address your demands to the Kremlin, and ask them now to cooperate with the rest of the world in preventing war. There is no one in Great Britain or America who wants war.[44]

The BPC and its allies not only relied on media events, but also had some success spreading the word about the peace drive within local trades councils, union branches, and Labour Party constituency organisations. Party and union leaders became uneasy with the rising number of resolutions and letters from their supporters that endorsed the peace petition.[45] Faced with these issues, the major political parties, the TUC and religious organisations launched vigorous propaganda campaigns against the Peace Partisans.[46] The Archbishop of Canterbury, fortified with IRD material on the Soviet treatment of religion, condemned in a widely reported statement the Partisans and any clergy foolish enough to support them.[47] Labour Party members and some trade unionists who consorted with the Peace Partisans were expelled, as were the few Conservatives who strayed.[48]

Within weeks of the British kick off the Peace Partisans decided to hold their second international congress in England, after the Italian government had blocked plans for a congress in Genoa.[49] It's not clear why the Partisan leadership chose England, but the British Foreign Office thought they knew. It would show the world that Britain – a major imperialist power – was impotent in the face of the Peace Partisans, thus undermining British status as a leader of anti-Communist forces around the world. Meanwhile, the congress would weaken Anglo-American links by inflaming American opinion against Britain for harbouring Communists and 'crypto-Communists'. And, of course, holding the congress in the West would obscure the degree of Communist control while energising the anaemic British peace movement.[50] The government mobilised friends and supporters for a stepped up campaign against the Peace Partisans and their congress, which was planned for Sheffield in November. As one diplomat explained:

> The attack on the Peace Campaign requires a network of contacts and a great amount of work directed towards enlisting the cooperation of many different non-official persons and organizations. Thus, we have succeeded in unleashing a campaign against the Campaign here which has involved the Labour Party, COMISCO, the TUC, the Liberal Party, the National Peace Council, the Conservative Party, the Confederation of Free Trade Unions and of course the Press and individuals in and out of the Government.[51]

Although the British government was united in its opposition to the Peace Partisans, it was divided about the proper tactics to use. From the beginning the Foreign Office and the Chiefs of Staff wanted legislation to ban the congress.[52] The US State Department strongly backed them, with Secretary of State Dean Acheson personally urging Bevin to 'throttle' the conference.[53] But Bevin's cabinet colleagues, especially Home Secretary James Chuter Ede, did not think they had the power to ban the congress, and argued that it would be better to cripple it through propaganda and visa restrictions on foreign delegates, especially the Communist leadership.[54]

Leaders of the Peace Partisans had expected complications. A full two months before the congress was scheduled to begin in England, organisers were arranging for back-up facilities in Warsaw.[55] They were having other problems as well. Comparatively few people in Britain were supporting the peace petition despite painful sacrifices for rearmament, rising anti-Americanism, and war fears.[56] Prominent endorsements melted away. The Communist leaders of the Electrical Trades Union had endorsed the petition, but their members, in widely covered balloting, refused to go along.[57] Left-wing Labour MP Ian Mikardo also withdrew his signature.[58] To compound their problems Konni Zilliacus, a leader of the international Partisan movement and a long-time fellow traveller, turned on them because of the Soviets' blatant use of the movement in their struggle with breakaway Yugoslav Communists.[59]

Meanwhile, after having failed to get a ban on the congress, Bevin began to characterise the Partisans as a direct threat to British security in order to persuade the cabinet to agree to wholesale visa denials. He mustered a litany of threatening quotes from Communists and their allies to try to prove that the movement was shifting away from a 'sentimental' appeal to pacifism toward concrete subversion and sabotage of military service, Western rearmament, and NATO itself.[60] The rest of the cabinet wanted to uphold liberal principles, yet avoid criticism from the public and the Americans for allowing leading Communists into the country. The solution was the creatively strict use of the rules of persona non grata to keep out large numbers of key Communists and fellow travellers in the major front organisations – without the public relations problems that might come from a wholesale ban.[61] The prohibition extended to almost anyone associated not only with the peace movement, but also with other Soviet 'front' groups.[62] With the Sheffield congress fast approaching, the government, Labour Party, trade unions, and some newspapers launched a blitz against the Peace Partisans in late October and early November.

British Prime Minister Clement Attlee's public relations adviser, along with the Ministry of Defence's spin doctor, arranged to meet London newspaper editors in mid-October.[63] Leading Quakers in contact with cabinet members publicly distanced themselves from the congress.[64] The *Observer*'s William Clark noted that he had been invited to be on the welcoming committee for the Sheffield peace congress, but refused to be involved. He juxtaposed the gentle face of the congress with what he saw as its violent, hate-filled true character.

> The invitation was as mild as a request to contribute to a sale of work for parish funds, and the note paper was covered with the names of kindly people of moderate fame who had apparently agreed to be associated.
>
> Perhaps it would interest them to know that the Czech delegation has announced its intention of presenting every member of the peace-loving Congress with an illuminated poem which makes the following kindly suggestions: 'Wherever the American G.I. sets foot he will be murdered, poisoned, set aflame, beaten, starved, baked as in hell, and this will happen in France, in Greece, in Bulgaria, in China, in fact everywhere.'[65]

Attlee had been advised to try to 'drown out' the congress with government-sponsored media events. For Attlee's own speech, his adviser and speechwriter Philip Jordan went to the IRD to get the inside dirt on the peace movement.

> Anything silly, malicious, or stupid that some of the leaders may have said or written would be useful, no matter whether such persons are British or foreign.
>
> I want the Prime Minister to be able not only to do irreparable damage to the Congress, but, if possible, to be able to make laughing-stocks of some of the persons on whom the organisers will rely for prestige: a judicious mixture, in fact, of serious exposure of sham and of ridicule for those who fall for or encourage it.[66]

Attlee, however, was true to his dry, laconic form – even with juicy IRD-provided titbits laced throughout the speech. He attacked the Sheffield Congress as a piece of deceptive, undemocratic Communist hypocrisy designed to subvert the West. The government would keep out foreign delegates who were threats, Attlee said, but would uphold civil liberties within Britain and not ban the congress.[67] The speech not only set the tone for British media discourse on the Sheffield Congress, but also sought to reassure the NATO allies that toleration of the congress was not a sign of British weakness.[68] The government persuaded the BBC to broadcast the speech in prime time in its home and overseas services, and most newspapers covered it prominently.[69]

The counter-campaign ran into trouble when the cabinet discovered that more than half the delegates were getting visas despite the restrictions. They decided to clamp down harder and started cancelling some delegates' visas and turning away other delegates when they tried to enter the country.[70] Some didn't even get that far: the Civil Aviation Ministry prohibited eight planeloads of delegates from landing in Britain.[71] Eventually about 500 foreign delegates were refused visas or turned away at British ports; others with valid visas did not even bother to come once it became apparent that the conference had been crippled.[72] This last minute clamp–down led to widely reported chaos as hundreds of delegates arrived at airports and channel docks only to be kept waiting for hours before being turned away. The scene in Sheffield was equally confused as British delegates arrived and a few foreigners trickled in, but Sheffield residents calmly ignored the world's spotlight, according to press reports.[73]

Organisers moved the conference to Warsaw after a brief but heavily reported rump session and press conference. The *Manchester Guardian* described the Sheffield gathering as a 'peace and quiet congress' and objectively reported organisers' statements.[74] The mass circulation *Daily Mirror* had sent acerbic columnist William Connor ('Cassandra') to Sheffield. He mocked celebrity delegates and Partisan leaders, verbally leered at the 'slim, pert personality of a certain Miss Kim' from North Korea, and ripped into the British organisers as pathetic, mindless fools.[75] A few days later the Pathé newsreel appeared in cinemas to further denigrate the congress. The newsreel story opened with a quick shot of a protester, followed by shots of milling crowds and close-ups of morose organisers. The narrator urged viewers to see the event as 'suspect kind of propaganda' and applauded the government action.

> For a peace congress it had strange ideas. From all over the world came the bewitched, but Britain couldn't be bothered and so now they're bewildered whilst their congress dances off to Warsaw. But still they come, to be told what to do next.[76]

The *Observer*'s diplomatic correspondent insisted that the peace movement 'has become the cover organisation for direct action, sabotage, and subversion in the non-Communist countries.'[77] But the *Manchester Guardian* and the *Daily Express* coverage focused on the damage to civil liberties and free speech, with the *Guardian* going so far as to describe treatment of foreign delegates as 'the methods of the Communist police states.'[78] Several complained about the debasement of the language through propaganda. The *Daily Express* cartoonist Giles poignantly illustrated that peace had become a 'wicked word' – even among children.[79]

The Reuters news agency's objective coverage of the peace movement, with factual quotes and descriptions, presented a special problem to the government. As the Commonwealth Relations Minister Patrick Gordon-Walker pointed out, intelligent British readers could easily see through the outrageous accusations and claims quoted in the factual Reuters dispatches, but unsophisticated readers in the former colonies could be fooled. The High Commissioner in Karachi had explained that Pakistanis trusted Reuters and believed what they read, because they were 'not sophisticated or capable of critical analysis.' Gordon-Walker demanded a meeting with Reuters leaders to discuss their coverage, but it is unclear whether they met or what emerged from the talks if they did.[80]

When the British Peace Partisans finished their canvassing in December, they tried to present their 1.3 million British signatures to the House of Commons. No one would accept them. After several days maverick Labour MP Sydney

Silverman, who had refused to sign the petition himself, finally agreed to introduce the petitions to parliament. They were ignored.[81]

Warsaw and Beyond

After the frenzy surrounding the aborted Sheffield congress, the Warsaw gathering was anti-climactic. British newspapers covered it extensively, but without
the emotion they displayed at Sheffield. Despite the scathing tones of some reporting, most stories could almost pass as anthropological studies of Western
fellow-travellers' behaviour in their native habitat – the subsidised congress.[82]
Daily Express reporter Sefton Delmer emphasised the way delegates were pam-
pered with rich food, copious alcohol, and 'dove of peace' knickknacks. His account of the 'beer and sausage congress' must have been galling to British readers
still struggling with food rationing.[83] But the highlight of the congress, for the
non-Communist news media, was the righteous and even-handed condemna-
tion of Soviet and American sins by US delegate John Rogge.[84] Unbeknownst to
newspaper readers, however, Rogge had been in close consultation with US State
Department and had been given advice ahead of time on how to best structure
and deliver his speech.[85] (The Peace Partisans also re-christened themselves at
Warsaw. The movement was now the World Peace Council – or WPC.)

After news of Sheffield and Warsaw disappeared from the headlines, the leaders of the British branch of the WPC took stock of the situation. They thought
Britain's back-breaking rearmament bills and the involvement of China in the
Korean War were pushing many people toward a 1930s-style 'popular front' of
left-wing forces opposed to the government's foreign policy. They pointed out to
the WPC's leadership that a Peace Aims group had formed among Labour back-
benchers and that the non-Communist National Peace Council, in cooperation
with the *New Statesman and Nation*, had set up a 'Peace With China Committee'
that had caught a wave of public support. Although this new committee shunned
the Communist-led peace group, WPC leaders believed they shared important
aims and should be encouraged as a 'transitional' group for people who were unhappy with British foreign policy, but were not prepared to risk political ostracism
by supporting the WPC.[86]

Despite their hopes at the beginning of the year, 1951 was not a success for
the World Peace Council. The WPC's next campaign – for a five-power peace
pact – did not capture the public's imagination the way the Stockholm Petition
had. British Communists had even less luck; party activists complained at an
October meeting about a sense of futility fuelled by unending petitions and the
failure to reach beyond the party faithful.[87] The Peace With China Committee
faced a virtual blackout in the mainstream press, a point noted by the *New
Statesman*.[88]

While the Peace With China Committee laboured in the dark, the WPC and
its Soviet backers were talking more and more about the how the WPC, not
the UN, truly represented the world's people. These statements led British and

American officials to suspect that the Soviets were trying to set up a situation in which the WPC could supersede the UN. The IRD leaked some of the details to its press contacts; it 'went over well' and resulted in articles in the *Observer* and *The Times*.[89]

British Quakers, however, were determined to reach out to the WPC, much to the IRD's dismay. The Quakers moved cautiously and met frequently with accommodating Foreign Office experts, who provided them with oral briefings and IRD material on the WPC.[90] With the Quakers primed the Foreign Office allowed several WPC leaders to enter the country for discussions, which went badly for the Quakers. The IRD's Peck concluded that either the Quakers did not know they were being dominated and manipulated '... or even worse, they realise that they are being imposed upon and do not seem to mind.'[91] The Quakers followed that meeting with a trip to the USSR, from which Foreign Secretary Herbert Morrison personally tried to dissuade them.[92] The Foreign Office feared a rapprochement between the WPC and the Quakers because it would end the WPC's isolation and give it public legitimacy, so officials continued to meet regularly with the Quakers, who remained distant from the WPC.[93]

The government still faced the problem of smaller gatherings of the peace movement and their rapidly proliferating allied front groups in Britain. In June 1951 the Home Office was considering admitting some foreign peace activists, all of whom had been on the blacklist at the Sheffield congress, to a WPC function in Britain.[94] The Foreign Office strongly objected, citing the salutary example of the Sheffield bans. 'This practical example did more than months of propaganda to bring home to the world the true nature of the movement and it was almost universally welcomed.'[95] Similar problems arose in rapid succession with WPC affiliates and associates in late 1951 and early 1952, and more were coming up.[96] Rather than deal with visa applications on an ad hoc basis the new Conservative government decided to adopt a policy in which foreigners would not be allowed into Britain for any event linked with the WPC. The Home Secretary made it clear that the British people were largely immune to Soviet-style peace propaganda, and that the banned foreigners were not security risks. But allowing the WPC to operate in Britain would undermine the Foreign Office's worldwide attempt to expose the peace council as 'an instrument of Soviet policy' and to encourage resistance to it.[97] The IRD was surprised at how well the British public 'including even the Liberals' accepted this illiberal policy.[98]

Throughout all this the propaganda continued to roll, and the IRD began to use its newly acquired book publishing capacity to attack in greater depth. An affiliated publishing firm, The Batchworth Press, published anti-Communist pocket books such as *Communists on Peace*, by tame journalist W. N. Ewer. The book assembled fifty-four quotations from leading Communists on the question of peace, drawing on the voluminous works of Lenin and Stalin as well as more esoteric sources.[99] Some of the more obscure quotes, including one from a Czech trade union journal and one from a Hungarian-language newspaper, had appeared earlier in IRD briefing material that Ewer regularly received.[100]

Within the Soviet Union years of intensive peace propaganda were having unintended consequences, with the Communist Party complaining behind closed doors in 1952 that the Soviet media were ignoring the 'intrigues of imperialist aggression' and drifting into irresponsible pacifism. The party criticised the press for getting 'carried away by outward symbols, publishing images of doves, primitive drawings and pacifistic stories and poems that have little value.'[101] Of course, they did not say that in public.

Outside of the Soviet bloc, activists associated with the WPC increasingly by-passed the organisation. Instead they used other long-established 'front groups' and created a plethora of professional and special interest peace groups – for artists, writers, teachers, veterans, and others. In Britain the government responded with a steady stream of IRD exposés and denunciations while allies in the Labour Party added them to their ever-growing list of proscribed organisations.[102]

But the WPC simply changed the subject, and in early 1952 joined the Chinese, North Koreans and Soviets in the propaganda assault alleging that the US had used bacteriological weapons against North Korea and China. (Recently discovered Russian documents indicate that the Communist campaign was based on fraud. There was no biological warfare, and Moscow knew it.)[103] When the accusations first surfaced in the spring of 1952 the British government quickly launched spin control, briefing journalists, commissioning articles from tame correspondents like W. N. Ewer, and sending out IRD-written rebuttals under pseudonyms. Early on the News Department 'obtained wide publicity for the Foreign Office line which was taken up by Reuters and all the main news agencies.'[104] By the summer the WPC had jumped into the controversy by sending a team of scientists, including prominent left-leaning biochemist Joseph Needham, to China to investigate the charges. Here the IRD launched a delicate operation to persuade leading British scientists to attack one of their own, but had little success with the leading members of the Royal Society.[105] They had more luck attacking Hewlett Johnson, the 'Red Dean of Canterbury Cathedral', who had visited Beijing in July and swallowed whole the Chinese allegations. Ecclesiastical and civil authorities tried, and failed, to punish Johnson.[106] The IRD turned to the Economic League's John Baker White, who represented Canterbury in parliament, to write an attack pamphlet *The Dean of Canterbury: An Analysis and Exposure* and distributed it widely throughout Europe and Asia.[107]

In December 1952 the WPC returned to the peace congresses circuit with the staging of the Vienna Peace Congress, which provoked the by-then ritualistic proscriptions and denunciations.[108] The Czech Communists had made the British propaganda job easier for their enemies by launching into a series of bloody, anti-Semitic purges of the party's top leaders. Journalist and former Attlee spin doctor Francis Williams linked that bigoted brutality with the attitudes of Western intellectuals, such as French writer Jean-Paul Sartre who attended the Vienna congress. 'They have the freedom to speak. If they wish to retain any of the respect that once was theirs let them do so now.'[109] They did not.

By 1953 the word 'peace' had been thoroughly debased in British political discourse, and non-Communist peace groups in Britain were at their low
point.[110] The general public associated most peace groups with the high-profile
Communist model – and stayed far clear of them. The British Peace Council
carried an even worse smell. Left-wing publisher Victor Gollancz advised keeping well away from it. 'Far from helping towards an understanding with Russia,
these Communist propaganda bodies, in my view, do the exact reverse.'[111]

But the peace movement and its myriad affiliates were still dangerous in the
eyes of the British government. The IRD had a separate desk to keep track of the
WPC and its allied organisations with the assistance of MI5, which had at least
one source high in the ranks of the WPC.[112] The IRD maintained a very tight
relationship with the non-Communist National Peace Council and its director,
Leslie Smith, and praised him for having 'cooperated admirably with us in the
exposure of the Peace Campaign.'[113]

Overseas the Foreign Office was pressing for NATO solidarity against the
WPC and encouraged NATO members to refuse to let these organisations have
headquarters, congresses or festivals on their territory. By 1955 the IRD was also
pushing to get Soviet-backed organisations such as the WFTU and the WPC
pushed out of neutral Austria so that 'they should be forced to sail under their true
colours by establishing themselves behind the Iron Curtain where they belong.'[114]

Post Script

By the mid-1950s a non-aligned peace movement emerged in response to public
worry about the next generation of nuclear weapons – the hydrogen bomb – and
internal problems in the Communist movement. The Americans' 1954 testing of
an extremely powerful hydrogen bomb, and the widespread radioactive contam-
ination it produced once again focused public attention on the nuclear threat.
Meanwhile, Communists and their friends in the WPC lost prestige and respect
in 1956 because of their pusillanimous response to the brutal Soviet repression of
Hungary, which closely followed Soviet leader Nikita Khrushchev's secret speech
on Stalin's crimes. Party membership slumped and even the leadership was in
confusion. This had an interesting effect on the peace movement as a whole. The
weakening of Communist-led peace movements removed some of the stigma
from peace activism, while many of the ex-Communists found a more agreeable
cause in the non-aligned Campaign for Nuclear Disarmament.[115] Despite the
Communists' reluctance to embrace the emerging peace movement – because
they could not control it – the British government regularly implied throughout
1957 that the non-aligned movement was, in fact, working for Moscow's interests
and stepped up counter-propaganda the next year.[116] The weapons forged for
dealing with Soviet interference were now used to attack British dissent.

Clearly the Communists must take a large share of the blame for discrediting
peace in the 1950s. Their ham-handed manipulation and shrill polemics frequently damaged their cause and alienated potential friends. But the Communists

alone could not manage to turn the word peace on its head in a few short years. They had plenty of help. Anti-Communist forces, like the British government, mobilised considerable power and influence to discredit the Soviet-backed peace movement. Fallout from those attacks hurt non-Communist peace groups as the public lumped all peace advocates together. Peace had become a dirty word.

Notes

1. PRO CAB130/65 (GEN341/1), Bevin to Attlee, 25 October 1950; PRO FO371/86758 NS1052/85, 'Summary of indications regarding Soviet Foreign Policy', 25 August 1950.
2. I will refer to the organisation as the Peace Partisans until the November 1950 re-christening as the World Peace Council.
3. Günter Wernicke, 'The Communist-led World Peace Council and the Western peace movements: the fetters of bipolarity and some attempts to break them in the Fifties and early Sixties', *Peace & Change*, Vol. 23, No. 3 (1998), pp. 266–7.
4. Guiliano Procacci (ed.), *The Cominform: Minutes of the Three Conferences, 1947–1948/1949* (Milan: Fondazione Giangiacomo, 1994), p. 651; Nataliia I. Egorova, 'Stalin's Foreign Policy and the Cominform', in Francesca Gori and Silvio Pons (eds) *The Soviet Union and Europe in the Cold War, 1943–1953* (London: Macmillan Press, 1996); David Holloway, *Stalin and the Bomb: The Soviet Union and Atomic Energy* (New Haven: Yale University Press, 1994), pp. 288–90; Lawrence Wittner, *The Struggle Against the Bomb, Volume One: One World or None, A History of the World Nuclear Disarmament Movement Through 1953* (Stanford: Stanford University Press, 1993), pp. 180–2; Marshall Shulman, *Stalin's Foreign Policy Reappraised* (Boulder: Westview Press, 1985), pp. 80–103.
5. PRO CAB130/65 (GEN341/1), 'Ministerial meeting on World Peace Congress', 30 October 1950; *FRUS, 1950*, Vol. IV, pp. 320–8.
6. Wittner, *One World or None*, pp. 319–20.
7. Martin Caedel, 'The first Communist "Peace Society": the British Anti-War Movement, 1932–1935', *Twentieth Century British History* 1 (1990).
8. Willie Thompson, *The Good Old Cause: British Communism, 1920–1991* (London: Pluto Press, 1992), pp. 68–70.
9. This quote was widely used in both British and American propaganda in the early Cold War. Most recently it was quoted in Wittner, *One World or None*, p. 172.
10. David Caute, *The Fellow-Travellers: Intellectual Friends of Communism* (rev. ed.), (New Haven: Yale University Press, 1988), pp. 316.
11. Ritchie Calder, *News Chronicle*, 25 August 1948.
12. PRO FO1110/112 PR1221/760/G, 'Working party on subversive movements; briefing of British delegates to international non-governmental congresses: note by joint secretaries', 13 January 1948; PRO CAB130/17 (GEN168/4th Meeting), 'Briefing of British delegates to international non-governmental conferences', 30 January 1949.
13. PRO FO1110/108 PR693/693, Cloake minute, 14 October 1948.
14. Manchester *Guardian Archives*, R/T19, Taylor to Wadsworth, 19 August 1948.
15. PRO FO1110/108 PR1171/693, T.A.K. Elliot minute, 30 December 1948, Murray minute, 4 January 1949. For examples of coverage, see 'A man named Taylor raps the world intellectuals', *Daily Express*, 27 August 1948.

16. PRO FO1110/271 PR749/92/G, Hankey minute, 18 March 1949; PRO PRO1110/114 PR785/785, Murray Note, 18 September 1948.
17. Ivor Montagu Papers, 5/2, 'Draft minute: reunion of signatories to the main Wroclaw Resolution held November 8, 1948, at Society for Visiting Scientists'.
18. PRO FO1110/108, Murray Note, 3 December 1948.
19. Procacci, *The Cominform*, p. 651. Also, see Egorova, 'Stalin's Foreign Policy.'
20. Shulman, *Stalin's Foreign Policy Reappraised*, p. 89.
21. Coleman, *The Liberal Conspiracy*, pp. 5–6.
22. Egorova, 'Stalin's Foreign Policy', p. 200.
23. PRO FO1110/271 PR749/92/G, Mayhew minute, 22 March 1949.
24. Cited in Wittner, *One World or None*, p. 283.
25. PRO FO1110/112 PR760/760, Circular, 23 September 1948; PRO FO1110/117 PR815/815, 'Notes on recent tactics experienced by United Kingdom representatives or individuals at certain international conferences', [n.d.].
26. 'Czechs protest to France', *Manchester Guardian*, 19 April 1949.
27. BBC WAC, Transcript of Home Service news bulletin, 22 April 1949.
28. 'Reds say it with a Picasso pigeon', *Daily Mail*, 22 April 1949. See also 'Led cheers for Nanking's fall', *Observer*, 24 April 1949.
29. PRO FO1110/202 PR2960/17/G, 'Foreign Office report to the Colonial Information Policy Committee', 3 October 1949.
30. PRO FO975/49, 'The Soviet Peace Campaign'.
31. Trades Union Congress, *Trade Unionists Stand Firm for Peace* ([London]: T.U.C. Pamphlet, [1950]), p. 15.
32. Labour Party Archives, International Department, Peace and Propaganda 1950 file, 'End the Veto on Peace' (Labour Party leaflet).
33. Ibid. Also see, 'The peace petition that passeth understanding', *Fact*, October 1950.
34. BBC WAC, Transcript of Home Service news bulletin, 9 November 1950.
35. *Time and Tide*, 25 November 1950, p. 1177.
36. *Manchester Guardian*, 24 March 1953; *News Chronicle*, 15 December 1952.
37. 'Profile: Pablo Picasso,' *Observer*, 12 November 1950.
38. 'Pocket Cartoon by Osbert Lancaster,' *Daily Express*, 13 November 1950.
39. Labour Party Archives, International Department, Peace and Propaganda 1950 file, Stockholm Peace Petition.
40. *FRUS, 1950*, IV, pp. 320–8.
41. PRO FO1110/346 PR87/34, Warner note, 18 May 1950, Undated, Unsigned note of Bevin's conversation; National Peace Council Papers, 8/1, National Peace Council minutes, 7 July 1950.
42. 'An important issue', *One World*, August–September 1949; 'NPC notes and news', *One World*, June–July 1952; 'Red letter boys', *Daily Worker*, 26 July 1950. See also Wittner, *One World or None*, p. 320.
43. '"British Peace Campaign" is launched', *Observer*, 23 July 1950.
44. 'Bevan asks Stalin: "Are you faithful?" ', *Observer*, 23 July 1950.
45. Labour Party, *National Executive Committee*, Minutes of 21 June 1950.
46. 'Beware phoney peace tactics, Co-ops warn', *Daily Herald*, 15 July 1950; 'Unions warned to shun these agents for peace', *Daily Herald*, 5 August 1950; 'You've been warned', *Daily Herald*, 29 June 1950; 'World Council of Churches', *Manchester Guardian*, 27 July 1950.
47. 'Archbishop on the peace petition', *The Times*, 29 July 1950.

48. For example, see '300 Socialists suspended', *Daily Telegraph*, 30 October 1950; 'Conservatives expel Woodard', *The Times*, 6 December 1950; 'Club requests resignation', *Daily Telegraph*, 2 October 1950.
49. *Daily Worker*, 18 August 1950.
50. PRO FO371/86758 NS1052/85, Summary of indications regarding Soviet Foreign Policy, 25 August 1950; Phillip Deery, 'The dove flies east: Whitehall, Warsaw and the 1950 World Peace Congress', *Australian Journal of Politics and History* 2002.
51. PRO FO953/637 P1013/120, Ashley-Clarke to Hoyer-Millar, 11 September 1950.
52. PRO FO371/86762 NS1053/26, Russia Committee minutes, 12 September 1950; PRO FO1110/348 PR87/234/G, D. P. Reilly minute, 11 October 1950.
53. NARA RG59, DF 740.5/9-2850, Memorandum of conversation (Bevin and Acheson), 28 September 1950.
54. PRO CAB128/18, 56 (50) 3, Cabinet minutes, 6 September 1950.
55. Ilya Ehrenburg, *Post-War Years, 1945–54* (London: McGibben and Kee, 1966), p. 224.
56. Communist Party Archives, CENT/EC/01/01, Report to October 1950 Executive Committee Meeting.
57. 'Union "peace" revolt', *Daily Herald*, 23 October 1950.
58. Labour Party, *National Executive Committee minutes*, Minutes of National Executive Meeting, 25 October 1950.
59. Konni Zilliacus, 'Letters to the Editor: the Sheffield Peace Congress', *Manchester Guardian*, 13 November 1950.
60. PRO CAB130/65 (GEN344/1), Bevin to Attlee, 25 October 1950.
61. PRO CAB130/65 (GEN341/1), Ministerial meeting, 30 October 1950.
62. PRO FO1110/349 PR87/269/G, 'Sheffield Peace Congress,' 30 October 1950.
63. PRO FO1110/348 PR87/244, Shinwell to Attlee, 12 October 1950.
64. 'Among the organizations', *One World*. August-September 1950. Also, Noel-Baker Papers, 4/121, Notes on Communism, Noel-Baker to Paul Cadbury, 8 November 1950, and Bailey to Paul Cadbury, 2 November 1950.
65. Pendennis Column, *Observer*, 29 October 1950.
66. PRO FO1110/348 PR87/227, Jordan to Peck, 12 October 1950.
67. 'Bogus peace congress/Prime Minister warns', *The Times*, 2 November 1950.
68. Attlee Papers, Box 111, Jordan to Attlee, 27 October 1950.
69. PRO PREM8/1150, Attlee to Morrison, 17 October 1950.
70. PRO CAB128/18, 72 (50) 8, Cabinet minutes, 9 November 1950.
71. 'Gvt. ban 18 Peace Congress planes', *Daily Mirror*, 10 November 1950.
72. *The Times*, 15 November 1950.
73. '"Peacemakers" call it a day at Sheffield', *News of the World*, 12 November 1950.
74. 'An "Iron Curtain" at Sheffield', *Manchester Guardian*, 14 November 1950.
75. William Connor, 'The peace men crash into reverse', *Daily Mirror*, 15 November 1950; William Connor, 'Red Congress switch brings fog and confusion', *Daily Mirror*, 13 November 1950.
76. WPA Film Library, Pathé Newsreel, Cannister 50/92, 16 November 1950.
77. 'Real aim of the "peace defenders"', *Observer*, 19 November 1950.
78. 'The illiberal Mr. Ede', *Manchester Guardian*, 13 November 1950; BBK, H/141, Christiansen to Beaverbrook, 17 November 1950.
79. Cartoon by Giles, *Daily Express*, 14 November 1950; 'London diary', *New Statesman and Nation*, 16 December 1950.

80. Layton Papers, Box 9, Gordon-Walker to Layton, 20 December 1950. There is no record of such a meeting in the Reuters Archive.
81. 'No champion for peace petition', *Manchester Guardian*, 8 December 1950.
82. See, Hugh Chevins, 'High-powered propaganda of hate at "Peace" Congress', *Daily Telegraph*, 29 November 1950.
83. Sefton Delmer, 'I might have been the Dean himself! . . . ', *Daily Express*, 20 November 1950.
84. BBC WAC, Transcript of Home Service news bulletin, 19 November 1950. Also, see '"Peace" Congress in Warsaw', *The Times*, 20 November 1950.
85. NARA RG59 Miscellaneous Records of the Bureau of Public Affairs, Lot 61 D 53, Box 72, John O. Rogge file, MacKnight to Rogge, 3 November 1950, and Memorandum of conversation (Rogge and MacKnight), 1 November 1950.
86. J. D. Bernal Papers, Box 3, Report to the Bureau of the World Peace Congress Meeting in Geneva, 10–11 January 1951.
87. Communist Party Archives, CENT/EC/02/03, minutes of Enlarged (CPGB) Executive Committee, 14–15 October 1951.
88. 'London diary', *New Statesman and Nation*, 2 December 1950; Clark Papers, Box 93, Clark to Martin, 13 January 1951.
89. PRO FO1110/453 PR114/1/51/G, Circular No. 6, 17 March 1951, Murray minute, 8 March 1951.
90. PRO FO1110/370 PR5/51/G, Peck minute, 7 April 1951.
91. PRO FO1110/371 PR51/132/G, 'Record of meeting between Minister of State (Younger) and delegation from Religious Society of Friends', 1 June 1951; PRO FO1110/371 PR5/133/G, Peck minute, 14 June 1951.
92. PRO FO1110/371 PR5/134/G, Peck note, 9 July 1951.
93. PRO FO1110/371 PR51/132/G, Peck minute, 2 June 1951.
94. PRO FO1110/371, Chuter Ede to Younger, 1 June 1951.
95. PRO FO1110/371, Peck note, 4 June 1951.
96. PRO FO1110/521 PR102/23/G, IRD Memo, 10 March 1952.
97. PRO CAB 129/50 C (52) 85, World Peace Movement, 26 March 1952; PRO CAB128/24, (52) 35 (8), Cabinet minutes.
98. NARA RG 59 Miscellaneous records of the Bureau of Public Affairs, 1944–62, Lot 58D 753, Box 2, British-memos of conversation 1952 file, US-UK meetings on information activities, 28 April 1952.
99. W. N. Ewer, *Communists on Peace* (London: Batchworth Press, 1953).
100. The original quotes in question can be found in PRO: FO975/33 'The Communist "Peace Offensive"', and FO975/68 'Congress of the Peoples for Peace: an examination of Communist tactics', [1953].
101. Draft Resolution of the Central Committee of the All-Union Communist Party (Bolshevik) (CC VKP(b)). Quoted in Nigel Gould-Davies, '"Pacifistic blowback?" New evidence on the Soviet peace campaign in the early 1950s', *Cold War International History Project Bulletin*, No. 11 (1998), pp. 267–8.
102. See, for example, PRO FO975/57 'The International Conference in Defence of Children'; PRO FO975/64 'Aspects of peace: study of Soviet tactics'; PRO FO975/73 'World Federation of Scientific Workers: aims and activities 1946–1953'.
103. 'Deceiving the Deceivers: Moscow, Beijing, Pyongyang and the Allegations of Bacteriological Warfare', *Bulletin of the Cold War International History Project* 11 (1998).
104. PRO FO1110/494 PR41/81, Tull minute, 25 March 1952.
105. PRO FO1110/494 PR41/366, Nutting to IRD, 5 December 1952.

106. Caute, *The Fellow Travellers*, pp. 260–5.
107. PRO FO1110/494 PR41/273/G, Wilford to Pitblado, 27 September 1952.
108. Labour Party Archives, Peace and Propaganda 1952 file, Labour Party Circular: Another Spurious Peace Campaign, October 1952.
109. Francis Williams, 'Are they ALL yes-men?' *News Chronicle*, 11 December 1952.
110. *News Chronicle*, 15 December 1952; *Manchester Guardian*, 24 March 1953; Wittner, *One World Or None*, pp. 328–9.
111. Gollancz Papers MSS.157/3/PAC/8/24, Victor Gollancz to Esther Edmonds, 3 February 1954.
112. PRO FO1110/861 PR152/52/G, MI5 Report, 13 November 1956.
113. PRO FO1110/613 PRG100/110, Peck to Selwyn Lloyd, 20 May 1953.
114. PRO FO1110/762 PR103/21, FO to Wallinger. In 1957 the Austrians closed down the WPC's world headquarters. Wittner, *Resisting the Bomb*, p. 100
115. Wittner, *Resisting the Bomb*, pp. 94–5.
116. Ibid. pp. 90–4, 121–4.

From the Inside Out: Defectors and the Gulag

Inside information on the Soviet Union's brutal and sordid side did not come easy during the late 1940s and 1950s. The IRD had built an industry out of finding and discreetly publicising the facts that they could find, and spent a great deal of effort on two types of stories that reflected especially badly on the USSR. Soviet defectors gave inside stories of incompetence, despotism and oppression, but the biggest blemish marring the USSR's international image was the vast system of internal forced labour known as the Gulag Archipelago. These offered the ultimate inside information and the ultimate betrayal of the worker's state, respectively, and were excellent material to destroy the 'Soviet myth'.

Defectors Tell their Stories

There were plenty of Soviet citizens available immediately after the war – the Germans had forced many of them to work for them and armed others to fight the USSR. But for the first two years after the war the British had regularly repatriated Soviet defectors and deserters. At the Foreign Office Christopher Warner was deeply involved in the forced repatriation of thousands of refugees, many of whom met unpleasant ends.[1] In 1947 British intelligence in Germany set up an office to handle defectors, and the IRD became interested the following year. Fresh defectors could offer the British valuable intelligence and once milked of their valuable information could be used for propaganda; by 1948 they were assiduously courted.[2]

At first British propagandists had to rely on other peoples' defectors. When Victor Kravchenko had defected in Washington in 1944 the Americans almost handed him back, but by 1946 he was useful.[3] Kravchenko wrote, with some help from a New York writer, a best-selling exposé *I Chose Freedom*, which detailed the full array of Soviet abuses from agricultural collectivisation to forced labour.[4] In Britain the FO's Warner was trying to expose the British public to the harsher realities of the USSR and put pressure on publisher Robert Hale to bring out a British edition more quickly (it was slated to come out in January 1947).[5] Soon afterward an 'anonymous donor' distributed free copies among British members of parliament.[6] The book was good anti-Communist propaganda, selling 400,000 copies in France alone. But more was to follow. When the French Communist weekly *Les Lettres francaise* claimed that the CIA had written it for him,

Kravchenko sued for libel. The trial became a major media event as Kravchenko brought witnesses from throughout Europe to support his claims. He won.[7]

In 1948 a great British opportunity – Soviet Lt Col G. A. Tokaev – walked through the door. Not only did Tokaev have top-level technical information (he was in charge of exploiting German rocket and aviation resources for the USSR), but he also was privy to a great deal of inside information on the workings of the Soviet state and Communist Party. After extensive debriefing by British intelligence, Tokaev was about to begin his career as a British propaganda asset. The department first arranged for literary agent and PWE veteran Cyrus Brooks to represent Tokaev.[8] The defector, however, was not willing to go along with the sedate pace that the IRD had chosen for him.

> Colonel Tokaev is now rather restive and there is some danger that if he is not soon guided into a position where he may appear publicly and publish his book, he may burst into publicity by some ill-judged action. He is not under any restraint here, and there is nothing to prevent him from approaching the Press on his own at any time.[9]

There were also worries that the Soviets could pre-empt Tokaev's announcement and put their own spin on his defection. The FO's Sir Orme Sargeant feared that he might be 'bumped off by Communist agents'.[10] Brooks approached left-wing publisher Victor Gollancz and Daily Herald editor Percy Cudlipp with Tokaev's story; Murray had insisted to Brooks that Tokaev make his debut 'as far to the left as possible'. Both Gollancz and Cudlipp were interested, but Cudlipp moved cautiously and said the Daily Herald would serialise Tokaev's book in October, but wanted an OK from Bevin first.[11] Bevin approved but insisted on no public FO connection.[12]

But the wait was too long for Tokaev. In late August he sent long letters to the New York Times, the Daily Telegraph, the Daily Herald and a Russian émigré newspaper in France. That led to questions about Tokaev's authenticity and credibility. To maintain the initiative Brooks arranged for a snap press conference.[13] An IRD Digest article on Tokaev was also rushed into print.[14] Murray lamented the turn of events:

> Unfortunately, Tokaev's precipitate action may cause his existence to go almost unnoticed because he will have to compete for space with the Moscow developments, French Government changes, Benes and Zhdanov obituaries. He could scarcely have chosen a worse moment, in fact.[15]

The press conference itself was a disaster. Nearly 100 journalists attended, including a number of Soviet journalists who abused Tokaev and passionately accused him of betraying his country – all in Russian. Tokaev refused to answer their questions and the conference ended in 'confusion'. The newspapers were able to quote from a six-page statement he released at the conference, in which he explained his defection and criticised the Soviet leadership for leading a traumatised country toward war. Other themes, such as the extent of forced labour, fitted nicely into the IRD's current themes.[16] An IRD post-mortem concluded that neither Tokaev nor Brooks were in the least bit prepared for the conference, which made a 'farcical and harmful' impression. The poorly edited translation of Tokaev's statement made him look foolish, while Brooks had completely misjudged Tokaev's ability to function in a press conference. He could not function at all. This all tended to detract from Tokaev's extremely serious and valuable material.

> It is in a totally different category from the ridiculous Gouzenko book, or from that of Kravchenko . . . On the contrary, it is – and this should in publicity be emphasised, made the basis of any statement – the story of a highly successful Soviet scientific expert who makes as impersonal as possible a survey of a system of centralised rule against which he has fought politically in the past as inhuman and inefficient, and against which he intends to fight politically in the future. It is the work of a Russian patriot, who is an émigré only because he is a patriot.[17]

Despite Tokaev's inauspicious debut Brooks told the Foreign Office he felt that further news conferences might be valuable. Brooks had already sold the rights to Tokaev's story in Sweden and France and wanted to drum up more interest.[18] Meanwhile, progress on Tokaev's book proceeded, but slowly. Tokaev's original 412-page manuscript was so disorganised and poorly written that the 'translator' had to re-write the entire book and add a great deal of new material. The translator then read the re-written sections back to Tokaev in 'a rough Russian translation' for his approval. But in order to make the book not appear to be too polished or give the impression of 'manufactured propaganda' a few sentences were left with 'a slightly Russian flavour' and quotes from Lenin and Churchill were taken translated from public Russian sources, rather than the existing English versions.[19]

By the end of 1948 enough was ready for the Foreign Office to translate, prepare and plant some excerpts in the *Sunday Express*, a mass-market Conservative newspaper.[20] The *Sunday Express* was hardly Murray's ideal of 'far left' but the *Express* did have several million regular readers and an overseas syndication service. The *Express* began the series on 2 January 1949 with the full sensationalistic treatment – screaming headlines, promises of secrets, and alarming predictions of war.[21] Not everyone in the Foreign Office was enthusiastic. Some dismissed the *Sunday Express* treatment as 'melodramatic' and 'highly coloured' but still thought the articles could be useful as propaganda.[22]

The BBC later broadcast Tokaev's story in a seven-part series. Those stories were later sent out through the regular IRD channels and got good reactions, especially in places like Turkey and Israel.[23] The story continued to churn when Tokaev filed a lawsuit against the *Daily Worker* for its reaction to the *Sunday Express* story. On 5 January 1949 the Communist newspaper had run a short item – under the headline 'Would you believe it?' – claiming that Tokaev was an impostor. Tokaev won in court and the *Daily Worker* agreed to withdraw its allegations and publicly apologise to him.[24] Tokaev remained doing 'varied work' for the British government through 1952 and had published three books of memoirs by the mid-1950s. The Foreign Office gave its seal of approval when former Moscow ambassador Sir David Kelly wrote the introduction to *Betrayal of an Ideal*. After 1952 Tokaev resumed his career in aeronautics and rocket science. He wrote prolifically on scientific topics, taught at the Northhampton College of Advanced Technology (later City University) and did theoretical work for the American Apollo space programme.[25]

The IRD's ultimate success with Tokaev encouraged a sustained push to encourage Red Army soldiers in Germany to defect. But Tokaev was an anomaly. The number of defections declined after 1948 – when eighty-three Soviets defected – as did the intelligence and propaganda value of the defectors. There were fewer defectors in 1949 and fewer still in 1950.[26] The IRD used the defectors to encourage more defectors via Russian-language broadcasts; the BBC expanded its reach by exchanging defector access, scripts and recordings with the American VOA.[27] It also used them to spread the bad news on the USSR to the rest of the world. Here are a couple of stories:

Soviet Major Vassili Michaelovitch Denisov had defected to the British but had developed an 'intransigent' attitude toward the usual channel for defectors, the BBC. Sheridan wanted to get some articles out of him so arranged for Denisov to sell three articles for the COI-controlled mass-circulation German magazine *Blick*.[28] Denisov 'has agreed to as much ghosting as necessary, which should make things easier for us.'[29] *Blick* published the first of the articles in March 1950 under the pseudonym Major Michailow.[30] The BBC then broadcast Denisov, but they also let him use a pseudonym, which Sheridan regretted as a 'great mistake, because it weakens the effects of his talks.'[31] Another Denisov story – 'Why I left the USSR' – appeared in the Berlin British-sector *Telegraf* newspaper about the same time. (The more-or-less transparent agency British Features handled the Denisov story, and the IRD-assisted story of a Russian named Borisov, apparently a defector under British protection in Germany, that appeared in the mass-circulation *Stern* magazine.)[32]

Some defectors had knowledge of the gulag, such as Red Army Lt Anatoly Alexandrovitch Baranov, who had defected from the Soviet zone of Germany. In the late 1930s he had been sentenced to three years corrective labour for returning five hours late from leave but in 1942 he was released and drafted back into the army. After his defection he made a series of broadcasts about his experience for the BBC to the Soviet Union and Eastern Europe. Then, with the assistance of Sovietologist and IRD client Edward Crankshaw, he wrote his experiences for the *Yorkshire Post* in which he highlighted his experience in forced labour camps. In his introduction Crankshaw plugged Baranov's objectivity on the issue by pointing out that he had been a Red Army officer for eleven years and a Communist Party member.

> His inside account of conditions in the forced labour camps most strikingly confirms in general and in detail eye-witness accounts by the many Poles who were amnestied in the early days of Russia's war with Germany, and whose stories are too frequently disbelieved.

Lieutenant Baranov can not be accused of anti-Russian bias, and to one who has spent a good deal of time in Russia during the period he covers in his story, his story has a truly authentic ring.[33]

By 1952 the British had a system. After 'tactical' and 'security' interrogations the IRD representative had a chance to interview the defector briefly 'with an eye to publicity'.[34] They hoped to be able to get wire services such as Reuters and 'above all DPA' to carry these interview stories without actually putting the correspondent in touch with the defector, instead using IRD staff to write them.[35] But the campaign for more defectors did not go that well. A survey showed fewer and fewer defectors, and pointed out that most of them deserted not out of ideology but to be with German women.[36]

In addition, the military wasn't enthusiastic about the BBC's approach; the War Office pointed out that even defectors didn't like many of the BBC defector broadcasts, which also may have stimulated tighter Soviet security.[37] By 1954 the overt defector campaign was at a crossroads. It had been reasonably successful, but any increase in propaganda would jeopardise the government's efforts to improve relations with the Soviet bloc. The JIC wanted a different grade of defector, scientists in particular, and felt that the campaign should be tailored for that market.[38] But by mid-1957 the defector programme had petered out, largely because of the lack of defectors.[39]

Exposing the Secrets of the Gulag

The attack on the Soviet forced labour system was more complex, with high level polemics at the United Nations backed by IRD preparation and follow up, and mid-level contacts with the trade union movement and human rights' campaigners. The Soviet regime's opponents had recognised its weakness on forced labour early on and had sought to publicise it in the face of obfuscation and denial by the USSR and its friends. For many supporters denying the existence of the camps was a matter of faith: the USSR was on the side of progress and humanity, therefore a massive forced labour system could not exist despite any evidence presented.[40] For the Soviets the massive system of forced labour in a state boasting to be the workers' paradise was a major contradiction and embarrassment.[41]

The existence of the gulag had been for years an open secret for those who cared to know. A steady stream of books and articles had been coming out since the 1920s, and accelerated with the coming of the Cold War and the testimony of refugees, ex-POWs, and others with firsthand knowledge. At the time non-Communist estimates on the total number of prisoners varied from 8 million to 14 million. Evidence from the Soviet archives now points at a total of roughly 2.5 million in the camps at the time of Stalin's death in 1953.[42]

The British government was just one of many players in the campaign to expose the Soviet gulag system. Research pioneers were frequently exiled Mensheviks, who often had had first-hand experience of the camps. Mensheviks David Dallin and Boris Nicolaevsky had collected as much documentary evidence and witness testimony as possible for their 1947 book *Forced Labour in Soviet Russia*. Their timing was good. Within months the book was being cited and debated at the UN, which led the authors to file a $1 million slander suit against Soviet representative Andrei Vyshinsky.[43] It made an impact on the British left as well, when Sovietologist Edward Crankshaw reviewed it favourably (with a few caveats) in the *New Statesman and Nation*. The vituperative letters that followed indicated that they had hit a nerve with British Communists and their friends.[44]

The American government and the vociferously anti-Communist American Federation of Labor also made many of the early public attacks on the forced labour issue at the UN. Ex-Communist Jay Lovestone was the driving force behind the AFL's attack. He used CIA money and his extensive international contacts to find and publicise the dark secrets of the Soviet gulag. Lovestone had German Social Democrat Toni Spender gather evidence from survivors of the gulag, which was then presented at the United Nations' Economic and Social Council in 1949.[45]

The British government held off on direct attacks until 1948, when the idea of a campaign against forced labour surfaced at a February Russia Committee meeting.[46] The IRD's strategy was not terribly innovative, but it did generate publicity. The IRD would identify a potential news peg, usually a speech at the United Nations, then supply information officers and trusted contacts around the world with background information, testimonials, statistics, and prepared articles to be released in conjunction with the speech.

The first British venture into the field was an October 1948 speech by Parliamentary Undersecretary Christopher Mayhew at the United Nations Economic and Social Council – possibly with help from Tokaev.[47] Mayhew quoted not only refugees and defectors, but also published statements from Soviet luminaries V. I. Molotov and Andrei Vyshinsky to establish the existence and extent of the forced labour system.

> It can no longer be denied that the Soviet Union is making use of large number of prisoner as forced labour in conditions denying to them the basic human rights; that these human beings, once deprived of their liberty, are maintained in conditions of wretchedness and undernourishment; that under the cloak of arrest for crimes and other offences against the regime, the Soviet Government has acquired for itself a vast body of cheap labour utterly without rights. That, in short, the Soviet Union has instituted a slave system recruited from among its own citizens which in scope has no parallel in history...[48]

The press reactions to Mayhew's speech were not inspiring. Despite extensive preparation, coverage was perfunctory in most of the European press. As the Rome embassy noted, the response was 'small and disappointing'.[49] In Britain *The Times* gave it four paragraphs and noted that Mayhew's accusations were backed by 'much documentary evidence, mostly from Soviet sources'.[50]

The campaign rolled into 1949 with the IRD gathering more evidence by combing British diplomatic missions and contacts around the world.[51] Mayhew again attacked at the UN in February 1949, this time backing up an American attack with evidence that Communists in Eastern Germany were taking over the old Nazi concentration camps. *The Times* noted pointedly that the Soviet delegate did not respond to the accusations.[52] The IRD's Murray was excited about the propaganda possibilities of forced labour; the Soviets were in a weak position as seen by their feeble and blustering responses to Mayhew's speech.[53] He also urged British representatives in the field, especially in the Commonwealth, to push for better coverage of UN speeches such as Mayhew's. 'These speeches provide one of the foundations of our work; and considerable importance attaches to their being widely reported.'[54]

The Foreign Office wrestled with presentation as well. As part of its overall campaign to manipulate words and images to draw unflattering comparisons between the Communists and the Nazis the officials tried to identify a few labour camps that could acquire the name recognition and instant repugnance of the Nazi concentration camps at Belsen or Buchenwald. Eventually they settled on Karaganda, the remote area of Central Asia heavily populated by labour camps, but largely failed to establish it in media discourse.[55]

The IRD also worried about overkill. By early 1949 there was already a risk that too much talk about forced labour at the UN would breed cynicism, leading to the impression that the Anglo–American attacks were nothing but a 'propaganda stunt'.[56] Another problem was compassion fatigue. Sheridan argued that after the horrors of World War II many people in Europe and the USA were bored with stories of atrocity, persecution, and prison. The IRD would have to do something original, or rely on a really big name to push forced labour into the public sphere and keep it there.[57]

The IRD's breakthrough came with a single document – the Corrective Labour Codex of the Russian Soviet Federated Socialist Republic. The Codex had been in print since 1936 and had been updated in 1941, but no one had used it as the basis for propaganda until the IRD hit upon the idea and backed it up with reams of evidence provided by British diplomatic missions around the world. The Codex basically laid out in detail the rules on why people were sent to what sort of labour camps and how they should be treated once there. As *The Times* summarised:

> The system is designed, the codex states, to defend the dictatorship of the
> proletariat against class-hostile and déclassé elements and unstable
> elements among the workers . . . The most severe punishment is
> deprivation of freedom with corrective labour, which seems to mean, in
> the main, 'mass-work' in colonies. Prisoners appointed to help in
> supervising the camps are to be drawn from the 'ordinary', i.e.
> non-political, prisoners.[58]

Unlike the Tokaev press conference fiasco the IRD was prepared this time. English and French versions of the text, articles and commentaries were ready for release by information officers around the world at a signal from London. On 22 July the Foreign Office released English and French translations of the Codex, as well as Photostats of the original Russian edition in London and at the United Nations Economic and Social Council meeting in Geneva, where the issue of forced labour was up for discussion.[59] Further activities in Geneva kept forced labour in the headlines in early August – first the Soviets acknowledged the existence of the system but argued that it was humane, and then the Americans called for a full-scale inquiry into forced labour.[60]

Despite the well-prepared information blitz the level of news coverage often depended more on the local circumstances and skill of the information officer. In the Netherlands where an energetic information officer had few obstacles he managed to send 250 translated copies of the information to his contacts. He telephoned the editors and foreign editors of all national papers to draw attention to the revelations. All national papers, with one exception, gave it front page coverage. The provincial and weekly press also covered it well.[61] In Turkey the country was saturated with news of forced labour after the recent serialisation of Dallin and Nicolaevsky's book on forced labour. The British news of the Codex passed relatively unnoticed.[62] In France the release was competing with news from the Tour de France bicycle race.[63] Things were more difficult in the Middle East. The Tehran embassy issued only an abbreviated version because the draconian conditions of the full Codex would only remind Iranian workers of their own abysmal conditions, while angering their employers.

> This is just one more illustration of the thesis that propaganda designed to work on fellow-travellers and trades unionists in democratic countries sometimes needs modification if it is to be directed at countries where neither political democracy nor the basic freedoms are firmly established.[64]

The revelations were news among most leading newspapers in Britain and continued with two weeks of follow-ups and new twists. The *Daily Telegraph*, *Daily Herald* and *Daily Mirror* made forced labour the lead story that day, with the *Daily Mirror* following up the story for three days.[65] The BBC Home and Overseas Services also covered the revelations extensively, with the IRD saying later that they 'did us proud'.[66] The IRD managed to remedy the lacklustre or downright dismissive coverage in *The Times* and *The Economist* by prompting friendly MPs to write letters to the editors with raw material it provided.[67] Once the letters were published, the IRD kept them in circulation by urging information officers to distribute them as part of their regular work.[68]

The IRD had other channels than the UN to keep the issue hot. It had supplied the *Daily Telegraph*'s Vienna correspondent with information on the camps that he then turned into a page-one story 'allegedly told by people who have escaped, but in fact all based on various I.R.D. papers'.[69] The *Daily Telegraph*'s story was riveting, starting with the claim that 'eye-witness accounts of conditions inside Russian forced labour camps were given to me to-day by a group of former inmates who have arrived here'. Curiously, he did not name his sources or quote them directly. The story went into depth on poor food, the imprisonment of non-Soviet nationals and details about a camp devoted to children as young as seven, most of whom had been taken away from parents suspected of 'bourgeois leanings'. The correspondent linked the Codex to those horrific stories, but qualified the attack by pointing out that the inmates did not provide any evidence of deliberate guard brutality. 'In this respect the Russian camps differ from the Nazi concentration camps, but the vitiation of human rights and dignity is nonetheless complete'.[70]

Seizing the Moral High Ground: Enter David Rousset

The Foreign Office's revelation of the Codex had attracted plenty of attention, but for keeping the forced labour issue in the public consciousness probably no one was as important as left-wing French journalist and activist David Rousset. Rousset was a vehement anti-Stalinist, a survivor of the Nazi concentration camps and the author of a widely acclaimed book on his experience at Buchenwald – *L'Univers Concentrationnaire*. His credentials were impeccably left – in the 1930s he fought against fascism in the streets of Paris, organised men and supplies for the Spanish Republic, and joined a dissident Communist movement. During the war he was in the Resistance, using propaganda to subvert German troops until he was caught and sent to Buchenwald in 1943. After the war he founded a short-lived anti-American, anti-Soviet political grouping with Jean-Paul Sartre – the Revolutionary Democratic Assembly.[71] And he had already shown his hostility toward the USSR by his organisation of the counter-demonstration to the 1949 Paris peace congress – the International Day of Resistance to Dictatorship and War.[72] The IRD could scarcely have invented a better ally, despite Rousset's awkward connections with the American embassy.[73]

For Rousset the Codex was the missing link that, coupled with refugee testimony, would prove once and for all the existence and nature of the Soviet forced labour system.[74] Several months after the release he took the propaganda offensive and announced in a 12 November *Le Figaro littéraire* article plans for veterans' of Nazi deportations to launch an investigation into forced labour. The USSR would be first because of its claims of social liberty.[75] He referred explicitly to the British publication of the Codex as being of 'monumental importance'.[76] This was an important move toward building an equivalency between the Soviet and Nazi regimes and legitimising the anti-Soviet campaign among left-wing Europeans. Deportees were closely associated with the resistance, which had come to symbolise heroism and a dedication to justice and liberty.

The non-Communist French and Belgian press covered Rousset's plans widely and favourably. The Communists were not amused and *Les Lettres françaises* attacked both Rousset and the authenticity of the Codex in the same manner the journal had attacked Kravchenko two years earlier. The gist of the Communist case against Rousset was that he falsified the Codex by leaving out one line, but supporters argued that this did not substantially change the sense of the paragraph.[77] The next day Rousset filed a libel suit and privately appealed to the British for help. Tennant, the British information officer in Paris, pointed out to the IRD in London that British credibility was at stake in this case and urged the IRD to help gathering witnesses, documentation and public support for Rousset. He also urged the government to allow inspections of prison labour in the British colonies to rebut Soviet accusations of forced labour there, a move that the Colonial Office adamantly opposed.[78]

The Foreign Office quickly gathered documentation and began lining up witnesses for Rousset.

> The speed and efficiency with which all the material was collected was remarkable, and the French lawyers handling the case for Rousset, with whom we had a conference yesterday, were profoundly grateful and amazed that all this work could be achieved in the short period of eight days'.[79]

In December Rousset came to London to rouse support for his cause among British socialists and other suitably left-wing anti-Communists. The IRD tried desperately to stay in the background, and mainly served as an introduction service – to the Labour Party's Denis Healey and Richard Crossman, as well as the editors of the *Tribune*, Polish exiles, and the BBC – as Rousset sought to build support for his case. Watson noted that Crossman and journalist Maurice Edelman, 'though not mouthpieces of this office, are good leftists who are doing useful anti-Communist work just now (esp. Crossman) and that Rousset should certainly see them both.'[80] For Soviet legal expertise the IRD steered them toward the London School of Economics' Leonard Schapiro and away from the University of Glasgow's Rudolf Schlesinger, whom they considered wobbly on the USSR. The IRD also helped find a publicity agency that set up a press conference for Rousset, attended by some thirty-five reporters including the big news agencies and the Westminster press corps.[81]

Rousset's left-wing credentials and French nationality were the ticket for the IRD. The department was not as enthusiastic about propaganda that associated their forced labour campaign with 'the wrong people'. A group of Polish émigrés was planning a touring exhibition of forced labour camp models and an additional model showing the Soviets carrying out the 1940 Katyn Forest massacre (of captured Polish officers). The IRD's Watson noted, 'The whole thing seems to me rather on the lines of Dr. Goebbels' publicity on the subject, and we have attempted to pour cold water on the scheme, through people like Mr. James Burnham, etc., who are in contact with the scheme'. The Italian Christian Democrats had been inspired by Rousset's campaign to propose their own campaign, but the IRD also discouraged them.

> (Rousset's) effectiveness would largely be destroyed, and indeed there might even be a revulsion in favour of the orthodox Communists, if it could be made to appear that the Catholic Church and the Demo-Christian Party in Italy were really behind the movement all the time.[82]

The lawsuit took a twist in February when *Les Lettres françaises* defendants Pierre Daix and Claude Morgan announced that the trial would proceed and that they would make no defence. Daix later explained that the party did not care about winning and saw the trial primarily as a propaganda exercise. To that end he wanted to discredit publicly the witnesses and shift attention from their testimony to their motivations – what he believed to be resentment and political hatred.[83] The controversy that Rousset kicked off generated massive publicity in Europe; an American journalist estimated that it had led to some 2,500 articles in the European press by April 1950.[84]

The trial began in November 1950, lasted nearly two months and offered abundant opportunities to examine and cross-examine witnesses to Soviet forced labour. Some of the witnesses had also appeared at the Kravchenko trial, including Margarete Buber, the wife of exiled executed German Communist leader Heinz Neumann and a survivor of both Soviet and Nazi camps. Neumann had fallen out of favour in 1932 and by 1937 was living in exile in Moscow under a cloud of suspicion. That year he was arrested and presumably killed; his wife was arrested the following year. In 1940 the Soviets turned her over to the Gestapo, perhaps in a gesture of solidarity during the Hitler–Stalin pact. The Nazis kept her in Ravensbruck concentration camp.[85] A new witness was Valentin Gonzalez, an anti-fascist hero of the Spanish Civil War better known as 'El Campesino'. Gonzalez had found a precarious refuge in the USSR after the fall of the Spanish republic but later escaped. As expected, Rousset won the judgment.

The IRD and others pushed hard for strong coverage overseas; in Israel the IRD representative persuaded the AFP representative to put out a full account.[86] But in London not everyone was excited about the trial's revelations. Sheridan thought that the only real new evidence was from 'El Campesino', dismissing the others as the 'usual cast of the "stage army" some of whom have already given evidence in the Kravchenko trial.'[87] Nevertheless, the testimony had raised unsettling questions and spread doubt about the Soviet Union among the Europeans, especially among the hard-to-reach French intellectuals. Many of those who had been willing to give the Soviet Union the benefit of the doubt were no longer willing to do so. Maurice Merleau-Ponty, in Les Temps modernes, admitted that Rousset's facts raised serious questions about the Soviet system. Simone de Beauvoir made the reactions to the revelations a scene in her novel Les Mandarins.[88]

The IRD and others were eager to publicise further the trial's revelations.[89] The French publishing giant Hachette was rushing out within weeks 40,000 cheap copies of the abridged and annotated trial record, with an introduction by Rousset; the Americans had approached Rousset about an English translation.[90] That prompted Sheridan to suggest leaving European distribution to Hachette, the English translation to the Americans and simply buying up the resulting English-language editions and shipping them off to the Far East for distribution.[91] But the Americans, in the form of the front group the Congress for Cultural Freedom, and its British affiliates were not having much luck in their push for a commercial British translation of Rousset's Pour la Vérité sur les camps concentrationnaires. They were turned down by Hamish Hamilton and Victor Gollancz.[92] Nevertheless, an English account of the revelations came out as Police-State Methods in the USSR in 1953.[93]

Rousset had set up a thirty-eight-member commission to investigate the camps in early 1950. A few months after the trial Rousset's commission got to work in Brussels. It had agreements in principle to visit Greek and Yugoslav prisons, but Spain was evasive and the Soviet Union vitriolic in its response.[94] The group kept an active publication schedule in the 1950s, with a monthly publication and books coming out on political prisoners in Tunisia, Greece and Spain, as well as the Soviet Union and China. The IRD continued to try to get distribution deals for Rousset's work, and Rousset kept on good terms with the department, visiting with IRD head John Rennie and regularly receiving IRD material both from Carlton House Terrace and the Paris Embassy.[95]

The post-Stalin thaw and Rousset's increasing focus on China as the Soviets greatly reduced their camp population led him into conflict with British realpolitik. The IRD had helped him when he made an investigative trip to Hong Kong in 1955.[96] This investigation was leading up to a planned formal hearing – to take place in Asia – with examination of witnesses. The results would then be forwarded to the ILO and ESOC in early 1956.[97] When Rousset wanted to hold a formal enquiry in Asia on forced labour, the Foreign Office was less helpful; colonial governments didn't want to host them fearing various problems.[98] At a later meeting, Reddaway explained to Rousset that there were not only local considerations, but also possible repercussions connected with the Geneva summit.[99]

Throughout the early 1950s the Foreign Office kept the focus on forced labour, gathering fresh information and funnelling it through various UN forums, trade union contacts, and regular propaganda channels.[100] The IRD thought the UN was 'the best publicity platform in the world' but argued that other branches of the government, such as the ministries of Labour and Education, were losing sight of the propaganda potential. The IRD had special venom for the Colonial Office, which consistently tried to avoid topics that could reflect poorly on colonial rule, such as forced labour.[101]

> Our main concern at the moment is the subject of Forced Labour; the Colonial Office in order to defend their nefarious activities in Kenya, are trying to get general adoption of the view that it was a mistake to have launched the Forced Labour operation against the Communist bloc in the first place. This is a complete heresy and should be treated as such.[102]

The British, American and non-Communist trade union representatives at the United Nations Economic and Social Council repeatedly called for an investigation into forced labour, bringing in new evidence with each appeal. Just as often the Soviets stonewalled.[103] Eventually, the UN approved an investigative committee that came out with a 671-page report in June 1953 that concluded that, indeed, a large-scale system of forced labour existed and was often used for punishing dissent.[104] But by that time the Soviet gulag was beginning to contract as Stalin's successors first faced rebellions in the camps, then the obvious bottom-line conclusion: the camps cost more than they were worth.[105]

The UN was not the only forum to attack forced labour; the IRD also funnelled information through the TUC and Labour Party to the ICFTU, which was preparing a report on the issue.[106] The ICFTU's September 1951 release of the scathing report, *Stalin's Slave Labour Camps*, kept the spotlight on forced labour at the UN and elsewhere.[107] In the short term it attracted plenty of media attention. In Britain the *Daily Telegraph* covered prominently, while the *Daily Mirror*'s William Connor ('Cassandra') summarised its horrors.[108] 'It is an appalling and horrible contrast to the political frisking of the squalid youths who still foment strikes in Britain and who raise the principles of the Red Flag in other lands.'[109]

The heyday of the forced labour campaign came to an end soon after the death of Stalin. His successors had to deal with the camps' economic inefficiencies, their inmates growing restiveness as well as the bad international public image they gave the USSR. They freed prisoners, closed camps and shrunk the gulag to a fraction of its former self. The IRD followed the Soviet lead, and forced labour became a much less prominent weapon in the anti-Soviet propaganda arsenal. After Khrushchev's anti-Stalin speech in 1956, the IRD shifted gears and downplayed forced labour and Soviet armaments in their propaganda, and played up other elements such as the distortions in the Soviet economy and foreign aid.[110]

Conclusion

Defectors had great potential for propaganda, especially after Tokaev's 1948 defection, but it was a largely unrealised potential. There were not many high ranking defectors, and few of the low-ranking ones came for any sort of ideological reasons thus cutting into their effectiveness. The BBC used them to encourage more defections, and the IRD used them to push their propaganda themes of Soviet incompetence, despotism and aggression, but overall it did not resonate as other themes did. Forced labour did resonate. For a workers' paradise nothing could be more shameful than millions of citizens working under armed guard, their only crime being political dissent. The British, the Americans and the AFL all hammered the theme in the United Nations, but it took left-wing Frenchman David Rousset to electrify the issue. At that point the IRD did what they did best, reinforce, supply and help from behind the scenes.

Historians have different conclusions about how effective it all was. Western gulag chronicler Anne Applebaum contends that the reality of the gulag never really sunk in for most Westerners, or even most former Soviet citizens.[111] But Russian historian Elena Zubkova argues that Stalin's successors were sensitive to international opinion and that that sensitivity was one of the major factors leading to the freeing of prisoners, closing of camps and the drastic shrinking of the gulag after 1953.[112] Zubkova's argument may lead us to believe that both British and American propaganda on the issue of forced labour, designed solely to score points in the Cold War, may have materially eased suffering within the Soviet Union.

Notes

1. Nicholas Bethell, *The Last Secret: The Delivery to Stalin of over Two Million Russians by Britain and the United States* (New York: Basic Books, 1974), pp. 15, 175–80.
2. Wesley Wark, 'Coming in from the cold: British propaganda and Red Army defectors, 1945–52', *The International History Review* 9 (1987), p. 56.
3. Aldrich, *Hidden Hand*, pp. 96–7.
4. Wall, *The United States and the Making of Postwar France*, p. 151.
5. Aldrich, *Hidden Hand*, p. 107.
6. 'The comedy of the Kravchenko trial', *Picture Post*, 26 February 1949.
7. Wall, *The US and the Making of Postwar France*, pp. 151–4; Tony Judt, *Past Imperfect: French Intellectuals, 1944–1956* (Berkeley: University of California Press, 1992), p. 113.
8. Garnett, *Secret History*, p. 128.
9. PRO FO1110/80 PR523/523/913G, Memo, 28 June 1948.
10. PRO FO1110/80 R523/523/913G, Sargent minute, 1 July 1948.
11. PRO FO1110/80 PR584/523/913G, Murray minute, 8 July 1948, F. A. Warner minute, 15 July 1948, R. C. McAlpine memo, 17 July 1948.
12. PRO FO1110/80 PR584/523/913G, F. A. Warner minute, 17 July 1948.
13. PRO FO1110/80 PR717/523/913/G, Murray minute, 1 September 1948.
14. Wark, 'Coming in from the cold', pp. 60–1.
15. PRO FO1110/80 PR717/523/913/G, Murray minute, 1 September 1948.
16. 'Colonel's flight from Russia', *Manchester Guardian*, 7 September 1948; 'Refugee Russian Colonel', *The Times*, 7 September 1948.
17. PRO FO1110/55 PR1116/265/913G, 'Some observations on the now completed 'Testament of a Russian Patriot' and the projected second book by the same author', 'Translator', H.D., 15 November 1948. Igor Gouzenko was a code clerk at the Soviet embassy in Ottawa, Canada, who defected in 1945 and later published an account of his life and defection, *This Was My Choice*.
18. PRO FO1110/115 PR796/796, Talbot to Murray, 15 September 1948.
19. PRO FO1110/55 PR1116/265/913G, 'Some observations on the now completed 'Testament of a Russian Patriot' and the projected second book by the same author', 'Translator', H.D., 15 November 1948.
20. BBK H/138, Gordon to Beaverbrook, 11 July 1950.
21. G. A. Tokaev, 'What Stalin intends to do: by a man who sat with him at the war-planning table in the Kremlin', *Sunday Express*, 2 January 1949. It continued in the same vein throughout the month.
22. PRO FO371/77609 N135/1024/38 and N241/1024/38.
23. Wark, 'Coming in from the cold', p. 61; PRO FO1110/277 PR28791/112/G, Appendix A: Progress report: Information Research Department'; PRO FO1110/318 PR46/6, Woodward to Murray, 6 June 1950.
24. 'High Court of Justice', *The Times*, 28 July 1950.
25. *Who's Who 1999*, Entry for Tokaty, Prof. Grigori Alexandrovich, p. 2014. Tokaev, obviously, had changed slightly the spelling of his surname.
26. For a partial account, see Wark, 'Coming in from the cold', and PRO FO1110/190.
27. NARA RG 59, Miscellaneous records of the Bureau of Public Affairs, Lot 58 D 753, Box 2, British-memos of conversation 1952 file, 'Memorandum of conversation (M. Gordon Knox, Peter Wilkinson)', 6 May 1952.

28. PRO FO1110/287 PR12/37/G, Sheridan to Murray, 9 February 1950.
29. PRO FO1110/287 PR12/37/G, MacLaren minute, 11 February 1950.
30. PRO FO1110/287 PR12/37/G, Welser (COI) to Sheridan, 1 March 1950.
31. PRO FO1110/287 PR12/37/G, Sheridan minute, 20 February 1950.
32. PRO FO1110/311 PRPR37/16, 'List of stories sold by British Features', April 1950; PRO FO1110/179 PR3645/5/G, Murray to Tennant, 8 December 1949.
33. Anatoly Baranov, 'Human cattle in Soviet labour camp', *Yorkshire Post*, 10 July 1950, 'Experiences in a Russian forced labour camp', *Yorkshire Post*, 17 July 1950.
34. PRO CAB176/38 JIC/2066/52, 'Defector operations in Germany', 5 September 1952.
35. PRO FO1110/377 PR12/65/51/G, Agenda for meeting with MacDonald [n.d.].
36. Wark, 'Coming in from the cold', pp. 64–6, 69–70.
37. PRO CAB159/13, JIC, 'Measures to encourage defection of members of the Soviet armed forces in Germany and Austria', 13 May 1953.
38. PRO CAB159/17 JIC (54), 81st meeting, 15 September 1954.
39. PRO FO1110/1005 PR1018/51, Rennie to Murray, 18 July 1957.
40. Judt, *Past Imperfect*, p. 114.
41. Elena Zubkova, *Russia After the War: Hopes, Illusions and Disappointments, 1945–57* (Armonk, NY: M. E. Sharpe, 1998), pp. 165–7.
42. Ibid., p. 165.
43. Andrew Liebich, 'Mensheviks wage the Cold War,' *Journal of Contemporary History* 30 (1995), pp. 254–7.
44. 'Review of Dallin and Nicolevsky's "Forced Labour in Russia" ', *New Statesman and Nation*, 15 May 1948.
45. Ted Morgan, *A Covert Life: Jay Lovestone: Communist, Anti-Communist, and Spymaster* (New York: Random House, 1999), p. 199.
46. PRO FO371/71687 N8166/765/38G, Russia Committee minutes, 19 February 1948.
47. Wark, 'Coming in from the cold', p. 61.
48. Quoted in Christopher Mayhew, *A War of Words: A Cold War Witness* (London: I. B. Tauris, 1998), pp. 134–6.
49. PRO FO1110/112 PR907/760/913, Rome to IRD, [October 1948].
50. 'Soviet "Slave System": Mr. Mayhew's Attack', *The Times*, 16 October 1948.
51. PRO FO1110/171-172.
52. 'US charges against Russia', *The Times*, 15 February 1949; 'Slave labour in Russia: demand for survey', *The Times*, 16 February 1949.
53. PRO FO1110/171. PR610/5/913, Murray to Tenant, [March 1949].
54. PRO FO1110/217 PR65/28/913, Murray to A. H. Joyce (CRO), 11 February 1949.
55. PRO FO1110/173 PR1450/5/G, Kirwan and Brimmel minutes, 26 May 1949; PRO FO1110/192 PR2122/14/G, Murray minute, 4 October 1949.
56. PRO FO1110/172 PR807/5/913, Murray to Tennant, 18 March 1949.
57. PRO FO1110/172 PR807/5/913, Sheridan minute, 27 April 1949.
58. 'Russian forced labour code', *The Times*, 23 July 1949.
59. 'Rigid Russian code for forced labor bared by Britain', *New York Times*, 23 July 1949.
60. 'U.S. urges inquiry into forced labor', *New York Times*, 4 August 1949; 'Forced labour inquiry postponed', *United Nations Bulletin*, 1 September 1949.
61. PRO FO1110/174 PR2114, Wright to IRD, 28 July 1949.
62. PRO FO1110/174 PR2176/5/913, Ankara to Foreign Office.

63. PRO FO1110/277, 'Progress report: Information Research Department' (Version for Caccia).
64. PRO FO1110/175 PR2217/5/913, Tehran to IRD, 8 August 1949.
65. 'Britain's proof: millions of Russians in the slave camps of the Soviet', *Daily Mirror*, 23 July 1949; W. N. Ewer, 'Soviet slave camp code shown to world', *Daily Herald*, 23 July 1949; 'Britain urged U.N. visit to Russian camps', *Daily Telegraph*, 23 July 1949.
66. PRO FO1110/277, 'Annexure 'D' reports on publicity about the forced labour Codex'.
67. PRO FO1110/174 PR2199/5/913, Watson to Reddaway, 3 August 1949, Reddaway to Watson, 4 August 1949; R. R. Stokes, 'Conditions at Aue: to the editor of *The Times*', *The Times*, 6 August 1949.
68. PRO FO1110/176 PR2271/5/913, IRD to Posts, 8 August 1949.
69. PRO FO1110/277, 'Annexure 'D' reports on publicity about the forced labour Codex'.
70. 'Russian network of slave camps', *Daily Telegraph*, 3 August 1949.
71. Sanche de Gramont, 'Two who bridge the generation gap,' in John E. Talbott (ed.) *France Since 1930* (New York: Quadrangle Books, 1972), pp. 212–4.
72. Saunders, *The Cultural Cold War*, pp. 68–9.
73. Wall, *The United States and the Making of Postwar France*, p. 153.
74. Émile Copfermann, *David Rousset: Une Vie dans le Siécle: Fragments d'autobiographie* (Paris: Plon, 1991), pp. 114–15.
75. Ibid. pp. 115–17.
76. PRO FO1110/179, Oliver Harvey to IRD, 17 November 1949.
77. 'Russian justice brought to trial', *Observer*, 17 December 1950.
78. PRO FO1110/179 PR3622/5/G, Tennant to Murray, 18 November 1949.
79. PRO FO1110/179 PR3812/5/G, Tennant to Murray, 3 December 1949.
80. PRO FO1110/179 PR3812/5/G, Watson minute, 7 December 1949.
81. PRO FO1110/179 PR3998/5/G, Murray to Tennant, 22 December 1949.
82. PRO FO1110/179 PR3659/5/913, Watson to Howard, 6 December 1949.
83. Pierre Daix, *J'ai cru au Matin* (Paris: R. Laffont, 1976), p. 257.
84. 'Former occupants wage war on Soviet slave labor camps', *Christian Science Monitor*, 24 April 1950.
85. Margarete Buber, *Under Two Dictators* (London: Victor Gollancz, 1949), pp. x–xii.
86. PRO FO1110/420 PR65/1/51, Woodward to Murray, 8 January 1951.
87. PRO FO1110/378 PR14/15/G, Sheridan minute, 9 January 1951.
88. Judt, *Past Imperfect*, pp. 112–15.
89. PRO FO1110/378 PR14/57/51, 'David Rousset's proposal for an investigation into Soviet forced labour camps,' January 1951.
90. PRO FO1110/378 PR14/19, Breene to Wilkinson, 17 January 1951.
91. PRO FO1110/378 PR14/19, Sheridan minute, 22 January 1951.
92. CCF Papers, Series II, Box 130, File 4, Goodwin to Bondy, 2 August 1951 and Sheila Hodges (Gollancz director) to Goodwin, 27 July 1951.
93. See, International Commission Against Concentrationist Regimes, *Police State Methods in the Soviet Union* (Boston: Beacon Press, 1953).
94. 'Prison visitors', *Observer*, 20 May 1951.
95. PRO FO1110/378 PR14/72, Paris Information Officer to IRD, 17 October 1951, IRD to Paris Information Officer, 15 November 1951; PRO FO1110/726 PR10123/7, Rennie to M. F. Cullis, 6 August 1955.

96. PRO FO1110/726 PR10123/2, Lewen minute, 24 May 1955.
97. PRO FO1110/726 PR10123/3, Rennie to Rayner, 30 June 1955.
98. PRO FO1110/726 PR10123/9, Mason to Meyer, 10 October 1955.
99. PRO FO1110/726 PR10123/9, 'Summary of discussions held in IRD on the 21st of October, 1955, with M. David Rousset of the Commission Internationale Contre le Régime Concentrationnaire'.
100. PRO FO1110/288 PR14/69/G, Circular to East bloc posts, 24 June 1950.
101. PRO FO1110/748. PR141/6/G, 'The interest of the IRD in United Nations Affairs (H. G. A. Overton)', 4 January 1955.
102. Ibid.
103. 'Forced labour in Russia: a vast economic enterprise', *The Times*, 1 March 1950; 'Soviet forced labour, *The Times*, 16 August 1950; 'Investigation of forced labour conditions in U.S.S.R. and satellites urged', *Department of State Bulletin*, 2 April 1951.
104. 'U.N.-I.L.O. Committee established existence of Soviet forced labor system', *Department of State Bulletin*, 10 August 1950.
105. Anne Applebaum, *Gulag: A History* (New York: Doubleday, 2003), pp. 484–526.
106. PRO FO1110/288 PR14/41/G, Watson minute, 8 March 1950.
107. Anthony Carew, et al., *The International Confederation of Free Trade Unions* (Bern: Peter Lang, 2000), pp. 202–3
108. Industrial correspondent (Hugh Chevins), 'Tenth of Soviet people work in slave camps', *Daily Telegraph*, 4 September 1951.
109. William Connor, 'Stalin stands condemned. . . by his own slave laws', *Daily Mirror*, 8 September 1951.
110. PRO FO1110/872 PR10111/90, Untitled note (H. T. A. Overton), 12 June 1956.
111. Applebaum, *Gulag*, pp. xv–xxiii.
112. Zubkova, *Russia After the War*, pp. 165–7.

Conclusion

The early Cold War is an instructive period, showing how media consensus and government manipulation operate in a democracy during an open-ended undeclared struggle, in this case against the Soviet Union and its Communist allies. There was government manipulation and occasional strong-arming, but much of the consensus came about through a gradual, negotiated revision of the media's common sense view of the world situation. Journalists, publishers, producers, politicians and government officials contributed in this informal process by which gallant allies became deceitful enemies – for the media changing acceptable sources, playing up or down information and choosing different questions to ask were just some of the factors in the switch. The IRD's under-the-table propaganda helped provide the detailed knowledge necessary to maintain this consensus in an adaptable and up-to-date form. Once Soviet intransigence, brutality, oppression and deceit were accepted as common sense, there was a ready made frame for a great deal of world and national news.

The British establishment showed some cracks during the Suez debacle in 1956. Afterward the government decided that it was not so much the policy that was at fault as it was the presentation. Dr Charles Hill came into the cabinet as de facto minister of information, tightening the links between propaganda and policy making and spending more money on propaganda.[1] The state-private network built to circulate IRD propaganda took on a life of its own, even after the department's 1977 closure. Former IRD clients and partners, like Brian Crozier, stayed in the network using many of the same methods to attack many of the same targets, but simply found other patrons to pay for it.[2] The hard edge of suppression faltered in the 1960s as journalists such as Chapman Pincher flouted the D-Notice system and others grew to distrust the clubby cooptation it represented. But continued prosecutions under the Official Secrets Act showed journalists what the consequences could be if they defied the state.[3]

This period also shows how global media channels built by the British in the nineteenth century persisted despite the country's twentieth-century decline as a world power. The government boosted Reuters with subsidies, supplemented it with covert news agencies such as the Arab News Agency, and kept the BBC External Services at a high level. The traditional role of London as a centre for world news allowed British propaganda to fit more-or-less unobtrusively into existing channels and be more likely to be accepted as legitimate news, and thus influence the creation of common sense overseas. Finally, the fact-based propaganda of the IRD and its cool, detached tone blended well into the Anglo-American journalistic tradition of facticity and objectivity. It almost seemed like news instead of propaganda.

During the 1950s, 1960s and into the 1970s Reuters continued to depend on government subsidies and hook-ups with various disguised news agencies – even cutting a deal for the Arab News Agency to distribute its dispatches in the Middle East. But in the 1970s Reuters returned to its roots of business news and capitalised on computerisation to make a very strong independent comeback. The BBC has gone through ups and downs, but has remained a strong player in global radio and television, while British publications such as the *Financial Times* and *The Economist* have become truly international media that are just logically based in London.[4]

Beyond the scope of the Cold War itself the exercise of this media power for anti-Soviet and pro-British propaganda strengthened the London-based system and residual British-dominated channels in a more generalised way. The IRD, LPS, COI, ANA and battalions of information officers kept up the flow of British news, the expectations of London as a news generator, and probably helped pre-empt or hobble other news agencies or other news systems. The legacy of empire and world power meant that London had the contacts, the journalistic talent pool, the technical expertise and the efficient and numerous travel and communication connections that are essential for a truly global media capital. And thanks to the American dominance of the post-1945 world, English has remained the language of power, thus giving the British a major advantage in the global news market. Finally, the harnessing of the British-based international media system for a global battle against Soviet Communism probably accelerated the process of media globalisation itself. In the interest of propaganda the British Foreign Office had eroded national media barriers based on routine and tradition, subsidised international news on hard-to-find topics and encouraged international media connections that served its interests.

Notes

1. Shaw, *Eden, Suez and the Mass Media*, pp. 195–6.
2. Crozier, *Free Agent*, pp. 187–95, 239.
3. Clive Ponting, *Secrecy in Britain* (Oxford: Blackwell, 1990), pp. 56–66.
4. Read, *Power of News*, pp. 326–32; Machin and Tunstall, *The Anglo-American Media Connection*, pp. 77–81.

Bibliography

Manuscript Collections

Archives of The Times, Times Newspapers Ltd, London.

Ralph Deakin Papers
Iverach McDonald Papers

Bodleian Library, Oxford.

Clement Attlee Paper
William Clark Papers
Conservative Party Archives, Records of the Conservative Central Office

British Library of Political and Economic Science, London.

J. D. Bernal Papers
Hugh Chevins Papers
Records of the National Peace Council
D. N. Pritt Papers

British Broadcasting Corporation Written Archives Centre, Caversham Park, Berkshire.

E1 – External Service Policy Records (Country Files)
E2 – External Service Policy Records
R1 – Board of Governors Minutes and Records
R28 – Radio News Records
R34 – Radio Policy Record
R51 – Radio Talks Records
Radio Contributor Files
Broadcast Scripts

Churchill Archives Centre, Cambridge.

Alexander Cadogan Papers and Diaries
William Haley Papers and Diaries
Ian Jacob Papers
Lord Noel-Baker Papers
Lord Francis-Williams Papers

Eisenhower Presidential Library, Abilene, Kansas.

C. D. Jackson Papers

Hoover Institution on War, Revolution and Peace, Stanford, California.

Malcolm Muggeridge Diaries

House of Lords Record Office, London.

Lord Beaverbrook Papers

Liddell Hart Centre for Military Archives, King's College, London.

Lord Ismay Papers

Modern Records Centre, University Library, University of Warwick, Coventry.

MSS.157 – Victor Gollancz Papers
MSS.220 – Federation of British Industry Records
MSS.292 – Trades Union Congress Records

National Archives and Record Administration, College Park, Maryland.

RG59 – State Department, General Records

National Film and Television Archive, British Film Institute, London.

Records of the Newsreel Association of Great Britain and Northern Ireland

Guardian Archives, John Rylands Library, University of Manchester, Manchester.

General Correspondence
A. P. Wadsworth Correspondence

National Labour Museum, Manchester.

Labour Party Archives:
  General Secretary's Papers
  International Department Records
Communist Party Archives:
  Communist Party Records
  Ivor Montagu Papers

Public Record Office, London.

CAB21 – Cabinet Office, Registered Files
CAB124 – Cabinet Office, Lord President's Committee Records
CAB130 – Cabinet Office, Miscellaneous Committee Records
CAB134 – Cabinet Office, Miscellaneous Committee Records
CAB128 – Cabinet Minutes
CAB129 – Cabinet Memoranda
DEFE4 – Ministry of Defense, Chiefs of Staff Committee Meetings
DEFE7 – Ministry of Defense, Registered Files
DPP6 – Department of Public Prosecutions, Policy and Procedures Files
FO366 – Foreign Office, Chief Clerk's Records
FO371 – Foreign Office, Political Departments' General Correspondence
FO800 – Foreign Minister Ernest Bevin's Private Papers
FO953 – Foreign Office, Information Services, General Correspondence
FO975 – Foreign Office, Information Research Department, Information Reports
FO1110 – Foreign Office, Information Research Department, General Correspondence
HO45 – Home Office, Registered Papers
INF8 – Central Office of Information, Monthly Division Reports
INF12 – Central Office of Information, Registered Files
LO2 – Law Officer's Department, Registered Files
PREM8 – Prime Minister's Papers, 1945–51
PREM11 – Prime Minister's Papers, 1951–64
T245 – Economic Information Unit Records

Joseph Regenstein Library, University of Chicago, Chicago.

Congress for Cultural Freedom Papers

Reuters Archives, London.

Records and Correspondence

The Tom Harrison Mass Observation Archive, The University of Sussex, Brighton.

Directive Replies
Diaries
File Reports
News Quotas
Topic Collections

Harry S Truman Presidential Library, Independence, Missouri.

Ralph Flynt Papers

Wheaton College Archives and Special Collections, Wheaton, Illinois.

Malcolm Muggeridge Papers

Newspapers

Daily Express, Daily Mail, Daily Mirror, Daily Herald, Daily Telegraph, Daily Worker, Evening Standard, Manchester Guardian, News Chronicle, New York Times, The Observer, Reynolds' News, Sunday Chronicle, Sunday Express, Sunday Times, The Times, Yorkshire Post.

Journals and Magazines

Department of State Bulletin, The Economist, Encounter, Fact, Labour Monthly, The Listener, New Statesman and Nation, Newspaper World, One World, Spectator, Time and Tide, United Nations Bulletin, World News and Views, World's Press News.

Interviews

Fisher, Norman. Interview by Author. Tape recording. London. 30 October 1996.
Junor, John. Interview by Author. Tape recording. London. 27 November 1996.
Mayhew, Christopher. Interview by Author. Tape recording. London. 24 July 1995.
Schaffer, Gordon. Interview by Author. Tape recording. London, 9 December 1996.
Tucker, H. H. 'Tommy'. Interview by J. Hutson. Transcript. 19 April 1996. British Diplomatic Oral History Project, Centre for the Study of Diplomacy, Leicester University, Leicester.

Published Primary Sources

Books etc.

British Security Coordination, *British Security Coordination: The Secret History of British Intelligence in the Americas, 1940–1945* (New York: Fromm International, 1999).
Cominform, *The Cominform: Minutes of the Three Conferences, 1947–1948/1949.* Giuliano Procacci (ed.) (Milan: Fondazione Giangiacomo, 1984).
Ewer, W. N., *Communists on Peace* (London: Batchworth Press, 1953).
Felton, Monica, *That's Why I Went* (London: Lawrence and Wishart, 1953).
Foreign Office Historians, *IRD: Origins and Establishment of the Foreign Office Information Research Department, 1946–48* (London: Foreign Office, 1995).
Gallup, George, *International Public Opinion Polls: Great Britain 1937–1975. Vol. 1, 1937–1964* (New York: Random House, 1976).
Garnett, David, *The Secret History of PWE: The Political Warfare Executive, 1939–1945* (London: St Ermin's Press, 2002).

Labour Party, *National Executive Committee: Minutes of the Labour Representation Committee, 1900–06, and the Labour Party Since 1906*. (Hassocks: Harvester Press. 1974). [Microfiche].

Marrett, Sir Robert, *Through the Back Door: An Inside View of Britain's Overseas Information Services* (Oxford: Pergamon Press).

Mass Observation, *Tom Harrisson Mass-Observation Archive: File Report Series* (Brighton: Harvester Press, 1983).

Mass Observation, *The Press and Its Readers* (London: Art & Technics, 1949).

Orwell, George, *As I Please, 1943–1945. The Collected Essays, Journalism and Letters of George Orwell*, vol. 3, Sonia Orwell and Ian Angus (eds) (London: Penguin Books, 1970).

Orwell, George, *In Front of Your Nose. The Collected Essays, Journalism and Letters of George Orwell*, vol. 4, Sonia Orwell and Ian Angus (eds) (London: Penguin Books, 1970).

Orwell, George, *Smothered Under Journalism, 1946. The Complete Works of George Orwell*, vol. 18, Peter Davison (ed.) (London: Secker and Warburg, 1998).

Orwell, George, *Our Job is to Make Life Worth Living, 1949–1950. The Complete Works of George Orwell*, vol. 20, Peter Davison (ed.) (London: Secker and Warburg, 1998).

Political and Economic Planning (for Arts Enquiry), *The Factual Film* (London: Oxford University Press, 1947).

Trades Union Congress, *Trade Unionists Stand Firm for Peace* ([London]: T.U.C. Pamphlet, [1950]).

UNESCO, *News Agencies: Their Structure and Operation* (Paris: UNESCO, 1953).

Williams, Francis, *Press, Parliament and People* (London: Heinemann, 1946).

Winnington, Alan, *I Saw the Truth in Korea* (London: People's Press Printing Society, [1950]).

Official British Documents

Annual Report of the Central Office of Information for the Year 1947–48. Cmd 7567. (1948).

Departmental Committee on Section 2 of the Official Secrets Act 1911 [Franks Committee], *Report of the Committee*. vol. 1. Cmnd 5104 (1972).

HMSO, *Documents on British Policy Overseas*, ser. 1, vols 1–7; ser. 2, vols 1–4 (1984–97).

Parliamentary Debates, 5th ser., vols 407, 478, 480, 489, 490, 491, 502, 503, 504.

Royal Commission on the Press, 1947–1949, *Report* (London: HMSO, 1949.)

White Paper on Broadcasting Policy. Cmd 6852 (1946).

Memoirs and Diaries

Barman, Thomas, *Diplomatic Correspondent* (London: Hamish Hamilton, 1968).

Brittain, Vera, *Testament of a Generation: The Journalism of Vera Brittain and Winifred Holtby* (London: Virago, 1985).

Buber, Margarete, *Under Two Dictators* (London: Victor Gollancz, 1949).

Burchett, Wilfred, *At the Barricades: Forty Years on the Cutting Edge of History* (New York: Times Books, 1981).

Clark, William, *From Three Worlds: Memoirs* (London: Sidgwick and Jackson, 1986).

Crozier, Brian, *Free Agent: The Unseen War, 1941–1991* (London: HarperCollins, 1993).

Daix, Pierre, *J'ai cru au Matin* (Paris: R. Laffont, 1976).

Ehrenburg, Ilya, *Post-War Years, 1945–54* (London: McGibben and Kee, 1966).
Hyde, Douglas, *I Believed: The Autobiography of a British Communist* (London: Heinemann, 1950).
Jameson, Derek, *Touched by Angels* (London: Ebury Press, 1988).
Mayhew, Christopher, *Time to Explain* (London: Hutchinson, 1987).
Mayhew, Christopher, *A War of Words: A Cold War Witness* (London: I. B. Tauris, 1998).
McDonald, Iverach, *Man of the Times: Talks and Travels in a Disrupted World* (London: Hamish Hamilton, 1976).
Muggeridge, Malcolm, *Like It Was: The Diaries of Malcolm Muggeridge*. Edited by John Bright-Holmes (London: Collins, 1981).
Nicolson, Harold, *Diaries and Letters, 1930–1964*. Edited and condensed by Stanley Olson (London: Collins, 1980).
Peet, John, *The Long Engagement: Memoirs of a Cold War Legend* (London: Fourth Estate, 1989).
Pritt, D. N., *The Autobiography of D. N. Pritt. Part 2, Brasshats and Bureaucrats* (London: Lawrence and Wishart, 1966).
Schaffer, Gordon, *Baby in the Bathwater: Memories of a Political Journalist* (Sussex: The Book Guild, 1996).
Williams, Francis, *Nothing So Strange* (New York: American Heritage Press, 1970).
Winnington, Alan, *Breakfast With Mao: Memoirs of a Foreign Correspondent* (London: Lawrence and Wishart, 1986).

Secondary Sources

Books etc.

Aldrich, Richard, *The Hidden Hand: Britain, American and Cold War Secret Intelligence* (New York: Overlook Press, 2002).
Aldrich, Richard, *Espionage, Security and Intelligence in Britain, 1945–1970* (Manchester: Manchester University Press, 1998).
Andrew, Christopher, *Her Majesty's Secret Service: The Making of the British Intelligence Community* (New York: Viking, 1986).
Applebaum, Anne, *Gulag: A History* (New York: Doubleday, 2003).
Ayerst, David, *The Guardian: Biography of a Newspaper* (London: Collins, 1971).
Barker, Elisabeth, *The British Between the Superpowers, 1945–50* (Toronto: University of Toronto Press, 1983).
Bell, P. M. H., *John Bull and the Bear: British Public Opinion, Foreign Policy and the Soviet Union, 1941–1945* (London: Edward Arnold, 1990).
Bethell, Nicholas, *The Last Secret: The Delivery to Stalin of over Two Million Russians by Britain and the United States* (New York: Basic Books, 1974).
Black, John, *Organising the Propaganda Instrument: The British Experience* (The Hague: Martinus Nijhoff, 1975).
Bloch, Jonathan and Patrick Fitzgerald, *British Intelligence and Covert Action: Africa, the Middle East and Europe since 1945* (London: Junction, 1983).
Bogart, Leo, *Cool Words, Cold War: A New Look at USIA's Premises for Propaganda*. Rev. edn (Washington, DC: American University Press, 1995).

Brewer, John, *Sinews of Power: War, Money, and the English State, 1688–1783* (Cambridge, MA: Harvard University Press, 1988).

Brewer, Susan, *To Win the Peace: British Propaganda in the United States during World War II* (Ithaca: Cornell University Press, 1997).

Briggs, Asa, *Governing the BBC* (London: British Broadcasting Corporation, 1979).

Briggs, Asa, *The History of Broadcasting in the United Kingdom, Vol. 4: Sound and Vision* (London: Oxford University Press, 1979).

Bullock, Alan, *Ernest Bevin: Foreign Secretary* (London: Heinemann, 1983).

Cain, P. J., and A. G. Hopkins, *British Imperialism: Innovation and Expansion, 1688–1914* (London: Longman, 1993).

Carew, Anthony, Michel Dreyfus, Geert Van Goethem and Rebecca Gumbrell-McCormack, *The International Confederation of Free Trade Unions* (Bern: Peter Lang, 2000).

Carruthers, Susan, *Winning Hearts and Minds: British Governments, the Media and Colonial Counter-Insurgency, 1944–1960* (London: Leicester University Press, 1995).

Carruthers, Susan, *Media at War: Communication and Conflict in the Twentieth Century* (New York: St Martin's Press, 2000).

Caute, David, *The Fellow-Travellers: Intellectual Friends of Communism*. Rev. edn (New Haven: Yale University Press, 1988).

Chalaby, Jean, *The Invention of Journalism* (Houndmills, England: Macmillan, 1998).

Chisholm, Anne, and Michael Davie, *Beaverbrook: A Life* (London: Hutchinson, 1992).

Clark, Sir Fife, *The Central Office of Information* (London: Allen and Unwin, 1970).

Cockerell, Michael, Peter Hennessy and David Walker, *Sources Close to the Prime Minister: Inside the Hidden World of the News Manipulators* (London: Macmillan, 1984).

Cockett, Richard, *Twilight of Truth: Chamberlain, Appeasement and the Manipulation of the Press* (London: Weidenfeld and Nicolson, 1989).

Cohen, Bernard, *The Press and Foreign Policy* (Princeton: Princeton University Press, 1963).

Cole, Robert, *Britain and the War of Words in Neutral Europe, 1939–1945* (New York: St Martin's Press, 1990).

Coleman, Peter, *The Liberal Conspiracy: The Congress for Cultural Freedom and the Struggle for the Mind of Postwar Europe* (New York: Free Press, 1989).

Copfermann, Émile, *David Rousset: Une Vie dans le Siécle: Fragments d'autobiographie* (Paris: Plon, 1991).

Crick, Bernard, *George Orwell: A Life* (London: Secker and Warburg, 1980).

Crofts, William, *Coercion or Persuasion: Propaganda in Britain after 1945* (London: Routledge, 1989).

Cull, Nicholas, *Selling War: The British Propaganda Campaign against American 'Neutrality' in World War II* (New York: Oxford University Press, 1995).

Cull, Nicholas, David Culbert and David Welch, *Propaganda and Mass Persuasion: A Historical Encyclopedia, 1500 to the Present* (Santa Barbara, CA: ABC/Clio, 2003).

Cunningham, Stanley, *The Idea of Propaganda: A Reconstruction* (Westport, CT: Praeger, 2002).

Curran, James, and Jean Seaton, *Power Without Responsibility: The Press and Broadcasting in Britain*. 6th edn (London: Routledge, 2003).

Darnton, Robert, *The Kiss of Lamourette: Reflections in Cultural History* (New York: Norton, 1990).

Defty, Andrew, *Britain, America and Anti-Communist Propaganda, 1945–1953: The Information Research Department* (London: Routledge, 2004).

Dorril, Stephen, *MI6: Inside the Covert World of Her Majesty's Secret Intelligence Service* (New York: Touchstone, 2000).

Edwards, Ruth Dudley, *The Pursuit of Reason: The Economist, 1843–1893* (London: Hamish Hamilton, 1993).

Engel, Matthew, *Tickle the Public: One Hundred Years of the Popular Press* (London: Victor Gollancz, 1996).

Gans, Herbert, *Deciding What's News:A Study of CBS Evening News, NBC Nightly News, Newsweek and Time* (New York: Vintage, 1980).

Gilbert, Martin, *Never Despair: Winston Churchill, 1945–1965* (London: Heinemann, 1988).

Gitlin, Todd, *The Whole World is Watching: Mass Media in the Making and Unmaking of the New Left* (Berkeley: University of California Press, 1982).

Gowing, Margaret, *Independence and Deterrence: Britain and Atomic Energy, 1945–1952*, Vol. 2 (New York: St Martin's Press, 1972).

Hallin, Dan, *The 'Uncensored War': The Media and Vietnam* (Berkeley: University of California Press, 1986).

Hart-Davis, Duff, *The House the Berrys Built* (London: Hodder & Stoughton, 1990).

Haslam, Jonathan, *The Vices of Integrity: E. H. Carr, 1892–1982* (London: Verso, 1999).

Headrick, Daniel, *Invisible Weapon: Telecommunications and International Politics, 1851–1945* (New York: Oxford University Press, 1991).

Hennessy, Peter, *The Secret State: Whitehall and the Cold War* (London: Penguin, 2003).

Hills, Jill, *The Struggle for Control of Global Communication: The Formative Century* (Urbana: University of Illinois Press, 2002).

Hobson, Harold, Phillip Knightley and Leonard Russell, *Pearl of Days: An Intimate Memoir of the Sunday Times, 1822–1972* (London: Hamish Hamilton, 1972).

Hollingsworth, Mark and Richard Norton-Taylor, *Blacklist: The Inside Story of Political Vetting* (London: Hogarth Press, 1988).

Holloway, David, *Stalin and the Bomb: The Soviet Union and Atomic Energy* (New Haven: Yale University Press, 1994).

Hooper, David, *Official Secrets: The Use and Abuse of the Act* (London: Secker and Warburg, 1988).

Hubback, David, *No Ordinary Press Baron: A Life of Walter Layton* (London: Weidenfeld and Nicolson, 1985).

Judt, Tony, *Past Imperfect: French Intellectuals, 1944–1956* (Berkeley: University of California Press, 1992).

Kent, John, *British Imperial Strategy and the Origins of the Cold War, 1944–49* (Leicester: Leicester University Press, 1993).

Klapper, Joseph, *The Effects of Mass Communication* (New York: Free Press, 1960).

Knightley, Phillip, *The First Casualty: From Crimea to Vietnam: The War Correspondent as Hero, Propagandist and Myth Maker* (New York: Harcourt Brace Jovanovich, 1975).

Kotek, Joël, *Students in the Cold War* (London: Macmillan, 1996).

Lashmar, Paul, and James Oliver, *Britain's Secret Propaganda War* (Stroud: Sutton Publishing, 1998).

Lawrenson, John, and Lionel Barber, *The Price of Truth: The Story of the Reuters £££ Millions* (London: Mainstream Publishing, 1986).

Lycett, Andrew, *Ian Fleming: The Man Behind James Bond* (Atlanta: Turner Publishing, 1995).

Mansell, Gerard, *Let Truth Be Told: 50 Years of BBC External Broadcasting* (London: Weidenfeld and Nicolson, 1982).

Margach, James, *Abuse of Power: The War Between Downing Street and the Media from Lloyd George to Callaghan* (London: W. H. Allen, 1978).

McDonald, Iverach, *The History of the Times. Vol. 5, Struggles in War and Peace, 1939–1966* (London: The Times, 1984).

McLachlan, Donald, *In the Chair: Barrington-Ward of 'The Times', 1927–1948* (London: Weidenfeld and Nicolson, 1971).

McLaine, Ian, *Ministry of Morale: Home Front Morale and the Ministry of Information in World War II* (London: Allen and Unwin, 1979).

McPhail, Thomas, *Global Communication: Theories, Stakeholders, and Trends* (Boston, MA: Allyn and Bacon, 2002).

Morgan, Kenneth, *Labour in Power* (Oxford: Clarendon Press, 1985).

Morgan, Ted, *A Covert Life: Jay Lovestone: Communist, Anti-Communist and Spymaster* (New York: Random House, 1999).

Nelson, Michael, *War of the Black Heavens: The Battles of Western Broadcasting in the Cold War* (Syracuse: Syracuse University Press, 1997).

Nicholas, Siân, *The Echo of War: Home Front Propaganda and the Wartime BBC, 1939–45* (Manchester: Manchester University Press, 1996).

Ogilvy-Webb, Marjorie, *The Government Explains: A Study of the Information Service* (London: Allen and Unwin, 1965).

Ponting, Clive, *Secrecy in Britain* (Oxford: Blackwell, 1990).

Potter, Simon J., *News and the British World: The Emergence of an Imperial Press System, 1876–1922* (Oxford: Oxford University Press, 2003).

Qualter, Terence, *Opinion Control in the Democracies* (New York: St Martin's Press, 1985).

Read, Donald, *The Power of News: The History of Reuters* (Oxford: Oxford University Press, 1992).

Rothwell, Victor, *Britain and the Cold War, 1941–1947* (London: Jonathan Cape, 1982).

Sadler, Pauline, *National Security and the D-Notice System* (Ashgate: Aldershot, 2001).

Saunders, Frances Stonor, *The Cultural Cold War: The CIA and the World of Art and Letters* (New York: New Press, 1999).

Schlesinger, Philip, *Putting Reality Together: BBC News* (London: Constable, 1979).

Schwartz, Herman, *States versus Markets: The Emergence of a Global Economy*, 2nd edn (Houndmills: Palgrave, 2000).

Shaw, Tony, *Eden, Suez and the Mass Media: Propaganda and Persuasion during the Suez Crisis* (London: I. B. Tauris, 1996).

Shaw, Tony, *British Cinema and the Cold War: The State, Propaganda and Consensus* (London: I. B. Tauris, 2001).

Shulman, Marshall, *Stalin's Foreign Policy Reappraised* (Boulder: Westview Press, 1985).

Stephens, Mitchell, *A History of News* (Fort Worth: Harcourt Brace, 1997).

Taylor, Philip, *Projection of Britain: British Overseas Publicity and Propaganda, 1919–1939* (Cambridge: Cambridge University Press, 1981).

Taylor, Philip, *British Propaganda in the Twentieth Century: Selling Democracy* (Edinburgh: Edinburgh University Press, 1999).

Thompson, Willie, *The Good Old Cause: British Communism, 1920–1991* (London: Pluto Press, 1992).

Tunstall, Jeremy, *Journalists at Work: Specialist Correspondents: Their News Organisations, News Sources, and Competitor-Colleagues* (London: Constable, 1971).

Tunstall, Jeremy and David Machin, *The Anglo-American Media Connection* (New York: Oxford University Press, 1999).

Wall, Irwin, *The United States and the Making of Postwar France* (Cambridge: Cambridge University Press, 1991).

Weiler, Peter, *British Labour and the Cold War* (Stanford: Stanford University Press, 1988).

West, Nigel and Oleg Tsarev, *The Crown Jewels: The British Secrets at the Heart of the KGB Archives* (London: HarperCollins, 1998).

Wilford, Hugh, *CIA, the British Left, and the Cold War: Calling the Tune?* (London: Frank Cass, 2003).

Wittner, Lawrence, *The Struggle Against the Bomb. Vol. 1, One World or None, A History of the World Nuclear Disarmament Movement Through 1953* (Stanford: Stanford University Press, 1993).

Wittner, Lawrence, *The Struggle Against the Bomb. Vol. 2, Resisting the Bomb: A History of the World Nuclear Disarmament Movement, 1954–1970* (Stanford: Stanford University Press, 1997).

Zubkova, Elena, *Russia After the War: Hopes, Illusions and Disappointments, 1945–57* (Armonk, NY: M. E. Sharpe, 1998).

Journals and Periodicals

Adamthwaite, Anthony, '"Nation Shall Speak Peace Unto Nation:" The BBC's Response to Peace and Defence Issues, 1945–58', *Contemporary Record* 7 (1993).

Anstey, Caroline, 'The Projection of British Socialism: Foreign Office Publicity and American Opinion, 1945–50', *Journal of Contemporary History* 19 (1984).

Caedel, Martin, 'The First Communist "Peace Society": The British Anti-War Movement, 1932–1935', *Twentieth Century British History* 1 (1990).

Cockett, Richard, '"In Wartime Every Objective Reporter Should be Shot." The Experience of British Press Correspondents in Moscow, 1941–5', *Journal of Contemporary History* 23 (1988).

Deery, Phillip, 'The Dove Flies East: Whitehall, Warsaw and the 1950 World Peace Congress', *Australian Journal of Politics and History* (2002).

Defty, Andrew, '"Close and Continuous Liaison": British Anti-Communist Propaganda and Cooperation with the United States, 1950–51', *Intelligence and National Security* 17 (2002).

Egorova, Nataliia I., 'Stalin's Foreign Policy and the Cominform' in Francesca Gori and Silvio Pons (eds), *The Soviet Union and Europe in the Cold War, 1943–1953* (London: Macmillan Press, 1996).

Fletcher, Richard, 'British Propaganda Since World War II – A Case Study', *Media Culture and Society* 4 (1982).

Foster, Alan, 'The Politicians, Public Opinion and the Press: The Storm over British Military Intervention in Greece in December 1944', *Journal of Contemporary History* 19 (1984).

Foster, Alan, 'The British Press and the Coming of the Cold War', in Anne Deighton (ed.), *Britain and the First Cold War* (London: Macmillan, 1990).

Foster, Alan, 'The Beaverbrook Press and Appeasement: The Second Phase', *European History Quarterly* 21 (1991).

Gould-Davies, Nigel, '"Pacifistic Blowback"? New Evidence on the Soviet Peace Campaign in the Early 1950s', *Cold War International History Project Bulletin* 11 (1998).

Grant, Mariel, 'Towards a Central Office of Information: Continuity and Change in British Government Policy, 1939–51', *Journal of Contemporary History* 34 (1999).

de Gramont, Sanche, 'Two Who Bridge the Generation Gap' in John E. Talbott (ed.), *France Since 1930* (New York: Quadrangle Books, 1972).

Hall, Stuart, 'The Rediscovery of Ideology: The Return of the Repressed in Media Studies', in Michael Gurevitch, Tony Bennett, James Curran and Janet Woolacott (eds), *Culture, Society and the Media* (London: Routledge, 1982).

Haslam, Jonathan, '"We Need a Faith": E. H. Carr, 1892–1982', *History Today* August (1983).

Hogenkamp, Bert, 'Not Quite Prepared for *Always Prepared*: Herbert Morrison and the Film of the 1950 East Berlin Youth Rally', *Contemporary British History* 12 (1998).

Jenks, John, 'The Enemy Within: Journalism, the State and the Limits of Dissent in Cold War Britain, 1950–51', *American Journalism* 18 (2001).

Jenks, John, 'Consorting with the Enemy: American Reporters and "Red Sources" at the Korean Truce Talks, 1951–1953', *Journal of Conflict Studies* 32 (2002).

Jenks, John, 'Fight Against Peace? British Propaganda and the Partisans of Peace, 1948–51', in Michael D. Kandiah, Gillian Staerck and Michael F. Hopkins (eds), *Cold War Britain, 1945–1964: New Perspectives* (London: Palgrave Macmillan, 2003).

Kennedy, P. M., 'Imperial Cable Communications and Strategy, 1870–1914', *English Historical Review* 86 (1971).

Kirby, Dianne, 'The Church of England and the Cold War Nuclear Debate', *Twentieth Century British History* 4 (1993).

Kirby, Dianne, 'Responses Within the Anglican Church to Nuclear Weapons: 1945–1961', *Journal of Church and State* 37 (1995).

Liebich, Andrew, 'Mensheviks Wage the Cold War', *Journal of Contemporary History* 30 (1995).

McIvor, Arthur, '"A Crusade for Capitalism": The Economic League, 1919–39', *Journal of Contemporary History* 23 (1988).

Merrick, Ray, 'The Russia Committee of the British Foreign Office and the Cold War, 1946–7', *Journal of Contemporary History* 20 (1985).

Morris, C. J., and W. Scott Lucas, 'A Very British Crusade: The Information Research Department and the Beginning of the Cold War', in Richard Aldrich (ed.), *British Intelligence, Strategy and the Cold War, 1945–51* (London: Routledge, 1992).

Palmer, Alasdair, 'The History of the D-Notice Committee', in Christopher Andrew and David Dilks (eds), *The Missing Dimension: Governments and Intelligence Communities in the Twentieth Century* (Urbana, IL: University of Illinois Press, 1984).

Pechatnov, Vladimir, 'The Rise and Fall of *Britansky Soyuznik*: A Case Study in Soviet Response to British Propaganda of the mid-1940s,' *The Historical Journal* 41 (1998).

Powell, Glyn, 'Turning Off the Power: The Electrical Trades Union and the anti-Communist Crusade 1957–61', *Contemporary British History* 18 (2004).

Rowley, Kelvin, 'Burchett and the Cold War in Europe', in Ben Kiernan (ed.), *Burchett Reporting the Other Side of the World, 1939–1983* (New York: Quartet Books, 1986).

Shaw, Tony, 'The British Popular Press and the Early Cold War', *History: Journal of the Historical Association* 83 (1998).

Shaw, Tony, 'The Information Research Department of the British Foreign Office and the Korean War, 1950–53', *Journal of Contemporary History* 34 (1999).

Smith, Lyn, 'Covert British Propaganda: The Information Research Department: 1947–77', *Millennium: Journal of International Studies* 9 (1980).

Taylor, Philip, 'Publicity and Diplomacy: The Impact of the First World War upon Foreign Office Attitudes towards the Press', in David Dilks (ed.), *Retreat from Power: Studies in British Foreign Policy of the Twentieth Century*, Vol. 1 (London: Macmillan, 1981).

Taylor, Philip, 'Censorship in Britain in the Second World War: An Overview', in A. C. Duke and C. A. Tamse (eds), *Too Mighty to be Free: Censorship and the Press in Britain and the Netherlands* (Zutphen: De Walburg Prees, 1987).

Taylor, Philip, 'The Projection of Britain Abroad, 1945–51', in Michael Dockrill and John Young (eds), *British Foreign Policy, 1945–56* (Houndmills: Macmillan, 1989).

Wark, Wesley, 'Coming in from the Cold: British Propaganda and Red Army Defectors, 1945–52', *The International History Review* 9 (1987).

Wernicke, Günter, 'The Communist-led World Peace Council and the Western Peace Movements: The Fetters of Bipolarity and Some Attempts to Break Them in the Fifties and Early Sixties', *Peace & Change* 23 (1998).

Wilford, Hugh, 'The Information Research Department: Britain's Secret Cold War Weapon Revealed', *Review of International Studies* 24 (1998).

Zametica, John, 'Three Letters to Bevin', in John Zametica (ed.), *British Officials and British Foreign Policy, 1945–50* (Leicester: Leicester University Press, 1990).

Unpublished Dissertations

Anstey, Caroline, 'Foreign Office Efforts to Influence American Opinion, 1945–49.' Ph.D. dissertation, London School of Economics and Political Science, 1984.

Jenks, John, 'Hot News/Cold War: The British State, Propaganda and the News Media, 1948–53.' Ph.D. dissertation, University of California-Berkeley, 2000.

Kirby, Dianne, 'The Anglican Church in the Period of the Cold War: 1945–65.' Ph.D. dissertation, University of Hull, 1990.

Index